THE CAMBRIDGE COMPANION TO
RUDYARD KIPLING

Rudyard Kipling (1865–1936) is among the most popular, acclaimed and controversial of writers in English. His books have sold in great numbers, and he remains the youngest writer to have won the Nobel Prize in literature. Many associate Kipling with poems such as 'If–', his novel *Kim*, his pioneering use of the short story form and such works for children as the *Just So Stories*. For others, though, Kipling is the very symbol of the British Empire and a belligerent approach to other peoples and races. This Companion explores Kipling's main themes and texts, the different genres in which he worked and the various phases of his career. As well as examining the 'afterlives' of Kipling's texts in postcolonial writing, and illustrations and film adaptations of his work, it also features a chronology and a guide to further reading.

HOWARD J. BOOTH is Lecturer in English Literature at the University of Manchester.

A complete list of books in the series is at the back of this book

D0985804

THE CAMBRIDGE COMPANION TO
RUDYARD KIPLING

EDITED BY
HOWARD J. BOOTH

CAMBRIDGE
UNIVERSITY PRESS

CAMBRIDGE UNIVERSITY PRESS
Cambridge, New York, Melbourne, Madrid, Cape Town,
Singapore, São Paulo, Delhi, Tokyo, Mexico City

Cambridge University Press
The Edinburgh Building, Cambridge CB2 8RU, UK

Published in the United States of America by Cambridge University Press, New York

www.cambridge.org
Information on this title: www.cambridge.org/9780521136631

© Cambridge University Press 2011

First published 2011

Printed in the United Kingdom at the University Press, Cambridge

A catalogue record for this publication is available from the British Library

Library of Congress Cataloguing in Publication data
The Cambridge companion to Rudyard Kipling / edited by Howard J. Booth.
p.   cm. – (Cambridge companions to literature)
Includes bibliographical references and index.
ISBN 978-0-521-19972-8 (hardback) – ISBN 978-0-521-13663-1 (paperback)
1. Kipling, Rudyard, 1865–1936–Criticism and interpretation.
I. Booth, Howard J. (Howard John), 1969– II. Title. III. Series.
PR4857.C36 2011
828'.809–dc23   2011020305

ISBN 978-0-521-19972-8 Hardback
ISBN 978-0-521-13663-1 Paperback

CONTENTS

FIGURES

CONTRIBUTORS

HOWARD J. BOOTH is Lecturer in English Literature at the University of Manchester. The author of many articles on nineteenth- and twentieth-century literature and culture, he has co-edited *Modernism and Empire* (2000) and edited *New D. H. Lawrence* (2009).

DAVID BRADSHAW is Reader in English Literature at Oxford University, a Fellow of Worcester College and Chair of Oxford's English Faculty Board (2010–13). Among other volumes, he has edited *The Hidden Huxley* (1994), *A Concise Companion to Modernism* (2003), *The Cambridge Companion to E. M. Forster* (2007) and, with Kevin J. H. Dettmar, *A Companion to Modernist Literature and Culture* (2006). He has also edited a wide range of novels and other texts from the modernist period and written many articles on authors such as Conrad, Huxley, T. S. Eliot, Woolf and Yeats. Current projects include a book on Woolf, a book on Huxley and, with Rachel Potter, a commissioned collection of essays on obscenity, censorship and fiction called *Prudes on the Prowl*.

PATRICK BRANTLINGER is James Rudy Professor of English (Emeritus) at Indiana University. A former editor of *Victorian Studies* (1980–90), his books include *Rule of Darkness: British Literature and Imperialism* (1988), *Crusoe's Footprints: Cultural Studies in Britain and America* (1990), *Dark Visionings: Discourse on the Extinction of Primitive Races, 1800–1913* (2003) and, most recently, *Victorian Literature and Postcolonial Studies* (2009).

LAURENCE DAVIES is Professor and Honorary Senior Research Fellow in English Literature at the University of Glasgow. For many years he taught for the Comparative Literature and other interdisciplinary programmes at Dartmouth College. He is co-author of a critical biography of R. B. Cunninghame Graham, the Scottish author and political campaigner. He succeeded the late Frederick R. Karl as general editor of *The Collected Letters of Joseph Conrad* (1983–2007), served as a volume editor for all nine volumes, and is president of the UK Joseph

Conrad Society and a member of the editorial board of the Cambridge edition of Conrad's works. Other academic interests include science and literature, speculative fiction, international Modernism, and the interactions of oral and literate cultures.

ROBERT HAMPSON is Professor of Modern Literature in the English Department at Royal Holloway, University of London. He is the author of three monographs – *Joseph Conrad: Betrayal and Identity* (1992), *Cross-Cultural Encounters in Joseph Conrad's Malay Fiction* (2001) and *Conrad's Secrets* (forthcoming) – and co-editor of *Conrad and Theory* (1998), *Ford Madox Ford: A Re-Appraisal* (1995) and *Ford Madox Ford and Modernity* (2003). He has edited Kipling's *Something of Myself* and *Soldiers Three* and *In Black and White* for Penguin.

JOHN McBRATNEY is Professor of English at John Carroll University in Cleveland, Ohio. He is the author of *Imperial Subjects, Imperial Space: Rudyard Kipling's Fiction of the Native-Born* (2002) and several articles on Kipling. He has also published articles on Dickens, Tennyson, Conan Doyle, Forster, Orwell and Paul Scott. His main scholarly interests include race, empire, ethnography, and detection in nineteenth- and twentieth-century British literature. He is currently working on a book on Victorian cosmopolitanisms.

JAN MONTEFIORE is Professor of Twentieth Century English Literature at the University of Kent, where she has taught in the School of English since 1978. The author of *Feminism and Poetry* (1987, 2004), *Men and Women Writers of the 1930s* (1996), *Arguments of Heart and Mind* (2002) and *Rudyard Kipling* (2007), she has edited *The Man Who Would Be King and Other Stories* for Penguin Classics (2011) and is currently editing a new collection, *In Time's Eye: Essays on Rudyard Kipling* (2011).

BART MOORE-GILBERT is Professor of Postcolonial Studies and English at Goldsmiths, University of London. He is the author of *Kipling and 'Orientalism'* (1987), *Postcolonial Theory: Contexts, Practices, Politics* (1997), *Hanif Kureishi* (2001) and *Postcolonial Life-Writing: Culture, Politics and Self-Representation* (2009). He has also edited *Writing India: British Representations of India, 1757–1990* (1996) and numerous articles and chapters in books on Kipling and colonial and postcolonial literature and theory.

KAORI NAGAI teaches at the University of Kent. She is the author of *Empire of Analogies: Kipling, India and Ireland* (2006) and has co-edited a collection of essays with Caroline Rooney entitled *Kipling and Beyond: Patriotism, Globalisation and Postcolonialism* (2010). She has also written an introduction and notes to

Kipling's Plain Tales from the Hills for Penguin Books (2011) and edited a special issue on 'Dream Writing' for the *Journal of European Studies* (2008).

JUDITH PLOTZ is Professor of English at George Washington University and a former president of the Children's Literature Association. She is the author of *Romanticism and the Vocation of Childhood* (2001) and has written frequently on children's books, nineteenth-century childhoods and Kipling. The editor of the forthcoming Penguin edition of the *Just So Stories*, she is currently completing a book on Kipling's non-canonicity entitled *Kipling and the Little Traditions*.

HARRY RICKETTS is Associate Professor in the School of English, Film, Theatre and Media Studies at Victoria University of Wellington, New Zealand, where he teaches nineteenth- and twentieth-century literature and creative non-fiction. His work on Kipling includes *The Unforgiving Minute: A Life of Rudyard Kipling* (1999), an edition of Kipling's poems, *Rudyard Kipling, The Long Trail: Selected Poems* (2004), and articles on Kipling's literary influence and on his parodic verse. He has also published a number of personal essays and eight collections of poems, most recently *Your Secret Life* (2005). His composite biographical study of a dozen First World War poets, *Strange Meetings: The Poets of the Great War*, was published by Chatto & Windus in 2010.

HARISH TRIVEDI is Professor of English at the University of Delhi, and has been visiting professor at the universities of Chicago and London. He is the author of *Colonial Transactions: English Literature and India* (Calcutta, 1993; Manchester, 1995) and has co-edited *The Nation across the World* (New Delhi, 2007; New York, 2008), *Literature and Nation: Britain and India 1800–1990* (London, 2000), *Post-colonial Translation: Theory and Practice* (London, 1999) and *Interrogating Post-colonialism: Theory, Text and Context* (Shimla, 1996; rpt. 2000, 2006). He has undertaken the introduction and notes to the new Penguin edition of *Kim* (2011) and contributed a chapter to the *Cambridge Companion to Gandhi* (2011).

MONICA TURCI is a Lecturer at the University of Bologna. The author of *Approaching that Perfect Edge: A Reading of the Metafictional Writings of Michael Ondaatje* (2001), she also co-edited *Language and Verbal Art Revisited: Linguistic Approaches to the Literature Text* (2007). She has written many articles on the relationship between text and image, and on literature and linguistics.

CHRONOLOGY

1865   On 30 December Joseph Rudyard Kipling born in Bombay
        to John Lockwood Kipling and Alice Kipling, born Alice
        Macdonald.

1868   Birth of sister Alice ('Trix'). Kipling's first visit to England.

1871   Kipling and Trix boarded in Southsea with the Holloway family.
        Kipling later called it 'The House of Desolation'. Kipling drew on
        this period in 'Baa Baa, Black Sheep', *The Light That Failed* and
        Something of Myself.

1877   Alice Kipling takes her son away from Southsea. Rudyard starts
        school at the United Services College, Westward Ho!, in Devon,
        later using his time there as the basis for the Stalky stories.

1881   A year of transition. Made editor of the school magazine. A first
        collection of his poems, *Schoolboy Lyrics*, privately printed by his
        parents without his permission. Returns to India and gets a job as
        assistant editor on the *Civil and Military Gazette* in Lahore.

1883   Verses published in *The Englishman* of Calcutta and in the *Civil
        and Military Gazette*.

1884   *Echoes by Two Writers*, a series of parodies by Kipling and Trix.

1885   *Quartette*, a Christmas Annual by all four members of the
        Kipling family.

1886   *Departmental Ditties*, comic poems about the English in India.

1887   Moves to work on the *Pioneer* in Allahabad. Some articles
        from this period later collected as 'Letters of Marque' (1891) in
        volume 1 of *From Sea to Sea*.

1888   *Plain Tales from the Hills* and the Railway Library series of short
        stories: *Soldiers Three, The Story of the Gadsbys, In Black and
        White, Under the Deodars, The Phantom Rickshaw, Wee Willie
        Winkie*.

1889   Kipling leaves India, travelling to Burma, Singapore, Hong Kong,
        Canton and Japan before crossing the Pacific and the United

States and arriving in London. Takes rooms in Villiers Street, off the Strand, and resolves to earn a living from his writing.

1890 After a nervous breakdown brought on by overwork and a broken engagement to Caroline Taylor, Kipling becomes very close to Wolcott Balestier. Writes the novel *The Light That Failed*.

1891 *Life's Handicap*, new and republished short stories. Collaborates with Wolcott Balestier on a novel, *The Naulahka*. After a further breakdown, travels via South Africa, Australia and New Zealand to spend Christmas with his family in India. Hearing of Wolcott Balestier's death, he returns straight away to London.

1892 Marries Wolcott's sister Caroline on 18 January. Decide to settle near the Balestier family in Brattleboro, Vermont. First child, Josephine, born in December. *The Naulahka* and *Barrack-Room Ballads and Other Verses* published.

1893 *Many Inventions*, a volume of short stories. The Kiplings move to 'Naulakha' – the word spelt correctly this time – a house they have built on land purchased from Beatty Balestier.

1894 *The Jungle Book*.

1895 *The Second Jungle Book*.

1896 Second child Elsie born. Leaves Brattleboro after a row with Beatty Balestier. A volume of verse, *The Seven Seas*.

1897 The Kiplings settle in Sussex, living first in Rottingdean. Son John born. American novel *'Captains Courageous'* published.

1898 Travels in South Africa and Rhodesia. Begins friendship with Cecil Rhodes. Volume of short stories *The Day's Work* published, as is *A Fleet in Being*, a series of articles about the Navy.

1899 On a trip to New York Kipling and Josephine develop pneumonia. Josephine, 'the Best Beloved', dies. Becomes involved with charitable work for those in the British military on the outbreak of the Second South African War (Boer War). Collected travel articles *From Sea to Sea* (2 vols.) and school stories *Stalky & Co.* published.

1900 In South Africa observing and writing about the war.

1901 *Kim*.

1902 The Kiplings buy and move into Bateman's at Burwash in Sussex. *Just So Stories for Little Children*.

1903 *The Five Nations*, a volume of verse. Includes 'Recessional' and 'The White Man's Burden'.

1904 *Traffics and Discoveries*. Short stories including '"They"', '"Wireless"' and 'Mrs Bathurst' show Kipling becoming a Modern in theme and technique.

1906   *Puck of Pook's Hill.* Children's stories and poems.

1907   Awarded the Nobel Prize in literature. Visits Canada.

1909   *Actions and Reactions*, short stories. *Abaft the Funnel*, previously uncollected early work.

1910   *Rewards and Fairies*, a sequel to *Puck of Pook's Hill.* Includes 'If–'.

1911   RK collaborates on *A School History of England*, with the historian C. R. L. Fletcher.

1913   Visits Egypt. Publishes *Songs from Books.*

1915   John Kipling missing in action during the Battle of Loos. Kipling becomes ill with what is diagnosed, many years later, as a gastric ulcer. War journalism collected in *The New Army in Training* and *France at War.*

1916   Further war journalism: *Sea Warfare* and *The Eyes of Asia.*

1917   Joins Imperial War Graves Commission. Volume of short stories, *A Diversity of Creatures*; includes 'Mary Postgate'. Articles about the Italian Front, *The War in the Mountains.*

1919   *The Years Between*, the last collection of poems. It includes 'Epitaphs of the War'. The Imperial War Graves Commission's *The Graves of the Fallen*, written by Kipling, appears.

1920   *Letters of Travel, 1892–1913.* Pieces on Japan, the United States, Canada and Egypt.

1923   *The Irish Guards in The Great War* (2 vols.), regimental history. (John Kipling was a Second Lieutenant in the Irish Guards.) *Land and Sea Tales for Scouts and Guides*, previously uncollected, and some new, fiction and verse.

1924   Surviving child Elsie marries George Bambridge.

1926   *Debits and Credits*, short stories. Includes 'The Wish House' and 'The Gardener'.

1927   Visits Brazil, where he writes a number of articles.

1928   *A Book of Words*, a volume of collected speeches.

1930   *Thy Servant a Dog*, narrated from a canine point of view. Spends an extended period in the Caribbean for Caroline Kipling's health.

1932   *Limits and Renewals*, final collection of short stories. Includes 'Dayspring Mishandled' and 'The Church That Was at Antioch'.

1933   *Souvenirs of France*, essays exhibiting Kipling's love of France.

1936   Dies after a short final illness on 18 January.

1937   *Something of Myself: for my Friends Known and Unknown* published posthumously. Written in Kipling's final year and edited for publication by Caroline Kipling and Alfred Webb-Johnson.

1937–9   Publication of the *Sussex Edition* of Kipling's works, which includes many of Kipling's own final revisions. Now rare, as many copies of the anyway limited edition were lost to bombing in the Second World War.

1939   Caroline Kipling dies. Bateman's left to the National Trust for Places of Historic Interest.

1940   The 'Definitive Edition' of *Rudyard Kipling's Verse* published.

HOWARD J. BOOTH

Introduction

There is no other literary career like Rudyard Kipling's. At the end of the nineteenth century he rapidly achieved a level of popularity that remains unique. Modern communications, mass education and a transformed publishing industry meant that he reached a worldwide audience, first in English and then in translation. More than a huge popular success, Kipling's work also received critical acclaim. The high point in terms of recognition came in 1907, when Kipling won the Nobel Prize in literature; he remains the youngest literature laureate. However, Kipling's reputation was already on the turn, mainly because of his strong views on the Empire and a preparedness, especially in his poetry, to use his writing for political ends. Kipling's late career is much debated: for one camp there is a marked decline, for another it benefits from a maturing vision.

Some critics have always simply dismissed Kipling. During the Second World War, five years after Kipling's death, H. E. Bates likened him to Hitler in his 'love of the most extravagant form of patriotism, flamboyant stage effects and sadistic contempt for the meek'. As for his style, that was all 'tinsel and brass'.[1] (Bates made no mention of Kipling's many warnings about German intentions in his last years.) Many, though, have found Kipling a spur to their own imagination and creativity. The French composer Charles Koechlin (1867–1950), who was a communist, first came across the *Jungle Books* in translation. From 1899, he wrote a series of symphonic poems and orchestral songs drawing on the stories. The project was not completed until the premiere of the full cycle in 1946.[2] Such marked variation in response can also be seen among postcolonial writers, who have both condemned and praised Kipling. However, many have refused to see the issue as a simple choice between an imperialist and a great artist whose attitudes and politics do not matter.

From early on it became clear that one-voiced attempts to describe and 'fix' Kipling were not going to work. A long line of major writers and critics – among them T. S. Eliot, George Orwell, Edmund Wilson, Randall

Jarrell, Edward Said and Salman Rushdie – have worked through their complex responses. The best modern criticism is willing to engage with the complexity and ambivalence found in Kipling. The task, as Jan Montefiore put it in her 2007 study, is to 'clarify its contradictions; not only the contradictions in his writing but in the ways he can be read'.[3] This means, as well, a preparedness to acknowledge all the elements in play in Kipling, whether they attract or shock. It is hard not to be taken over by the way *Kim* portrays the 'Great Game' on the 'Road of Life', but it is also necessary to acknowledge those who are excluded and demeaned in his texts, where this can extend to the people of entire religions, races, nations and continents (including Hindus, Jews, the Irish, Germans and Africans). To read a Kipling text for the first time is often to feel suspense in terms of the attitudes that are about to be expressed as well as the plot. One does not know what is coming next – a negative judgement against an individual and their kind, or a powerful expression of human sympathy from a writer on intimate terms with illness and loss.

Kipling can be used to challenge a popular assumption about literature and colonialism. This is that imperialists were all unthinking and vulgar, where anyone with intelligence, responsiveness and literary talent must always be on the side of the opponents of empire. Would this were so: colonialist writing can be powerful and effective. Like Amit Chaudhuri, many others who have attacked him roundly have had to acknowledge that 'Kipling is a very great writer.'[4]

The tenth and eleventh of Kipling's 'Letters of Marque' can serve as an example here. These were first part of a series of travel letters from the Punjab that appeared in the *Pioneer* of Allahabad between late 1888 and early 1889. Later they were collected together in the first volume of *From Sea to Sea*. The first of these two letters is mainly taken up with the history of Chitor (now Chittorgarh), and the second with an account of Kipling's visit to the ruined city and the recessed spring he called Gau-Mukh. One can alight on the way the text registers feelings of 'desolation',[5] 'an apprehension of great evil' and a sense of the 'uncanny' (102). Along with historical narratives of the inevitable fall of empires, this might lead us to expect the kind of crisis of self and in the authority to govern found later, as Harry Ricketts has pointed out, in E. M. Forster's *A Passage to India* (1924).[6] Whatever actually happens in the caves in the Marabar Hills, Forster seeks to capture the stripping away, in Indian conditions, of a confident western subjectivity.[7]

Many further possible intertexts and approaches to these letters can be suggested, however. The number of dead in the historical account – which makes parts of the approach 'a reeking, ruined slaughter-pen' (89) – and the description of approaching the spring ('Oh, horror! in that unspeakable

Gau-Mukh!' (104)) suggest a comparison with Joseph Conrad's *Heart of Darkness* (1899, 1902). Kipling's transport to and from the site on a less than well-trained elephant can be compared with the relationship between colonial and animal found in Orwell's famous essay 'Shooting an Elephant', from 1936. There killing the animal, and being observed doing so, is used by Orwell to describe his growing awareness of what maintaining colonial rule really involved. A psychoanalytic reading could do much with the references to gender and sexuality in these two letters. In the historical narrative there are women who are idealised in their beauty and resolve, committing suicide rather than falling into the hands of their enemies. The women who surprise Kipling in the ruins, though, are both disturbed and disturbing, with the entry to those ruins described in a language that suggests both a womb and vagina. The male body is addressed more directly. There is a 'red daubed *lignum* ... It is a piece of frieze, and the figures of the men are worn nearly smooth by time. What is visible is finely and frankly obscene' (94). We learn of the tower that 'most abhorrent of all [was] the slippery sliminess of the walls always worn smooth by naked men' (98), where this is seen in racial terms as 'he felt ... he were treading on the soft, oiled skin of a Hindu' (101). The suggestion of ascents into knowledge and descents into the pit suggest the possibility of a structuralist analysis. These two letters can also be seen in terms of the spatial dislocation that Fredric Jameson noted in modern literature after 1885, in which writing registers the difficulty of representing a global imperial system at the level of form and style.[8] Chitor resembles a 'black bulk' in the 'form of a ship' (82), and the transport to the nearest settlement is a 'railway track running off into the infinite' (91).

And yet the problem is that, with the possible exception of the sexual references, these hardly constitute the 'unconscious' of the text. Kipling is creating these effects and he is not seeking to bring colonialism into question. Order is reasserted and the traveller continues on his way. The (female) elephant is brought to order by beating it over the knuckles, and while the initial explanation of the disturbance in Gau-Mukh is unconvincing – 'choke-damp' (102) – the resolution is formed to go straight back down to the spring again in the moonlight. The tone describing the experiences is knowing, often seeking to turn events to comic effect. Kipling's strategy of calling himself 'the Englishman' and using the third person creates a sense of ironic distance – for example, 'The Englishman endured as long as he could – about two minutes' (101). The references to English poetry, including Browning's 'Childe Roland to the Dark Tower Came' (1855), serve to domesticate the scene. The aim is to craft something Anglo-Indian readers will respond to, and not to seek to overthrow their world.

When climbing the tower, 'the Englishman' wonders whether his feelings about it are induced by the builder's design:

> The Englishman fancied presumptuously that he had, in a way, grasped the builder's idea; and when he came to the top story and sat among the pigeons his theory was this: To attain power, wrote the builder of old, in sentences of fine stone, it is necessary to pass through all sorts of close-packed horrors, treacheries, battles and insults, in darkness and without knowledge whether the road leads upward or into a hopeless *cul-de-sac*. (98)

Readers, too, must wonder whether they are being led by the writing to take on a related perspective in these chapters. The message seems to be: do not let engagements with cultural difference and the consequences of colonial conquest disturb; if that should happen, then laugh it off, confront it, and most of all carry on and let the future take care of itself. Just because we do not share or are shocked by Kipling's attitudes does not mean that we cannot recognise the force and power of the writing. What is at issue is how these effects are achieved, and how the text resonates with its readers.

The volume builds on the excellent scholarly and critical work on Kipling from the last twenty years. This includes a six-volume selection of his letters, edited by Thomas Pinney; a new bibliography; editions of Kipling's autobiographical texts and his writings on writing; and a remarkable, ongoing online project to annotate Kipling's entire output, *The New Readers' Guide to the Works of Rudyard Kipling*. This Companion has three sections: the first looks at themes in Kipling, the second at texts, forms or chronological periods, and the third at responses to the author.

In the first essay in the collection Robert Hampson looks at the period after Kipling's arrival in London to begin a full-time literary career. His novel *The Light That Failed* examines, Hampson notes, the 'tensions and frustrations' Kipling experienced at the start of the fin-de-siècle and 'explores (though in a much more confused way) tensions and frustrations relating to sexuality and gender that Kipling also encountered'. In his chapter on Kipling, India and empire, John McBratney surveys Kipling's responses to British colonialism over the course of his career. He stresses the significance of analogy to Kipling, where a small group is said to suggest the whole, with all the strains and contradictions that attend on maintaining such correspondences. Making a claim for the significance of America for Kipling, Judith Plotz argues that though Kipling turned against the United States, it had a central role in his main relationships and his writing. It is wrong to say that he ever left the country wholly behind.

Laurence Davies explores Kipling's deep interest in technology and science. He unpacks the apparent paradox of a conservative writer fascinated by modernisation and discovery, concluding with an investigation of Kipling's contributions to the genre of science fiction. Science in Kipling is a male world, and Kaori Nagai explores both his interest in homosocial bonds and what she calls 'the role which Kipling assigns to all women'. They support men, indeed make them whole, but they are also expected to leave them free to enjoy the male worlds of work and leisure.

A writing task that the young Kipling could never have predicted he would undertake was the pamphlet *The Graves of the Fallen* (1919), written for the Imperial War Graves Commission. It set out, in a respectful and clear prose, the Commission's initial conclusions on how the cemeteries and monuments to the dead of the First World War were to look. As a member of the Commission, this was for Kipling public work with a very personal motivation. He had lost his son John at the Battle of Loos in 1915. David Bradshaw charts Kipling's changing response to war and conflict in his chapter. The writer who first sought to depict the speech and everyday lives of the ordinary 'Tommy' had later to reflect on the destruction of his kind in the industrialised killing of the Western Front.

Such topics as empire and war seem a long way from the Kipling who is one of the most popular of writers for children. And yet the topics have often been related by those who see Kipling as trying to inculcate in his young readers a sense of duty to both nation and Empire. There is much in this, but if it were all that could be said of these books it would be hard indeed to account for their enduring popularity. Jan Montefiore explores the *Jungle Books* and finds – *pace* much writing on the genre – that they offer a space in which children can discover, through a creative use of their imaginations, both the boundaries and possibilities of life.

Pleasure, energy and sheer memorability are often said to characterise Kipling's poetry. Harry Ricketts surveys Kipling's career and the key responses it has received from, in particular, T. S. Eliot, Craig Raine and Jan Montefiore. He also points out that acknowledging the depth and thoughtfulness of Kipling's reading in English poetry can add much to both the readings of individual poems and our sense of Kipling as a poet. Continuing the section devoted to particular texts, periods or forms of writing, Patrick Brantlinger explores Kipling's most famous novel – and probably his masterpiece – *Kim*, with a particular focus on the novel's Anglo-Indian context. Much less has been written about the short fiction Kipling wrote after the turn of the century than on *Kim*. My chapter looks at Kipling's stories for how they comment on the new and changing world from a position in his extended 'late career'.

The final set of chapters looks at responses to Kipling. Within a wide-ranging though precise piece, Bart Moore-Gilbert explores the responses of postcolonial, specifically South Asian writers; one point he makes is that Kipling laid down a powerful image of India as a plural nation. Monica Turci looks at Kipling and the visual, and the relationship between text and image in the illustrations of his texts, focusing on illustrations by Lockwood Kipling and Kipling himself. She also engages with a number of the major film adaptations of Kipling, exploring how Kipling's texts have been re-imagined for different media in new conditions. If the Disney film based on the *Jungle Books* meant that Kipling's creations were widely disseminated around the world, Harish Trivedi concludes the volume by drawing attention to the boundaries of Kipling's readership. While a particular image of Kipling has often stood in for the British in India – indeed, for imperialism as a whole – Trivedi points out that the vast majority of Indians have not read Kipling. Readers of serious literature in English constitute only a tiny percentage of the population, where Kipling is yet to be translated into many of the other Indian languages. While Trivedi's observation that 'interpretation from distinctly "Indian" points of view' is still awaited shows the limits of Kipling's reach, it also reminds us that the story of his reception has not yet ended. New readers will engage with the works in the future, where their reactions will take forms as yet unknown.

Notes

1 H. E. Bates, *The Modern Short Story: A Critical Survey* (London: Thomas Nelson, 1941), pp. 111, 117.

2 Robert Orledge, *Charles Koechlin (1867–1950): His Life and Works* (Chur, Switzerland: Harwood, 1988), pp. 96–7.

3 Jan Montefiore, *Rudyard Kipling* (Tavistock: Northcote House, 2007), p. 1.

4 Amit Chaudhuri, 'A Feather! A Very Feather Upon the Face!', *London Review of Books*, 22:1 (6 January 2000), p. 21.

5 Rudyard Kipling, 'Letters of Marque', in *From Sea to Sea and Other Sketches, Letters of Travel, Volume 1* (London: Macmillan, 1900), p. 103. Subsequent references are in brackets in the text.

6 Harry Ricketts, *Rudyard Kipling: A Life* (1999; New York: Carroll & Graf, 2000), pp. 105–6. See also Nigel Messenger, 'Imperial Journeys, Bodily Landscapes and Sexual Anxiety: Adela's Visit to the Marabar in *A Passage to India*', *Journal of Commonwealth Literature*, 33:1 (March 1998), pp. 99–110.

7 It is indeed possible to wonder whether, at some level, Forster was thinking of the 'Letters of Marque' when he wrote his novel. There is evidence that Forster knew his Kipling. See E. M. Forster, 'The Poems of Kipling' (1908) and 'Some books: Hilton Brown on Kipling; Keenan, Wilson and Welty' (1945) in *The Creator as Critic and Other Writings by E. M. Forster*, ed. Jeffrey M. Heath (Toronto: Dundurn, 2008), pp. 26–40, 299–302.

8 Fredric Jameson, *Modernism and Imperialism* (Derry: Field Day, 1988).

I

ROBERT HAMPSON

Kipling and the fin-de-siècle

'*Fin de siècle*', murmured Lord Henry with languid anticipation in the 1891 version of Oscar Wilde's novel *The Picture of Dorian Gray*. Wilde's novel first appeared in *Lippincott's Magazine* in June 1890.[1] Six months later, the same headlining position was occupied by the periodical version of Kipling's 'The Light That Failed'. That version and the first English edition of *The Light That Failed* (1891) would seem to be a long way from Wilde's work and his 'Wardour Street aestheticism'.[2] However, both novels involve artworks and artists, and both show how sexual identity has become problematic (and a subject for analysis) at the end of the century.[3] Kipling's novel explores what he calls the 'good love' between men and the much more difficult territory of male–female relations. One of the complicating factors, for Kipling, is women's refusal to play the role that men expect. In Maisie and 'the red-haired girl', Kipling presents his version of the 'New Woman'. At the same time, Kipling's novel serves to remind us that 'empire-building' was also part of the fin-de-siècle. He attempts to project a masculinist ideology within, and as part of, an imperialist vision. However, the attempt to assert a military model of masculinity is constantly subverted from within by traces of homoeroticism within the homosocial bondings, disquieting elements of sadism, and the haunting sense that male separateness might be a limitation rather than a strength.

Kipling in London

In Chapter 4 of *Something of Myself* (1937), Kipling describes his return to England in 1889 and his taking up residence in London. The life he describes operates on a topographical axis that he expresses as 'from Piccadilly to Villiers Street'.[4] His rooms in Villiers Street, just off the Strand, overlooked Gatti's Music-Hall, where he listens to music-hall songs in the company of an elderly barmaid, with soldiers singing 'at his elbow' (*SM* 85). The 'primitive and passionate' demotic life of the Strand (*SM* 82) is not unconnected with the 'shifting, shouting brotheldom' (*SM* 85) that characterised the Strand and Haymarket in this period. 'Piccadilly', by contrast, means the Savile Club, a gentleman's club for writers, journalists and publishers, to which he had been invited by Andrew Lang. As Elaine Showalter notes, 'A significant aspect of the construction of masculinity was the institution of "Clubland"': these clubs were 'primarily extensions of the male communities of the public schools and universities' and were predicated on the exclusion of women.[5] Where the 'smoke' and 'roar' of Gatti's represents 'the good fellowship of relaxed humanity' (*SM* 81), the more exclusive world of the club provided 'very good talk' (*SM* 90) with the likes of Besant, Gosse, Hardy and Haggard. Kipling compares this talk to 'the careless give-and-take of the atelier when the models are off their stands, and one throws bread-pellets at one's betters' (*SM* 83). Having demonstrated his familiarity with popular culture, Kipling celebrates his access to the literary establishment, but the comparison he uses asserts intimacy with the more suspect world of the artist's studio, which he then recuperates through the reassuring shared memory of public-schoolboy boisterousness. The artist's studio and the public school, with their very different cultures, were two other axes around which his early life revolved.[6]

Despite this display of his familiar acceptance by diverse communities, the chapter is punctuated by repeated allusions to emotional crises. He notes, for example, how once he 'faced the reflection of [his] own face in the jet-black mirror of the window panes for five days' (*SM* 84), and then adds, without comment, how after the fog thinned he watched a man cutting his throat in the street below his window.[7] Later, he explicitly mentions 'depression', though only glancingly, as part of the breakdown resulting from overwork combined with the excitements and distractions of the city that caused his departure from London. In the latter half of the chapter, after he has left England, he describes himself seeking out male company in the homosocial groupings of empire. In South Africa, he is introduced into 'the Naval society of Simon's Town', and in Australia he interested himself in 'the middle-aged men who had spent their lives making or managing the land' (*SM* 90–1). The chapter concludes with his encounter with General Booth, the founder of the Salvation Army, while sailing from Adelaide to Colombo, and an anecdote which ends with the judgement that Booth was 'at sea among women' (*SM* 94). The implication is that Kipling is not, but this serves only to draw attention to the peripheral position of women in the chapter. It had begun with observing the new experience of 'white women' who 'stood and waited on one behind one's chair' (*SM* 79). After that, there was only the company of 'the elderly but upright barmaid' (*SM* 81) at the music hall, the improvised monologues of the female music-hall performers, the prostitutes in the streets, and the glimpse of a woman on a boat at Adelaide with her skirt rucked up 'to her knees' (*SM* 94). It is this glimpse of leg that embarrasses Booth and leads to Kipling's judgement on Booth's lack of expertise.

The chapter does refer to one other woman: it begins with Kipling's meeting with the explorer Mary Kingsley, his invitation to her to come up to his rooms, and her realisation that this wasn't permissible in England. Andrew Lycett suggests that the meeting took place some years later – the placing of the memory at the start of the chapter implies that it occurred shortly after Kipling's arrival in England – and that Kipling has turned the story around: 'The local geography indicates that he simply accompanied Miss Kingsley a few hundred yards from Warwick Gardens to her flat in Addison Road where, with his diffidence, he probably declined to go to her rooms because he was a married man.'[8] Kipling also omits any description of his accommodation in Villiers Street. According to Lycett, 'the walls were papered in a dull green, interwoven with a gold that had lost its sheen'; and the rooms were furnished with a white sheepskin rug, Persian carpets, and 'a sofa spread with a large posteen rug, bordered with astrakhan and embroidered in rich yellow silks'.[9] This recalls Captain Sholto's chambers in Queen Ann Street, with their 'big divan covered with Persian rugs and cushions', which are presented as an example of how 'a man of fashion would live now' in James's 1885 novel *The Princess Casamassima*.[10] Kipling masculinised the rooms with military pictures on the walls. However, his tall Japanese screen and morning attire of a Japanese dressing gown suggest other, perhaps unexpected, affinities.[11] Despite this concession to orientalist aestheticism, Kipling famously expressed his impatience with London's aesthetes.[12] However, neither this impatience with London's artistic circles nor his discomfort with educated middle-class women are mentioned in this chapter.

Two more significant omissions are his engagement to Carrie Taylor and his renewed acquaintance with Florence Garrard. He had become engaged to Carrie Taylor, the sister of his friend Edmonia Hill, during his 1889 visit to America, but by early 1890 this unofficial engagement was over. He had first met Florence Garrard when he had visited his sister at the 'House of Desolation' in Southsea in 1880. He had fallen in love with her then, and she had been the inspiration for some of his early verses. In 1887, she had finished her final year at the Slade and had then moved on to another art school, the Academie Julian in Paris.[13] After their chance meeting in London early in 1890, Kipling's interest in her revived and he visited her in Paris, where she was living with Mabel Price, another painter at the Academie Julian. This became the basis for his novel *The Light That Failed*.

The Light That Failed

The Light That Failed was written in 1890 and first published in *Lippincott's Magazine* in a short version of twelve chapters. The first English edition was published by Macmillan in March 1891 (in a longer version of fifteen chapters).[14] The opening chapter is very reminiscent of Kipling's earlier work 'Baa Baa, Black Sheep' (1888), which was a fictional account of his early years at Southsea. The novel introduces Dick Heldar as an orphan staying with a young widow, Mrs Jennett, and his friendship with another orphan, Maisie. In Chapter 2, Dick is taken on as a war artist with the Nile Expedition of 1884–5. He then moves to London and sets himself up in chambers in Villiers Street, in the same Embankment Chambers that Kipling was actually living in at the time of writing. He then sets about building on the success he has had as an illustrator in magazines. This part of the novel is quite clearly a transposition of Kipling's own success as a writer and a fictionalisation of his own move to London.

The rest of the novel is divided between Dick's relationship with Maisie (who now reappears in his life) and his work as an artist. Maisie, by this time, has also become a painter, and Dick has apparently determined to court and marry her. As he puts it later, 'whether she liked it or not she should be his wife' (*LTF* 176). Maisie herself, however, shows no interest in marriage: like Dick, she is committed to her painting. In the context of what is presented as Dick's unhappy love for Maisie, he paints his masterpiece, his *Melancolia*: a work on which he expends the last of his failing sight, the result of the head wound he received during the Nile expedition. Unknown to Dick, this masterpiece has been comprehensively defaced by Bessie, a servant-girl cum prostitute whom he has used as a model, to avenge herself on Dick for preventing her relationship with his friend Torpenhow. Kipling, in other words, has produced a kind of sex-war version of Balzac's 'The Unknown Masterpiece' (1831). In the magazine version, the story ended with the tearful return of Maisie to Dick's rooms and their imminent marriage. In the book version (where the brief Preface asserts that it is the story as 'originally conceived by the Writer'), Maisie refuses to give up her painting to become Dick's nurse; Dick takes in Bessie for a while as a substitute for Maisie – until she confesses that she destroyed the painting; and Dick then goes on one last campaign, despite his blindness, to die in the arms of his friend Torpenhow.

The two versions of the novel have a curious counterpart within the novel itself. In Chapter 4, Dick offers his conception of 'Art': 'Give 'em what they know, and when you've done it once do it again.' He offers, in illustration, the story of the two versions of his sketch 'His Last Shot'. In the first version, he depicts 'a flushed, dishevelled, bedevilled scallawag, with his helmet at the back of his head, and the living fear of death in his eye' (*LTF* 49). But the art manager for the weekly magazine that was going to reproduce the work thought this was too 'brutal and coarse and violent' for the magazine's subscribers. Dick then produces a second version: the soldier is now dressed in 'a lovely red coat without a speck on it', with polished boots, clean rifle and pipeclayed helmet. For this he gets paid 'twice as much as for the first sketch' (*LTF* 49). Dick's cynical response to editorial criticism and to the pressures of the literary-artistic marketplace draws from Torpenhow the warning: 'you will fall under the damnation of the check-book, and that's worse than death' (*LTF* 51). However, while Dick changed his painting from a realistic representation to an idealised picture that matched his audience's expectations, the publication history of *The Light That Failed* suggests that although Kipling might be content to supply a happy ending for an American magazine, he insisted on a harsher and more brutal ending for book publication in England.

If *The Light That Failed* explores the tensions and frustrations that Kipling experienced in his new career as a professional writer in London, it also explores (though in a much more confused way) tensions and frustrations relating to sexuality and gender that Kipling also encountered. The oddness of this aspect of the novel was picked up in early reviews. Edmund Gosse, for example, commented on *The Light That Failed* 'with its extremely disagreeable woman, and its far more brutal and detestable man'.[15] In the same article, Gosse also drew attention to a recurrent figure in Kipling's fiction, what he calls the 'devouring female'. Similarly, the following year, Lionel Johnson was very critical of Kipling's cult of 'Strong Men': he complained that Kipling's 'glorification of the Strong, the Virile, the Robust, the Vigorous' was 'fast becoming as great a nuisance and an affectation as were the True and the Beautiful years ago'.[16]

Johnson might have had in mind lines such as the following from 'The Ballad of East and West', which first appeared in *Macmillan's Magazine* in December 1889:

> *Oh, East is East, and West is West, and never the twain shall meet,*
> *Till Earth and Sky stand presently at God's great Judgement Seat;*
> *But there is neither East nor West, Border, nor Breed, nor Birth,*
> *When two strong men stand face to face, though they come*
> *from the ends of the earth!*

The first line is, of course, very familiar and often quoted, but the second couplet offers a significant qualification, and its conception of the mutual respect and recognition of 'strong men' as a bonding that transcends 'race', creed, colour or class is a trope that recurs not only in Kipling but in the work of his friend Henry Rider Haggard, and in other imperialist writings.[17] This trope has its roots, in this period in England, in the athletic culture of the public schools. Together, these figures, the 'devouring females' and 'Strong Men', also point to recurrent concerns of the fin-de-siècle.

We are men

The Light That Failed creates a distinctively 'male' world: it is a world of action and adventure and male friendship that offers a distinctly militaristic construction of masculinity. While the first chapter revolves around the young Dick and Maisie playing with a pistol, our first sight of Dick as an adult, in Chapter 2, presents him 'in action' with the British army in Egypt as one of 'the New and Honourable Fraternity of war correspondents' (*LTF* 21). Dick is thus initiated into a doubly homosocial environment: he is part of a freemasonry of war correspondents within the larger male world of the army. And, lest one might think that war correspondents were marginal or peripheral to the military action, the narrative asserts that the correspondents 'sweated and toiled' with the soldiers (*LTF* 18). More than that, in the description of the surprise attack by the Mahdi's forces, the distinction between soldiers and civilians very quickly disappears (*LTF* 26–7). As Dick joins in the fighting, the writing conveys very clearly a sense of the excitement of killing and also hints (for example, through the use of the slang phrase 'collar low') at the continuity between school games and military action.

Dick's domestic arrangements in London reproduce this atmosphere of militaristic masculinity. Because of the nature of his paintings, his studio is decorated with 'felt-covered water-bottles, belts, and regimental badges' (*LTF* 45). His role as a military painter, in other words, justifies the conspicuous display of signs of 'masculinity' and distances him from any suggestion of epicene artiness. This is emphasised at the exhibition of his paintings through the appreciative responses of 'two artillerymen' to his picture of a field battery. Heldar's painting, like many of Kipling's early stories (such as 'Black Jack' in *Soldiers Three*), displays a special, technical knowledge, knowledge that is derived from a specifically male sphere of activity, and asserts the artist's place in this male world.

This dialogue between the artillerymen is also the summation of a series of motifs in earlier chapters. It can be seen, for example, as a direct response to the discussion about 'Art' in the previous chapter. But it also goes back to the start of Chapter 2, which not only placed Dick in the masculine setting of the British army in Egypt but also showed how he asserted his identification with that world in opposition to the world of 'the British public'. He expresses there the malicious wish that 'a few thousand of them' might be 'scattered' among the rocks of the desert with the soldiers, and he engages in the equally malicious fantasy of the 'regulation householder ... frizzling on hot gravel' (*LTF* 15). In both cases, not only is the military world celebrated but the celebration of that world is set against a criticism of the non-military world. This is explored most fully in Chapter 3 in Dick's encounter with the head of the Central Southern Syndicate, for which he has been working. In his argument with this man over his drawings, Dick imports into the metropolitan centre the behaviour he has developed at the frontiers of the Empire. Indeed, Dick brings the encounter to a solution that is satisfactory for him precisely because he adopts colonial manners in the metropolitan context. He concludes the meeting with a series of imperatives in English, Arabic and Afrikaans, positioning his employer as if he were a servant from a subject people. There was another significant exchange at an earlier point in this argument, when Dick ran his hand down the man's 'plump body': 'My goodness!' said he to Torpenhow, 'This thing's soft all over – like a woman' (*LTF* 42). The contrast between military and civilian, between colonial and metropolitan male, is presented here as a contrast between hardness and softness, which is shadowed and inflected by the contrast between male and female. Again, when Dick puts his hand on his opponent's body, he also, effectively, puts his opponent in the female position in a male/female hierarchical binary opposition. His subsequent dismissal of his opponent, using the language 'appropriate' to a colonial inferior, aligns the female other and the colonised other as in parallel subject positions. The white ruling-class male is positioned as the central reference point of an epistemology built on a system of binary oppositions in which he always occupies the privileged position; in this case, that central reference point is occupied by a specifically militaristic construction of masculinity.

The male world of Dick's domestic life is also the setting for an unselfconscious assertion of male love: 'the austere love that springs up between men who have tugged at the same oar together and are yoked by custom and use and the intimacies of toil' (*LTF* 73). The assertion that this is 'a good love' might seem to imply that there is also a 'bad love', and it is, perhaps, significant that Dick immediately after goes on to think of Maisie. The 'good love' between Dick and Torpenhow is certainly used to examine what are to Dick (and Kipling, too) the much more puzzling relations between men and women. The imagery used to describe that good love ('tugged at the same oar') gestures, once again, towards male athleticism and shared school days. The only problem is that, in rowing as a sport, the oarsmen don't actually tug 'at the same oar'. The technical imprecision is part of a fuzzy nostalgia for schooldays, and that in turn subtends nostalgia for a world of simple competition, simple loyalties, simple hostilities. This structure of feelings is manifested in the boisterous horseplay that characterises the social life of Dick and his friends (*LTF* 142) and in the representation of the various 'rows' in which these men are keen to play a part. In these 'rows', Dick's team plays an opponent who offers fierce opposition but is also marked down as inferior. The most striking instance of this juvenile structure of feeling occurs in the final chapter when Dick's train comes under attack and responds with machine guns (*LTF* 279). The world becomes a playground in which everything is subordinated to the desires and pleasures of the imperial subject. More than that, the world has been divinely appointed so that Dick's pleasure is more important than the self-defence or self-determination of other peoples.

Sea-devils and sea-angels

A basic feature of Dick's thinking is his sense of sharply divided gender roles. For Dick, the world of women is complementary – though, of course, not equal – to the world of men. Where men are soldiers (or, at least, war correspondents), women are assigned the role of nurses. Where men are painters, women can have a role as their models. The only problem is that the most important woman in the novel won't accept these roles. Thus, his friend the Nilghai offers his male fantasy: 'I've often thought, when I've seen men die out in the desert, that if the news could be sent through the world, and the means of transport were quick enough, there would be one woman at least at each man's bedside' (*LTF* 197). Maisie, however, is not interested in nursing Dick – as the men expect her to do. With much reduced expectations, Dick is obliged to turn to Bessie: 'The girl can't care … but if money can buy her to look after me she shall be bought' (*LTF* 248).

Similarly, in Chapter 8 Dick tells the story of his voyage from Lima to Auckland and how he painted a picture on the lower deck using as his model the ship's other passenger, 'a sort of Negroid-Jewess-Cuban; with morals to match': 'the woman served as the model for the devils and the angels both – sea-devils and sea-angels, and the soul half-drowned between them' (*LTF* 131–2). Despite the somewhat anxious overtones to this image, Dick presents this as an idyllic experience, with the over-defined but under-characterised 'Negroid-Jewess-Cuban' figuring as both artistic model and object of desire. Again, Maisie has a problematic relationship to these roles. In the first place, Maisie, like her friend, the red-haired girl, is a painter rather than a model, even though neither is ever taken very seriously in this role. Dick, for example, complains about the problem of visiting Maisie in her studio: 'I shall be wanting to kiss her all the time, and I shall have to look at her pictures' (*LTF* 72). To justify his low valuation of her painting, he claims that she shirks the 'hard work' of art (despite his opposite complaint that she has no time for him because of the hours she puts in at her painting). More technically, he criticises her work on the grounds that she neglects the line and 'form'. The narrative generally supports his dismissive attitude towards 'Woman's Art'. Her commitment to her art is presented as selfishness and obstinacy, and there is always the suggestion that her efforts are futile (for example, in the emphasis given to her working and re-working the chin in a single picture). A concern for the line is understandable in an artist whose drawings are destined for magazines and illustrated newspapers, but is out of touch, as Kipling must have known, with contemporary developments in French visual art.[18]

The treatment of the red-haired girl repeats this dismissive attitude towards 'Woman's Art'. To begin with, she is given a minimal role in the novel: she is never given a proper name; and, although she is called an 'impressionist', she is never allowed to discuss aesthetics with Dick or to contest his championing of realism. All the aesthetic teaching is directed by Dick towards Maisie. However, there is a certain turbulence around the red-haired girl insofar as, rather than providing a model for Dick, she takes him as the subject for the only piece of her work we see: 'It was the merest monochrome roughing in of a head, but it presented the dumb waiting, the longing, and, above all, the hopeless enslavement of the man, in a spirit of bitter mockery' (*LTF* 81). However, she doesn't take this piece of work very seriously as art, and it gradually becomes clear that her art is ultimately not the most important thing in her life. One of the few ironies in the novel is that, while Dick sees her as a rival, she is represented as being in love with him. Dick regards her as 'unwholesome' and fantasises about poisoning her on his wedding day (*LTF* 83). But this muted recognition of lesbianism is very securely contained by the narrative's own broad hints about her love for Dick. Indeed, as the narrative proceeds, her main function in the novel becomes to suggest the 'normal' response by which to judge Maisie. Thus, in Chapter 13, when Maisie delays returning to London, the red-haired girl chides her: '*I* should go back to London and see him, and I should kiss his eyes, and kiss them and kiss them until they got well again' (*LTF* 214).

The red-haired girl has one other function in the narrative, which is to prompt Dick to produce his masterpiece. At the start of Chapter 9, Maisie mentions her plan to produce a 'fancy head', contrary to all Dick's instructions to her to concentrate on 'line-work'. The red-haired girl then reveals that this plan was inspired by her reading to Maisie the description of

Melancolia from James Thomson's *The City of Dreadful Night* (1874), and she reads the relevant passages to Dick:

> 'The forehead charged with baleful thoughts and dreams,
> The household bunch of keys, the housewife's gown,
>   Voluminous indented, and yet rigid
>   As though a shell of burnished metal frigid,
> Her feet thick-shod to tread all weakness down.'

There was no attempt to conceal the scorn of the lazy voice. Dick winced.

(*LTF* 149)

Dick's appropriation of this idea for his own *Melancolia* thus enacts a complex revenge on both women. He takes over the subject in which Maisie 'means to embody herself' (*LTF* 150), and replaces her self-expression through art with his own objectification of her through his art. It is hinted later that his picture of 'a full-lipped, hollow-eyed woman who laughed from out of the canvas' with 'a sort of murderous, viperine suggestion in the poise of her head' (*LTF* 183) is based on Maisie. Dick's account to Torpenhow of his intention in this work gives a further twist to his revenge. He sees his painting of this female head as addressed to other men as a collective revenge against the women they see as having caused them to suffer: 'He shall see his trouble there, and, by the Lord Harry, just when he's feeling properly sorry for himself he shall throw back his head and laugh, – as she is laughing' (*LTF* 184). In this context, Bessie's vengeful destruction of the painting can be seen as the final term in a dialectic of revenge, and this dialectic of revenge can be seen to constitute the underlying pattern for the heterosexual relationships in the novel. Torpenhow's judgement on Bessie's attack is thus significant: 'Only a woman could have done that!' (*LTF* 186).

The men in the novel assume or assert a heterosexual orientation, but the narrative seems to find it difficult to find a form for it. Thus, for example, Dick's account of his relations with the 'Negroid-Jewess-Cuban' presents her as the object of sexual desire, but this is represented largely in terms of the jealousy of the ship's captain. The account of Dick's stay 'in Cairo, Alexandria, Ismailia, and Port Said' similarly gestures towards sexual activity by reference to the 'iniquity' and 'vices' (*LTF* 30–1) to be found there. But again Dick seems to have spent his time painting and merely watching as 'the naked Zanzibari girls danced furiously' (*LTF* 33). Thirdly, there is the curious sketchbook that Dick produces in Chapter 8:

> In it Dick had drawn in his playtime all manner of moving incidents, experienced by himself or related to him by the others, of all the four corners of the earth. But the wider range of the Nilghai's body and life attracted him most.

When truth failed here he fell back on fiction of the wildest, and represented incidents in the Nilghai's career that were unseemly, – his marriages with many African princesses, his shameless betrayal, for Arab wives, of army corps to the Mahdi, his tattooment by skilled operators in Burmah, his interview (and his fears) with the yellow headsman in the blood-stained execution-ground of Canton, and finally, the passings of his spirit into the bodies of whales, elephants, and toucans. Torpenhow from time to time had added rhymed descriptions, and the whole was a curious piece of art, because Dick decided, having regard to the name of the book, which being interpreted means 'naked', that it would be wrong to draw the Nilghai with any clothes on, under any circumstances. (*LTF* 126)

What these three incidents testify to is, first of all, the link between empire and sexual adventure; but, also, there is a clear tendency to locate sexual desire or sexual fantasy in this realm of the other. These women are, in fact, doubly other – in terms of both 'race' and gender – just as Dick's world, as I suggested earlier, is doubly homosocial. This explains the insistence on otherness in the multiply overdetermined designation of the 'Negroid-Jewess-Cuban'. At the same time, the exotically exogamous nature of these objects of sexual fantasy contrasts significantly with the curiously incestuous nature of Dick's relationship with Maisie. Thirdly, what is claimed explicitly in the third instance is that it is the male body that has been the source of inspiration, and it is the Nilghai's nakedness that recurs throughout the sketchbook.

Given all this, it is not surprising that the novel seems to be as confused as Dick about the primary heterosexual relationships it presents, and that it fails to find a form for the heterosexual orientation it asserts. On the one hand, there is Dick sending Torpenhow away to save him from the temptation of living with Bessie, and on the other, there are Torpenhow's anxieties about Dick's relationship with Maisie. In Chapter 6, he complains to the Nilghai: 'She'll spoil his hand. She'll waste his time, and she'll marry him, and ruin his work for ever. He'll be a respectable married man before we can stop him, and – he'll never go on the long trail again' (*LTF* 93). In Chapter 8, he goes so far as to warn Dick against marriage (*LTF* 138). At the same time, the novel presents Maisie's unresponsiveness to Dick as reprehensible. Similarly, the novel presents an image of hard, isolated masculinity as something admirable ('Dick had never asked anybody to help him in his joys or his sorrows' (*LTF* 172)), but, just occasionally, it presents this life as emotionally deprived: '"It gives a lonely man a sort of hankering doesn't it?" said Torpenhow, piteously' (*LTF* 165), as he talks of watching Bessie moving about his rooms. And yet the narrative can find no place for women except as a housekeeper or nurse – the two roles that Bessie plays.

The novel is most confused about Maisie. The first chapter already suggests some of the problems she poses for Dick. His first response is significant: he 'mistrusted her profoundly, for he feared that she might interfere with the small liberty of action left to him' (*LTF* 4). This anticipates the response of Torpenhow, but the problem that Maisie poses for Dick is, in fact, exactly the opposite. Her standing up to Mrs Jennett shows the strength of Maisie's will, and what the narrative tries to present as Dick's 'love' for Maisie comes across more often as a conflict of wills. When they meet again in Chapter 5, for example, Dick observes: 'It's the same Maisie, and it's the same me ... We've both nice little wills of our own, and one or other of us has to be broken' (*LTF* 71). In other words, Maisie's separate identity seems to be a threat or a challenge to Dick. Certainly, his 'love' for her tends to express itself as the desire to impose a role upon her. Thus it is perhaps significant that this 'love' for Maisie first reveals itself at the moment he learns that she is planning to leave Mrs Jennett's. His immediate response is to cast her into the stereotyped role of the 'beloved': he begins to call her 'darling'; he helps her down a slope, 'a descent that she was quite capable of covering at full speed' (*LTF* 11); and he feels compelled to comment on the 'prettiness' of her hands. Similarly, in Chapter 5, he contemplates how he might 'adorn Maisie barbarically with jewellery' – 'a thick gold necklace round that little neck, bracelets upon the rounded arms, and rings of price upon her hands' – even though he knows that the real Maisie 'would laugh at golden trappings' (*LTF* 73). Not only does he feel compelled to act out a role that he knows to be inappropriate, but also, interestingly, as the word 'barbarically' suggests, he partly recognises that he is attempting to convert the sisterly Maisie into an exotic other. By contrast, later, when he is talking seriously to Maisie, he almost apologises to her: 'you're so like a man that I forget when I am talking to you' (*LTF* 107). Clearly Maisie and the red-haired girl represent the 'New Woman' who breaks the rigid categorisation of 'masculine'/'feminine' by which Dick lives. His response to this challenge is, as we have seen, first to try to impose a stereotyped 'feminine' role upon her, that treats her as a kind of invalid; then he plays briefly with the idea of seeing her as exotically other; then he tries to deny that she is 'a woman' (*LTF* 108); and, finally, like the novel itself, he accepts her as a woman but presents her as destructive. Thus the accident with the gun in the first chapter ('Oh, Dick! have I killed you?') ironically foreshadows what the novel presents as Maisie's ultimate role in Dick's life: Dick's final journey to the battlefield can be read as suicide, but it is also the suicide to which Maisie has driven him.

In the end, the novel seems to share Dick's confusion: the sense that only 'damned obstinacy' keeps Maisie from accepting Dick's love, and that

Maisie is selfish to reject him. The novel's conclusion is permeated by a tone of male self-pity in relation to women, and the final chapters can be read as a celebration of male comradeship as Dick finds refuge at last in the world of men.

Conclusion

In the novel's blaming of women – of Maisie for her selfishness, of Bessie for her destructiveness – one female is exempted. The novel presents Dick as an orphan, and its first criticism of Mrs Jennett is that she was 'supposed to stand in the place of a mother' but didn't. It might be argued, however, that she stands 'in the place of a mother' in quite another sense. Kipling's own mother, of course, wasn't dead, but very much alive, when he was left behind in the house at Southsea. In 'Baa Baa, Black Sheep', there is one break in the impersonal narrative of Punch and his sister, and this occurs in the account of the night before they are to be sent back to England. The parents are described as watching their sleeping children: 'They were standing over the cots in the nursery late at night, and I think that Mamma was crying softly.' As other critics have noted, it is very difficult to read the tone and significance of that 'I think'. *The Light That Failed* carries a dedicatory poem which has the refrain 'Mother o' mine, O mother o' mine'. The poem concludes:

> If I were damned of body and soul,
> I know whose prayer would make me whole,
> *Mother o' mine, O mother o' mine!*

And curiously, in Chapter 15, when Torpenhow and the others have gone off to war, Dick gets Alf Beeton to sing him eight verses of 'A Boy's Best Friend is His Mother'.

The opening chapter presents very clearly a situation of extreme emotional deprivation. The mother who is no mother has her failings detailed in what seems an echo of the words of St Francis of Assisi:

> Where he had looked for love, she gave him first aversion and then hate. Where he ... had sought a little sympathy, she gave him ridicule ...

The narrative decides that the result of all this is that Dick acquired 'the power of living alone' (*LTF* 3). In other words, the opening chapter describes a damaging childhood, but the narrative subsequently never considers that Dick might actually have been damaged by it. It notes that Dick learned self-sufficiency, but never questions whether that characteristic, which he has acquired through neglect and abuse, might be a factor in his difficulties with women. There is a lack of reflexivity in the narrative, and part of the explanation for this is ideological. In a culture in which 'the power of living alone' is valued as an aspect of 'masculinity', it is difficult to see that this 'power' might have more to do with emotional damage and compensation for emotional damage – with weakness, in short – than with strength.[19] Another part of the explanation, of course, is that this particular construction of masculinity was reinforced by subsequent experiences – and, in particular, by his time at public school. The narrative notes that this 'power' was of service to him 'when he went to a public school and the boys laughed at his clothes, which were poor in quality and much mended' (*LTF* 3). In a similar turning of abuse into valued experience, Dick suggests to Maisie that the beatings he has had at school have put Mrs Jennett's beatings into perspective: '"She doesn't hurt," he explained' (*LTF* 5). However, the sentences that follow immediately after this betray exactly how he has been 'hurt': the recurrent description of Dick as 'savage in soul' suggests one of the side effects of his 'living alone'. This 'savagery' was manifested at school in the way he would hit the smaller boys 'cunningly and with science' (*LTF* 5). And this skill and connoisseurship in beating is not restricted to school. The passage continues: 'The same spirit made him more than once try to tease Maisie, but the girl refused to be made unhappy' (*LTF* 5). In the serial version, Maisie was unable to maintain this resistance. When she returns to Dick at the end and surrenders to him, she says: 'Afterwards you shall beat me. I think it would do me good. I wants to be beated. Oh, Dick, I have been such a bad, double-bad villain!' Dick clearly seems to have acquired a certain sadistic tendency through the emotional neglect and the regime of beatings at Mrs Jennett's and at school, which the serial text reads as normal heterosexuality; conversely, when it comes to tender or softer emotions, as the narrator observes, 'he had no knowledge to put his feelings in words' (*LTF* 9) and, at the start of the novel and the end of the serial text, he required Maisie to help him out.

The opening chapter, then, presents the picture of a severely damaged child, but the subsequent narrative never connects this damage with the adult's personality, and it fails to do this largely because that personality is assumed to be merely normal 'masculinity', since it corresponds to a construction of masculinity that is ideologically presented and socially reinforced within the culture. At the same time, the connection between the childhood experience and the adult personality is blurred in part because the narrative elides the period of public school training as it jumps from Maisie's departure from Mrs Jennett's to Dick's presence in Egypt. The account of those schooldays needed to be told, but had to wait until *Stalky & Co.* By then the focus on empire had taken over from other fin-de-siècle concerns.

Notes

1 Oscar Wilde, *The Picture of Dorian Gray*, ed. Isobel Murray (Oxford University Press, 1981), p. 179. Oscar Wilde, 'The Picture of Dorian Gray', *Lippincott's Magazine*, 46:271 (July 1890), pp. 3–100. For an account of the textual history of Wilde's novel, see Donald Lawler, *An Inquiry into Oscar Wilde's Revisions of 'The Picture of Dorian Gray'* (New York, Garland Publishing, 1988).

2 Unsigned review of 'Dorian Gray', *Daily Chronicle*, 30 June 1890, p. 7.

3 Sexological works of the period included Havelock Ellis's *Man and Woman* (London: Walter Scott, 1894) and his collaboration with John Addington Symonds, *Sexual Inversion* (first published in German translation by Georg H. Wigands Verlag, Leipzig, in 1896). For a discussion of the similarities between *The Picture of Dorian Gray* and *The Light That Failed*, see D. C. Rose, 'Blue Roses and Green Carnations: Three Rudyard Kipling and Oscar Wilde Textual Interactions', *Kipling Journal*, 76 (June 2002), pp. 28–38.

4 Rudyard Kipling, *Something of Myself*, ed. Robert Hampson (Harmondsworth: Penguin, 1987), p. 84. All subsequent references in this chapter are to this edition and in the text as *SM*.

5 Elaine Showalter, *Sexual Anarchy: Gender and Culture at the Fin de Siècle* (London: Virago, 1992), pp. 11–12.

6 Like Ford Madox Ford, Kipling had had a Pre-Raphaelite childhood: three of the Macdonald sisters had married artists: Edward Burne-Jones, Edward Poynter and Lockwood Kipling. Kipling escaped from Southsea for a month each year to the home of his uncle, Edward Burne-Jones.

7 For Kipling's sensitivity to the weather in England, see his letter to John Addington Symonds (15 October 1889): 'There is no light in this place, and the people are savages living in black houses.' Quoted by Andrew Lycett, *Rudyard Kipling* (London: Weidenfeld & Nicolson, 1999), p. 199.

8 Lycett, *Rudyard Kipling*, p. 268.

9 *Ibid.*, pp. 186–7.

10 Henry James, *The Princess Casamassima* (New York: Harper & Row, 1968), p. 183.

11 Lycett, *Rudyard Kipling*, p. 187.

12 See, for example, his poem 'In Partibus' with its nostalgia for men of the Indian army. Andrew Rutherford (ed.), *Early Verse by Rudyard Kipling, 1789–1889: Unpublished, Uncollected and Rarely Collected Poems* (Oxford University Press, 1986), pp. 470–2.

13 Of the private schools, the Academie Julian reproduced most faithfully the discipline of the Beaux-Arts. If one wanted access to the most successful artists of the day, it was the place to enrol. The school's brochure prided itself upon its segregated classes, where 'in an atmosphere of impeccable character and advanced technical values,' a woman could acquire 'a professional attitude …' See Carolyn Burke, *Becoming Modern: The Life of Mina Loy* (New York: Farrar, Straus and Giroux, 1996), p. 75. As Burke notes, when Mina Loy became an art student in Paris in 1900, female art students were still regarded ambivalently (p. 74).

14 Rudyard Kipling, *The Light That Failed* (London: Macmillan, 1899). All subsequent references in this chapter are to this edition and in the text as *LTF*.

15 Edmund Gosse, 'Rudyard Kipling', *Century Magazine*, 42 (October 1891), pp. 901–10. See Roger Lancelyn Green, *Kipling: The Critical Heritage* (London: Routledge and Kegan Paul, 1971), pp. 105–24, p. 116.

16 Lionel Johnson, Review of Rudyard Kipling, *Barrack-Room Ballads*, *Academy*, 40 (28 May 1892), pp. 509–10. See Green, *Kipling: The Critical Heritage*, pp. 98–103, p. 102.

17 Consider, for example, the account of the hiring of Umbopa in *King Solomon's Mines*. See Henry Rider Haggard, *King Solomon's Mines*, ed. Robert Hampson (Harmondsworth: Penguin, 2007), p. 40.

18 Impressionism had been establishing itself since the early 1860s. The eighth and last Impressionist exhibition took place in Paris in 1884, and, with the founding of the New English Art Club in the same year, Impressionist influences were beginning to be felt in England.

19 For an account of Conrad's fiction in relation to 'a utopian masculine identity' as an 'ideal of detached freedom', see Scott McCracken, '"A Hard and Absolute Condition of Existence": Reading Masculinity in *Lord Jim*', *The Conradian*, 17.2 (Spring, 1993), pp. 17–38, p. 33.

2

JOHN McBRATNEY

India and empire

The writings of Rudyard Kipling are thematically more various than the single topic of empire to which they are often reduced. Nonetheless, the British Empire of the late nineteenth and early twentieth centuries stood as the dominant concern of his prose and poetry throughout much of his career. He came of age as a writer when Britain was awakening to the advent of the 'new imperialism' – that phase of British imperial history, from 1882 to 1906, during which Britain, prompted by the rise of European imperial rivals and by the outbreak of nationalist uprisings throughout the Empire, came to adopt a more self-conscious imperial policy.[1] During that time, Kipling emerged as the unofficial laureate of empire, the writer who most clearly articulated the spirit of imperial consolidation and who most deeply inspired proponents of a more deliberately conceived and energetically prosecuted imperial project. When the new imperialism began to fade in popularity after Britain's indecisive victory in the Second South African War (1899–1902), he continued to advocate an assertive imperialism, but with increasing pessimism – less as a tonic for British expansionism than as an antidote to the national degeneration that he and others saw in Britain's inept performance in the war against the Boers. In the last two decades of his life, when imperial Britain was clearly waning, a bitter Kipling largely forsook his vision of a wide and powerful empire.

That vision had its origins in his early experience in India. Born in 1865 in Bombay, he spent the first six years of his life in that city, more attuned to Indian than to English ways. Although his parents were Anglo-Indian, he nonetheless spoke Hindustani as his first language and spent much of his time playing with the family's Indian servants, moving fluidly between indigenous and colonial cultures in ways that were to inform his art and vision of empire profoundly. As his memoir, *Something of Myself* (1937), reveals, as part of his cross-cultural play he devised a game in which he 'set up business alone as a trader with savages':

My apparatus was a coconut shell strung on a red cord, a tin trunk, and a piece of packing-case which kept off any other world. Thus fenced about, everything inside the fence was quite real, but mixed with the smell of damp cupboards. If the bit of board fell, I had to begin the magic all over again ... The magic, you see, lies in the ring or fence that you take refuge in.[2]

Although he was torn from the pleasures of a childhood in India to spend a decade at school in England, he returned to the subcontinent as a sixteen-year-old, this time to Lahore and Allahabad, to work for seven years as a journalist for two Anglo-Indian newspapers. It would be untrue to say that, at this point in his life, he possessed a comprehensive conception of the Empire; observing and writing about official and indigenous life in north-west India, he was too immersed in the parochial affairs of that part of the imperial world to entertain such broad views. According to *Something of Myself*, it was only when he settled in London in 1889, while working on 'The English Flag', that he began to think about answering, as fully as possible, what became the key question in that poem: 'What do they know of England who only England know'?[3] Thus, he came upon the 'notion of trying to tell to the English something of the world outside England – not directly but by implication'. As he fleshed out the idea:

Bit by bit, my original notion grew into a vast, vague conspectus – Army and Navy Stores List if you like – of the whole sweep and meaning of things and effort and origins throughout the Empire. I visualised it, as I do most ideas, in the shape of a semi-circle of buildings and temples projecting into a sea – of dreams.[4]

In the succeeding years of his career, it was the vastness of Kipling's rendering of empire that fired his readers' sense of wonder. The reviewer Andrew Lang spoke for a generation of readers when he proclaimed, 'There has, indeed, arisen a taste for exotic literature: people have become alive to the strangeness and fascination of the world beyond the bounds of Europe and the United States.'[5]

As the descriptions of both his childhood play and his imperial dream suggest, Kipling's imagination was fundamentally spatial in character. Taken together, the two descriptions may seem to present antithetical impulses of spatial configuration, the boy wishing to cordon off magical enclaves of intercultural exchange and the adult desiring to project imperial architecture into a visionary sea. The two, however, can be seen to work together in the writer's envisioning of empire, the child's small performance of cross-cultural rapprochement suggesting, by way of analogy, the adult's vast structure of imperial enlargement. As I hope to show, this pattern of analogy – of small suggesting large – served as a key structural figure within his artistic conception of empire, one that had significant ramifications for both his personal sense of self and his understanding of Britain's imperial identity. Analogy functions in his work primarily as a means of integrating the various parts of a far-flung empire, but as the strain in joining tiny to grand suggests, a central tension threatens to disrupt his attempts at integration. As Kipling sought in his art to connect the small with the large, he found resistances within that project that took two forms: a tendency among imperial insiders to promote ethnic or racial exclusivity and a tendency among imperial outsiders to cling to forms of national particularism. As I move through the main geography of Kipling's unfolding imperial oeuvre, passing from India to 'Greater Britain' to South Africa and finally briefly to England, and discussing with each a representative work, I will emphasise both the large ambition and the persistent complications of his imperial dream.[6]

India

To understand the function of analogy in Kipling's imperial works, it is necessary to look more closely at the magical ring of play to which he was drawn as a child in India. As a version of that play, Kipling recalls in his memoir that as a child he accompanied Meeta, his bearer, into 'little Hindu temples where, being below the age of caste, I held his hand and looked at the dimly seen, friendly Gods'.[7] As Angus Wilson has argued, this experience, in which the young, casteless Rudyard was able to enter freely into Indian spaces off-limits to Anglo-Indian grown-ups, constituted a kind of 'Paradise' to which he as an adult wished to return but from which he was barred.[8] The sense of being cast out of Eden, when he and his sister were left by their parents with guardians in England to attend school, burdened him with an abiding sense of dislocation – of not knowing to which society he belonged. When he returned to India as a young man to work as a newsman for the Lahore *Civil and Military Gazette*, he enjoyed an uncertain relationship to the Anglo-Indian establishment. Although the *Gazette* was an official newspaper, Kipling, as a subeditor, was left off the Civil List, which established the status of most Britons in India.[9] Moreover, as a bright, curious reporter who revelled in exploring 'native' haunts that no respectable Anglo-Indian gentleman would be caught entering, he was regarded as a figure of suspicion in some quarters. Yet he also wanted ardently to belong to 'the inner Ring',[10] the coterie of expert professionals who did the hard, practical, day-to-day work of running an empire and who embodied what Kipling called 'the Law', that set of moral principles that formed the bedrock order of the British Raj, and, by extension, western civilisation. The sometimes irritating knowingness so prevalent in the narrators of his youthful fiction can be seen as a form of compensation for his inability to feel himself a secure member of the inner Ring. Unwilling to go native and yet unable to attain the status of a pukka sahib, he felt stranded between the unofficial world of the indigenous and the official realm of Anglo-India.

Freemasonry – he was a Mason all his adult life – represented a means by which he could achieve the sense of belonging he craved. With its secret rituals, communal loyalty and ethic of universal brotherhood, it fed his need for inclusion and mutuality. Kipling first joined the Masons in 1885, becoming a member of the only lodge in Lahore that admitted Britons and Indians together as equals. Although outside the walls of the lodge racial and political differences divided these members, inside they met, as Kipling's poem 'The Mother-Lodge' attests, as '"*Brother*[s]" ... *upon the Level*'.[11] In ensconcing a rare egalitarianism within an enclave of ritual, the lodge in Lahore was able to blend together the parts of his Indian experience that he could not combine in the real world: cross-cultural 'play' within a fenced-off arena; intimacy with Indians within a casteless, edenic realm; and membership within an inner Ring of adult worthies. Throughout his fiction, Kipling was drawn to delineating these Masonic-like spaces of magical fraternity – what I have called elsewhere 'felicitous spaces'[12] – not only to enact psychological integration for the individual but also to represent possibilities of cultural integration for the Empire. We can see these possibilities most clearly in felicitous realms like the spy ring of the *Sat Bhai* ('Seven Brothers') in *Kim*, where the eponymous hero and Hurree Mookerjee meet as rough equals. There Kipling was able to depict characters of hybrid identity and broad cross-cultural knowledge who might serve as models of a new, more savvy and effective imperial servant. Throughout his writings, Kipling offered these small magical rings of egalitarianism, cosmopolitan understanding and efficacious service as analogies for a larger empire of comparable unity and strength. Yet these writings also suggest the ethical and ideological ambiguities to which the use of analogy can give rise. A reading of one of his finest Indian stories, 'The Man Who Would Be King' (1888), reveals these uncertainties.

The tale concerns the tragic adventures of Daniel Dravot and Peachey Carnehan, two ex-soldiers, loafers and confidence men, who journey into remote Kafiristan in north-eastern Afghanistan, establish themselves as kings of that region, and then, through Dan's hubristic desire to rule as a god, fall from power. Although Dan is killed by the Kafirs, Peachey lives to return to Lahore, where he tells his story to the newspaper editor who had helped the two travellers launch their conquest of Kafiristan three years earlier. The story is a frame-narrative, in which the editor serves as the 'I' narrator of the frame and Peachey as the narrator of the central, framed tale.

Although the exploits of Dan and Peachey are clearly fantastical, they are nonetheless based, as Edward Marx has shown, on Kipling's careful study of the accounts of British travellers who had either heard about or actually visited Kafiristan (now known as Nuristan).[13] These accounts revealed the inhabitants to be a fair-skinned, pre-Islamic people supposedly descended from Alexander the Great, whose army had settled for a time in this secluded region. The accounts also discussed this frontier population as a possible buffer between the British and Russian empires. As 'The Man Who Would Be King' bears out, Kipling was acutely aware of the geopolitical realities that form the context for his protagonists' activities in Kafiristan. As Dan, at the height of his grandiosity, dilates upon the empire he and his comrade hope to found, he imagines the great army they will gather for British India's protection: 'Two hundred and fifty thousand men, ready to cut in on Russia's right flank when she tries for India!'[14] Later, when the Kafirs are closing in on Dan and Peachey to punish them for their arrogance, Dan laments, 'This business is our Fifty-Seven' – a clear reference to the Indian 'Mutiny' of 1857–8.[15] These two passages taken together suggest British India's greatest strategic concern during the 1880s. While Britain was consolidating its own empire, Russia was also expanding its imperium, establishing the state of Turkestan in Central Asia and building a railroad to the edge of the Anglo-Russian frontier – actions that Britain interpreted as a possible prelude to a military thrust southward that, when combined with a second Indian rebellion, might result in the overthrow of British rule in India.

Given the clear setting of 'The Man Who Would Be King' within a world of imperial rivalry, many of its readers have seen in the rise and fall of Dan and Peachey's dream of conquest an analogy with the fortunes of the British Empire in India.[16] These readers, however, have failed to agree on what this analogy means. In their grand ambition and surprising resourcefulness, are Dan and Peachey, despite their lowly status, meant to be heroic embodiments of what a revitalised British India could be? Or are they prideful fools who emblematise what the British Empire may become if she disregards the constraints of the Law? It is hard to say. Because of its ingenious frame-structure and its indeterminacies of tone and point of view, the story 'changes its prevailing colour, like an opal, whenever it is read'.[17] Yet it is possible to see in the tale a paradoxical, 'double' analogy: both a call to action and a cautionary tale directed at the governors of British India.

As the former, it is the story of two 'strong men', men of independent action who, throughout Kipling's verse and fiction, are seen to bend the Law in order to strengthen it.[18] They are in a sense throwbacks to the 'Punjab style' of John and Henry Lawrence, whose success within the 'non-regulation' province of the Punjab during the 1840s inspired Anglo-Indians of the

1880s, including Kipling, to yearn for a rejection of the administrative style of impersonal, centralised governance dominant at the time in British India and a revival of the personal, decentralised rule of the Lawrence brothers.[19] Although some readers doubt that Kipling would have ever intended that tramps like Dan and Peachey be seen as heroes, in *From Sea to Sea* he semiseriously recommends a period of vagabondage as useful field instruction for trainees in the Intelligence and Political Department.[20] The jest of 'The Man Who Would Be King' is that it is precisely the raffish Dan and Peachey who bring a modicum of order and justice to Kafiristan. Impatient with the timid, complacent, rule-bound government of British India, Kipling seems to be suggesting that what the Empire needs is more Dans and Peacheys let loose upon the North-West Frontier.

Yet the story of these strong men is also minatory. It is one thing to practice a tactical irregularity within the broad limits of the Law; it is another thing entirely to violate the Law outright, embodied, in Dan and Peachey's case, in their 'Contrack'.[21] Although Dan falls ostensibly because he disobeys the contract's injunction to abstain from contact with women (his bride's nuptial bite draws the blood that belies his divinity), he in fact stumbles because he trespasses against the code's first commandment: that he and Peachey *'will settle this matter* [of governing Kafiristan] *together'*.[22] Dan's defiance of the need for mutual regard between his partner and himself points to an even more fundamental abuse of the need for mutual respect between the two Englishmen and their Kafir counterparts, demonstrated by Dan's flouting of the Masonic ritual that the Englishmen and their subjects mysteriously share. It is Dan's ability to produce the Masonic 'Master's Mark' in the nick of time that seals his fraudulent identity – and outrageous performance – as Alexander's godly descendent. By manipulating the Masonic ritual for his own gain, Dan corrupts the space of felicitous, intercultural exchange that stood for Kipling as the desideratum of a successful empire. Unlike Kim, Dan lacks the imagination to engage in the generous give and take across cultures that for his creator formed the basis of the ideal imperial servant. Kipling implies that the brand of exclusionism that Dan practices – his refusal to include Kafir strong men honourably within his rule – is, in miniature, what the British Indian government practices, too. Ironically, as his imperial vision matures, Kipling will come to endorse a form of the exclusionism that he reveals in Dan.

Greater Britain

In 1891, the American writer Brander Matthews visited Kipling in London. While the two were discussing 'the insularity of the British', Kipling remarked,

'Well, I'm not an Englishman, you know; I'm a colonial!'[23] Louis Cornell has observed that, for the rest of his life after India, Kipling remained, in some sense, 'a returned Anglo-Indian'.[24] Yet at the same time he had, as we have seen, 'two / Separate sides to [his] head'.[25] On his return voyage from India in 1889 through East Asia and North America, and on his visit to South Africa, Australia, New Zealand, Ceylon and India in 1891, Kipling saw much more of the world, and particularly of the British Empire, than he had ever glimpsed before. With this greater grasp of global realities, he drew up that 'vague, vast conspectus' of empire to which he dedicated much of his life and work thereafter. In drafting this survey, he began to adjust his sense of both national audience and imperial identity. While in India, his primary readership had been Anglo-Indian; even then, however, he had also been eying his growing audience in England. In setting up shop in London, Kipling came to see these readers as his new main audience. As Brander Matthews suggests, he often fumed at the provincialism of the English, but he was determined, as the laureate of empire, to arouse in them a more intense awareness of their membership within 'Greater Britain':[26] the white, English-speaking nations of Great Britain, South Africa, the Australian colonies, New Zealand and Canada.

In 1896, Kipling published *The Seven Seas*, a volume of poems whose title referred implicitly to the ocean journeys that had transformed his vision of empire.[27] Many of these poems feature the actors who made this enlarged vision possible. One set, replacing the soldiers of his earlier works, comprises the seamen who sail forth from Great Britain to extend the reach and power of the Empire. Another set includes colonials from the so-called 'white settler' nations who call upon the English to recognise their shared commitment to imperial unity. The poem 'The Native-Born' (1895) combines agents from both these sets. Like 'The Man Who Would Be King', it is written with a keen sense of the real imperial world from which it originates and to which it speaks. In 1884, in response to the rise of large, unified, imperial nation states such as Russia, the United States, Germany and Italy, the Imperial Federation League had been founded in London to promote the political and economic integration of the Empire. Although it was disbanded in 1893, the issues it raised continued to be debated.[28] In September 1895, the debate centred on whether the self-governing colonies ought to help fund the Royal Navy; a month later, Kipling published 'The Native-Born' in enthusiastic support of the idea.[29] Like 'The Man Who Would Be King', the poem rests on the idea that the actions of a small group of men might analogise the activities of an empire. As in the short story, the use of analogy in the poem gives rise to some perplexity.

In 'The Native-Born', Britons born and bred in 'the Four New Nations' (Australia, New Zealand, Canada and South Africa) toast the queen, their

'English brother' and themselves, pledging to join in hauling the '*cable-tow*' of the imperial ship of state.[30] The ceremony of the toast and the warm familial language suggest the egalitarian ambiance of Freemasonry. In turn, the lodge-like gathering of men stands as a simulacrum of the larger Empire. Yet tensions divide the fraternity even within the ritual space of the toast, for despite the efforts of the native-born to befriend their English brother, 'he does not understand'. Like many writers, historians and politicians in the latter part of the nineteenth century, Kipling believed that, if the Empire were to be rehabilitated, the healthy imperial margins would have to assist the sickly imperial core. In 'The Native-Born', it is the men from the imperial periphery who take the initiative in urging federation. Yet the insular Englishman responds either in confusion or with indifference.

But the difficulty goes deeper. If the English brother balks at the invitation of his country-born brethren to unite, these brethren are, in their own way, reluctant to sever ties to their indigenous lands:

> They [the native-born] change their skies above them,
>   But not their hearts that roam!
> We learned from our wistful mothers
>   To call old England 'home' ...

Ambiguities abound here. Pronouns shift uncertainly between the third and first person. The hearts that 'roam' suggest a restlessness at odds with the fixity of their affections. The mothers are 'wistful' either for England or for sons whose allegiance has strayed beyond the colonial family to the extended imperial family. And finally the inverted commas around 'home' imply its fraught status: drawn to the land of their birthplace, the native-born can embrace the idea of an English home only awkwardly. Although the poem ends with a rousing cheer for a common endeavour – '*By the might of our cable-tow (Take hands!)*' – the poem reveals attitudes that resist a sense of imperial commonality: the ethnic exclusivity of the uncomprehending English and the national particularism of the provincial native-born.

The poem also reveals an element of authorial self-suppression: the native-born Kipling's exclusion of his own birthplace, India, from the 'New Nations'. During the 1890s, Kipling's conception of empire had clearly changed from one based on an intimate relationship with India to one based on an abstract racial community among Anglo-Saxons: in the words of the poem, '*six white men arow*'. The gains and losses of this shift were clear. If he had at last joined an inner Ring of white men, he had in effect abandoned the world of Meeta, his childhood bearer. Moreover, if his geographical sense of empire had widened, his cultural sense of the imperial – his entertainment of the possibility of inter-imperial dialogue among persons of different ethnic or racial backgrounds – had shrunk. In 'The Native-Born', the device of integrative analogy – the toast among six men as a sign of future federation among six nations – operates with mixed results not only within the narrow limits of the albocracy the poem sketches but also in the larger empire whose diverse peoples the author is unwilling to affirm.

South Africa

Having in a sense become the citizen of a white empire, Kipling nonetheless hankered after a home in some corner of it. In 1900, the mining magnate and imperialist politician Cecil Rhodes, with whom Kipling had become close friends, built a home, The Woolsack, on his estate in Cape Town, South Africa, for the Kipling family, and every English winter from that year to 1908 they stayed there happily. Yet South Africa never became the home Kipling craved, nor did he write about it, as his South African friends hoped he might, in the way he wrote about India – with a deep, complex sense of its people and their history.[31] Rhodes, who had invited his friend to love the land and its inhabitants, had also asked him to value the country as a salient part of the British Empire; it was finally in the latter way that Kipling was attracted. Although he wrote sensitively about South Africa's open, arid landscape, he rarely wrote compellingly about its people, whether the Afrikaners or the English. (Indigenous Africans are entirely absent from his stories and poems.) At the turn of the century, it was South Africa as the new linchpin of empire – as a guardian of the long sea-route to India; as a rich land ripe for English mining and farming; and, in Rhodes's dream, as the southern terminus of a Cape-to-Cairo railway that would neatly divide the French and German empires in Africa and thus secure the continent for Britain – that finally inspired him.

When war broke out between the Boer republics and Great Britain in 1899, Kipling was sanguine about a British victory and, with it, the inclusion of the Afrikaner states of the Transvaal and the Orange Free State within a federated British South Africa. Although he was disgusted by Britain's prosecution of the war and sickened by the peace treaty of 1902, which, in his eyes, ceded too much political control to the vanquished Boers, he was buoyed by the contribution of colonial soldiers from Australia, New Zealand and Canada to the war effort. Like his friends the 'constructivist' politicians Alfred Milner and Joseph Chamberlain, he believed that strong colonial assistance during the war portended firm colonial sympathy for imperial cooperation, including reciprocal tariff preferences and shared military expenses, after the war.

The Five Nations (1903), which collected many of the poems he wrote about the war, spoke to Kipling's hopes for post-bellum collaboration between Britain and its white settler colonies. In 'The Parting of the Columns' (1903), he returns, with renewed confidence, to a theme broached in 'The Native-Born': imperial federation. The later poem represents the mirror image of the earlier, for in it the English implicitly apologise to their overseas brethren for their former narrow-mindedness and, in their newly enlightened condition, acknowledge the power of those brethren to re-energise the imperial centre. In the poem, a group of English soldiers extend a hearty farewell to their colonial comrades-in-arms as they leave for their homelands in Australia, New Zealand and Canada. They thank the colonials for teaching them 'how to camp and cook 'an steal a horse, and scout'.[32] They are also grateful to the colonials for stirring their imaginations with stories about their home countries. They hint, too, that they will regard the colonies differently in future, reading the newspapers with a fresh eye to 'all those friendly dorps where you was born an' nursed' and promising that, after the war, they will chase 'the girls your side the drift'. In this teasing threat, the poem holds out the possibility of emigration to the colonies – for Kipling, one of the most promising means of linking the imperial periphery to Great Britain. The poem ends with the familiar analogy of small implying large: 'The world's no bigger than a kraal. Good-bye – good luck to you!'[33] Within the poem, we find many of the elements associated with the Masonic lodge – camaraderie, ritual performance (here of leave-taking), membership within a ring and unity in diversity – that we have seen elsewhere in Kipling's delineation of empire.

In 'The Parting of the Columns', the impediments that clog fraternal intimacy in 'The Native-Born' seem to have melted away in the bonhomie of soldierly *esprit de corps*. Yet the seeds of an obstructive particularism are nonetheless there. In the English soldiers' estimation of the colonials ('All independent, queer an' odd, but most amazin' new'), the poem unconsciously hints at tendencies within the white Dominions that, in the post-war period, came to impede broad inter-imperial agreement on tariff preferences and military spending. In their nationalism, invigorated ironically by their spirited contribution to the fighting in South Africa, the colonials were too 'independent' to cater for the economic and political plans of English constructivists like Milner and Chamberlain. Busy with federalising their own nations, intent on protecting their own national economies, interested in commercial ties with nations nearer to home than Great Britain, they were too wary, after the war, to commit themselves wholeheartedly to metropolitan ideas about imperial cooperation.[34]

Conclusion

In September 1902, shortly after the end of the South African War, the Kiplings moved into Bateman's in Sussex. Excited by their new home, Kipling wrote to a friend, 'England is a wonderful land. It is the most marvelous of all foreign countries that I have ever been in.'[35] The irony is telling. Although this house, which he dearly loved, would be his last, his idea of home always carried an undercurrent of willed attachment. Nonetheless, he felt he belonged in Sussex, and with his thoughts centring more and more on England, he gradually abandoned his original dream of empire. In *Puck of Pook's Hill* (1906) and *Rewards and Fairies* (1910), two of his finest short story collections written after the South African War, one might argue that he continued to ponder imperial themes, but he did so through the medium of time rather than that of space, introducing an elegiac tone into his tales that muffles their imperial point. In both collections, the narrator Puck takes his children-auditors, Dan and Una, back into the English past so that they may claim it as theirs. In both sets of tales, Kipling again uses analogy to underscore an imperial message. In 'On the Great Wall' in *Puck of Pook's Hill*, for example, the efforts of the centurion protagonists, Parnesius and Pertinax, to protect the Roman Empire's northern frontier represent, in miniature, Britain's endeavour to defend the margins of its present-day empire, whether in India or in South Africa. The meeting of the two native-born soldiers, Parnesius from Gaul and Pertinax from Britain, within the temple of the sun god Mithras, recalls the Masonic encounters of cosmopolitan egalitarianism, enacted within a felicitous ring, that we have encountered elsewhere in Kipling. Their friendship represents the possibility of a more integrated empire and a more capacious imperial identity, not simply for ancient Romans but also for today's Greater Britons. 'On the Great Wall', however, carries a hint of impending doom; because of internal and external threats, Rome is withdrawing from its imperial outposts, and Parnesius and Pertinax will soon retire to their farms.

Kipling might have been describing his own retirement from imperial affairs to his Sussex estate. He was still capable of writing and speaking out forcefully on empire, but these pronouncements lacked the sustained energy and optimism of his earlier work. He had given up on South Africa, which by 1910, despite its continued presence within the Empire, had fallen under Afrikaner control. He was hysterical on the matter of India, writing to a friend that, with the establishment of a nationalist government, *suttee*, armed gang robbery and mass store closings accompanied by rampant murder would ensue.[36] Shortly after Kipling's death in January 1936, his friend Michael O'Dwyer recalled:

More than once in recent years I urged him to come forward and expose the dangers of the policy of surrender, arguing that his name and authority would compel people to think.

His reply was to this effect: 'I have been forty years before my time in uttering the warning. For over thirty years I have been trying to hammer into the heads of certain British public men the elementary facts about India. I have had no success.'[37]

With this, he uttered his final verdict on his 'vast, vague conspectus' of empire. Yet he never laid his particular spatial imagination entirely to rest. In the final image of *Something of Myself*, a description of his working-desk, he again couples the snugly small with the vast, this time as if looking wistfully into a post-imperial age: 'Left and right of the table were two big globes, on one of which a great airman had once outlined in white paint those air-routes to the East and Australia which were well in use before my death.'[38]

Notes

1 Bernard Porter, *The Lion's Share: A Short History of British Imperialism, 1850–1983*, 2nd edn (London: Longman, 1984), pp. 74–195.
2 Rudyard Kipling, *Something of Myself: For my Friends Known and Unknown* (London: Macmillan, 1937), pp. 9–10.
3 *Ibid.*, p. 90.
4 *Ibid.*, pp. 90–1.
5 Andrew Lang, 'Mr Kipling's Stories', in *Essays in Little* (1891). Reprinted in Roger Lancelyn Green (ed.), *Kipling: The Critical Heritage* (London: Routledge, 1971), pp. 71–2.
6 I had initially hoped to include a section on Ireland, but considerations of space finally made this impossible. On Ireland in Kipling's writings, see Kaori Nagai, *Empire of Analogies: Kipling, India and Ireland* (Cork University Press, 2006).
7 Kipling, *Something of Myself*, p. 2.
8 Angus Wilson, *The Strange Ride of Rudyard Kipling: His Life and Works* (New York: The Viking Press, 1977), p. 4.
9 Philip Mason, *Kipling: The Glass, the Shadow and the Fire* (New York: Harper & Row, 1975), p. 49.
10 C. S. Lewis, 'Kipling's World', in *They Asked for a Paper* (1963). Reprinted in Elliot Gilbert (ed.), *Kipling and the Critics* (New York University Press, 1965), p. 115.
11 Rudyard Kipling, 'The Mother-Lodge', in *Rudyard Kipling's Verse: Definitive Edition* (London: Hodder and Stoughton, 1940), p. 445.
12 John McBratney, *Imperial Subjects, Imperial Space: Rudyard Kipling's Fiction of the Native-Born* (Columbus: The Ohio State University Press, 2002). Women are largely unwelcome in these spaces.
13 Edward Marx, 'How We Lost Kafiristan', *Representations*, 67 (1999), pp. 44–66.

14 Rudyard Kipling, 'The Man Who Would Be King', in *Wee Willie Winkie, Under the Deodars, The Phantom Rickshaw and Other Stories* (London: Macmillan, 1969), pp. 238–9.

15 *Ibid.*, p. 248.

16 See among others Paul Fussell, 'Irony, Freemasonry, and Humane Ethics in Kipling's "The Man Who Would Be King"', *English Literary History*, 25 (1958), p. 232; Jeffrey Meyers, 'The Idea of Moral Authority in *The Man Who Would Be King*', *Studies in English Literature*, 8 (1968), pp. 717, 719, 723; and Zohreh T. Sullivan, *Narratives of Empire: The Fictions of Rudyard Kipling* (Cambridge University Press, 1993), p. 100.

17 J. M. S. Tompkins, *The Art of Rudyard Kipling* (London: Methuen, 1959), p. 234.

18 Kipling, 'The Man Who Would Be King', p. 214. The phrase 'strong men' appears most famously in 'The Ballad of East and West', a poem that declares that East and West shall never meet except when *'two strong men stand face to face, though they come from the ends of the earth!' Rudyard Kipling's Verse*, p. 234.

19 On the Punjab style, see Lewis Wurgaft, *The Imperial Imagination: Magic and Myth in Kipling's India* (Middletown, CT: Wesleyan University Press, 1983), pp. 32–41; and Andrew St John, '"In the Year '57": Historiography, Power, and Politics in Kipling's Punjab', *Review of English Studies*, 51 (2000), pp. 62–79.

20 Rudyard Kipling, *From Sea to Sea and Other Sketches*, Bombay edn, 26 vols. (London: Macmillan, 1913), vol. IV, p. 97.

21 Kipling, 'The Man Who Would Be King', p. 214.

22 *Ibid.*, p. 217.

23 Quoted in Harold Orel (ed.), *Kipling: Interviews and Recollections*, 2 vols. (Totowa, NJ: Barnes and Noble Books, 1983), vol. I, p. 140.

24 Louis L. Cornell, *Kipling in India* (London: Macmillan; New York: St. Martin's Press, 1966), p. 165.

25 Rudyard Kipling, 'The Two-Sided Man', in *Rudyard Kipling's Verse*, p. 587.

26 Charles Dilke coined the term in *Greater Britain: A Record of Travel in English-Speaking Countries during 1866 and 1867* (London: Macmillan, 1872).

27 On *The Seven Seas*, see among others Peter Keating, *Kipling the Poet* (London: Secker & Warburg, 1994), pp. 89–120.

28 E. H. H. Green, 'The Political Economy of Empire, 1880–1914', in Andrew Porter (ed.), *The Oxford History of the British Empire: The Nineteenth Century* (Oxford University Press, 1999), pp. 347–8.

29 Andrew Lycett, *Rudyard Kipling* (London: Weidenfeld & Nicolson, 1999), p. 281.

30 Rudyard Kipling, 'The Native-Born', in *The Seven Seas* (London: Methuen, 1896), pp. 49–54.

31 On Kipling's South African writings, see among others Paula M. Krebs, *Gender, Race, and the Writing of Empire: Public Discourse and the Boer War* (Cambridge University Press, 1999), pp. 156–73; and Andrew Hagiioannu, *The Man Who Would Be Kipling: The Colonial Fiction and the Frontiers of Exile* (Houndmills: Palgrave Macmillan, 2003), pp. 117–35.

32 Rudyard Kipling, 'The Parting of the Columns', in *The Five Nations* (London: Methuen, 1903), pp. 175–8.

33 *Ibid.*, p. 178.

34 For a comprehensive analysis of the failure of the constructive imperial vision, see Green, 'Political Economy', pp. 346–68.

35 *The Letters of Rudyard Kipling, Volume 3, 1900–10*, ed. Thomas Pinney (Iowa City: University of Iowa Press, 1996), p. 113.

36 *The Letters of Rudyard Kipling, Volume 5, 1920–30*, ed. Thomas Pinney (Iowa City: University of Iowa Press, 2004), p. 575.

37 Quoted in Orel, *Kipling*, vol. i, p. 90.

38 Kipling, *Something of Myself*, p. 231.

3

JUDITH PLOTZ

Kipling's very special relationship: Kipling in America, America in Kipling

> Let there be no misunderstanding about the matter. I love this people
> and if any contemptuous criticism has to be done I will do it myself.
> My heart has gone out to them beyond all other peoples.[1]

It is evident, even notorious, that Kipling was committed to an Anglo-American 'special relationship' long before Winston Churchill coined the term. No work of Rudyard Kipling's is more celebrated or imperative than 'The White Man's Burden' (1899), that injunction to the US to assume imperial power in the Philippines.[2] The most cursory reader recognises Kipling's demands for Anglo-Saxon solidarity between the great English-speaking nations. But for all the political clarity of Kipling's international demands on the US, he had a more complex relation to the country, a bonding that emerged from his life as a Vermont householder. If Kipling had lots of clear opinions, he also harboured deeply confused feelings. The clarity made him a famous polemicist but the feelings made him an American writer.

The American ark: home at Naulakha

The newly married Caroline and Rudyard Kipling built the house called 'Naulakha' in 1892–3 on a hillside in Dummerston, Vermont, overlooking the Connecticut River Valley and facing Mount Wantastiquet. The name meant their 'Jewel Beyond Price', their 'Treasure' and betokened '*The* House' to be happy in.[3] For a few years they were happier than ever again in their lives. After they left Naulakha because of an explosive family feud with Carrie's brother Beatty, they never again inhabited so comfortable a house or enjoyed such family happiness.

During the four years, 1892–6, that Rudyard Kipling lived in America, he put down roots whose extirpation cost him dear: 'There are only two places in the world where I want to live –', he wrote in 1898, 'Bombay and Brattleboro. And I can't live at either.'[4] That Kipling bonded blissfully to India in childhood is well known, but some retrospective bitterness about the States (e.g. as an 'atmosphere ... to some extent hostile') has masked his heartsick homesickness for Vermont.[5] The depth of his attachment to America is clearly evident in the very lineaments of this intensely loved house, a masterpiece of the uniquely American Shingle Style.

Designed to the Kiplings' specifications,[6] Naulakha was the first and fullest home for a man who had never before had a permanent home and who longed to be a 'householder'. Kipling repeatedly applies this resonant Indian term – strongly connoting the founding of a family – to himself during the American years.[7] In its quirky idiosyncratic beauty, Naulakha synthesises the mixed experiences of Kipling's earlier unfixed and wandering childhood and young manhood: his constant voyaging is replicated in its ark shape; India in its furnishings, design and garden; England in its Arts and Crafts aesthetic; and New England in its materials, furniture, landscape and atmosphere.[8]

It was for good reason that Kipling called Naulakha 'my ship' and others likened it to an ark, which was Kipling's chosen anagram.[9] As befits a man who had spent much of his adult life on one steamship line or another (nine trans-Atlantic or trans-Pacific crossings between his seventeenth and his twenty-eighth years) passing from one temporary sojourning place to another, the first and only house he built was a ship-shaped structure, strongly resembling both a Kashmiri house boat and a Mississippi river boat.[10] Long and narrow, Naulakha is one room wide. The prow of the house faces south, with Kipling's study, like the captain's cabin, opening onto a porch shaped like the captain's deck. The four porches of the house all resemble decks on a liner – there are two forward decks (Kipling's verandah on the first floor and the children's porch on the second); a long side deck, the 'loggia', on the portside facing east; and a small orlop deck (a summer picnic porch off the kitchen) portside and close to the stern.[11]

The four decks also resemble the verandahs of the Indian bungalows Kipling knew so well. Indeed, the Kiplings called them 'verandahs' except for the side 'loggia' – an indoor-outdoor room which was shielded by wooden shades in summer and protected by outsize windows in winter. There is a famous photograph of three-year-old Josephine sitting on a tiger-skin-draped cane chair in the loggia, a photograph that evokes India as much as Brattleboro.[12] There is a similar synthesis of India and Vermont in the Kiplings' summer pergola, a stone-built gazebo reached by an arched rhododendron walkway, a Himalayan mountain plant used in Simla for similar purposes.

Inside the house, the furnishings and colours are post-Victorian and elegant, belonging to the Arts and Crafts Movement of the 1890s. Such simplicity of line and design was not to the taste of their Vermont neighbours, who found the house 'by any standards … ugly' with 'meager furnishings' not very adequately improved 'by cotton hangings from India'.[13] To a modern eye, however, the house is welcoming and beautiful, vigorously hybrid: it combines American country carpentry and cabinet-making with an Arts and Crafts aesthetic in its muted colours (walls of café-au-lait, olive, light yellow; Tiffany glass in amber) and with many Indian elements – fabrics, metalwork lamps and woodcarvings.

The house is physically comfortable, light and airy but also warm. The large well-screened windows, curtained not draped, ensured the summer breezes. Against the Vermont winter, the Kiplings installed an enormous coal-burning 'octopus' furnace that consumed 'about a ton of coal every ten days plus six fireplaces' and kept the house very warm.[14] The furniture too was comfortable (the Kiplings left most of it behind and it is still used today by guests in Naulakha) – for example, the yielding soft leather sofa in Kipling's study and the several softly pillowed easy chairs. The atmosphere and the furnishings are thus in marked contrast with those at Bateman's, the handsome but uncomfortable Caroline country house the Kiplings inhabited for much of their lives in England – a cold dark house in a damp valley filled with famously unyielding furniture – not one comfortable chair in the house, Elsie Kipling complained.

That Kipling was deeply engaged in householding at Naulakha is plain: he assiduously read seed catalogues in the hope of perfecting the several gardens he planned (see his poem 'Pan in Vermont'); he personally planted an avenue of white pines (now grown magnificently to almost one hundred feet tall). He snapped endless photographs of the house, the garden, and 'Bo' (Josephine) with his little Kodak. A facsimile of the family album is still on display: 'These are pictures of Bo in the flower garden at Naulakha in the summer of 1896 when she went barefooted. In the two top ones you can just see a glimpse of Father's verandah.' These are momentary snaps, just idyllic random moments of family happiness: 'Bo in a summer garden' and 'Father on his skis'.

But the idyll ended abruptly. The Kiplings left Naulakha forever in August 1896 taking this album, the books, some rugs and pictures, the nursery furniture, and one desk. Everything else was left behind. After the hasty departure from Vermont in 1896, Kipling returned to the United States just once. In January 1899 the Kiplings took the North Atlantic crossing to New York, where both father and elder daughter fell ill and where Josephine, the 'best Beloved', died of pneumonia. The loss of 'my American daughter' shattered Kipling, who could never again face returning to the place he thenceforth associated with 'my chiefest joys and sorrow'.[15] To leave a place so deeply loved so hastily and utterly behind suggests a decision made in pain and rage. The mix of Kipling's feelings suggests how complicated his view of America was, how much he felt both outsider and insider.

American punditry

Kipling's commentary on America is extensive and antithetical,[16] but it is not complex. Indeed, his most celebrated pronouncement on the United States, the call to imperial responsibility over the Philippines in 'The White Man's Burden', justly epitomises his long-term political assessment of the US: potentially estimable if an imperial partner and co-equal of Imperial Britain; potentially contemptible if selfishly evading the burden under cover of democracy.[17] This is the pattern of Kipling's explicitly public and polemical writings on America from his first setting foot on the American ship *City of Peking* ('This is America')[18] in November 1889 until the close of his life. In a note written to a Washington journalist just days before his death, Kipling recalls composing a critical poem about the United States, 'The American Spirit', but cites it as a demonstration of his commitment: 'As the nigger said in Court "If Ah didn't like de woman, how cum I'd take de trouble to hit her on de haid".'[19] (This casual racism that here uses black Americans as mere comic props reveals Kipling's characteristic discomfort with an anglophone society that is not Anglo-Saxon.)

Kipling arrived in the US from colonial India and looked at the USA through a comparative colonial eye. Kipling sees the US, because Anglo-Saxon in heritage, as destined to fulfil that ancestry imperially (and thus to become a rival or an ally) or else to fail by lapsing into mere democracy. Insofar as the US can itself become imperial rather than narrowly republican, it is recognisable and tolerable either as an attractive and licensed enemy or as an ally. Kipling becomes most critical of the elements in US culture that will deflect from an outward-looking international politics and most appreciative of those that promote it.

From first sight, Kipling judges the United States as one who speaks for an older, more wisely governed imperial civilisation but speaks in the all-knowing tone of a young journalist already famous. Kipling was twenty-three when he first arrived in North America, travelling from west to east on his way to England from India. The letters in *From Sea to Sea*, first published in the Allahabad *Pioneer* in 1889–90, are emphatic with condescension, doubly determined by the routine superiority of nineteenth-century British visitors such as Dickens and Fanny Trollope, but also by a personal exasperation at American literary piracy that robbed Kipling and other English writers of their legitimate royalties. Thus his spirited curse on America:[20]

Because you steal the property of a man's head, which is more his peculiar property than his pipe, his horse or his wife, and because you glory in your theft and have the indecency to praise or criticise the author from whom you steal, and because of your ignorance ... you shall be cursed with this curse from Alaska to Florida and back again. Your women shall scream like peacocks when they talk and your men shall laugh like horses when they laugh. You shall call 'round' 'raoound' and 'very' 'vury' and 'News' 'Noose' till the end of time.[21]

Kipling makes the routine English traveller's complaints. American manners are crude, they grub rather than eat: 'The American has no meals. He stuffs for ten minutes thrice a day.'[22] Americans chew and spit, a topic to which Kipling endlessly recurred: 'For God's sake. Let's stop talking about spittoons,' the visiting Arthur Conan Doyle begged Kipling years later.[23] American servants are insolent – especially the Irish, especially the Negroes – because of the poisonous democratic assumption of equality for non-equals. Americans are violent; 'the accepted lawlessness of life' is the norm.[24] So is hyperbole: Americans are boastful, all 'Blatherumskite and bunkum', always praising themselves as 'the greatest, freest, sublimest, most chivalrous and richest people on the face of the earth'.[25] Americans are impatient, hasty builders of gimcrack settlements and flimsy mines, tunnels and bridges. Kipling is appalled by unregulated sprawl and, especially, speeding railroad traffic: he delivers a rant against unregulated free enterprise: 'you have nothing to be proud of ... What you call your freedom is just the desolate freedom of the wild ass ... Wait till your country fills up and you have to unlearn all your pleasant little theories of doing as you darn please if you are strong enough.' American journalists are nosey, importunate, ignorant. Americans are both too democratic and too corrupt to be democratic since the vaunted American democracy is for sale: 'If I had money enough,' he quotes a native informant, 'I could buy the Senate of the United States, the Eagle, and the Star Spangled Banner complete.' Less routine are his scathing comparative observations on the genocidal treatment of native Americans and the American assumption that the British in India (actually up-lifters of 'the Aryan') are 'exterminating the native in the same fashion'.[26]

Kipling's ten intense American years from 1889 to 1899 coincide with a cusp period in Anglo-American relations, the period in which an older mistrust gives way to a commonality of imperial Anglo-Saxon blood brotherhood and expansionism. Until late in the nineteenth century, in the West, South and agricultural regions of the US, Britain was considered the once and future enemy. 'America will hate England', editorialised the *New York Times* in 1865, 'until the last American now living goes to his grave.' As late as 1895, a boundary dispute between Venezuela and British Guinea provoked fears of British incursions in the western hemisphere and the resulting calls for war with Britain and the immediate invasion of Canada.[27] But by the end of that decade, John Hay, Kipling's friend and Teddy Roosevelt's Secretary of State, could declare: 'The fight of England is the fight of civilization and progress and all our interests are bound up in her success.'[28]

Upon landing in California, Kipling at first sight considers the United States in the light of a rival power and potential military threat to the British hegemony in the Pacific. Thus, he jokily sizes up San Francisco harbour in 1889 as a splendidly vulnerable naval target for 'two gunboats from Hong Kong'.[29] When the American press stirred up war fever against Britain over the Venezuela–British Guinea Border dispute in 1895, Kipling thought war conceivable between the United States and Britain. That same year Kipling visited Washington and heard a Senator's wife boast of her husband's 'twisting the Lion's tail' in an inflammatory speech.[30] But on that same Washington trip, Kipling befriended John Hay, Henry Cabot Lodge and Theodore Roosevelt, strong proponents of a trans-Atlantic system of alliances, men whose masterminding of the Spanish–American War and whose securing of the Panama Canal catapulted the US to world power and empire. If the acquisition of the Philippines was principally engineered by Roosevelt, Lodge and Hay, it was certainly also ennobled by Kipling's powerful 'The White Man's Burden', sent to Roosevelt for publication in the American press on the very eve of the Senate's vote to ratify the treaty securing the Philippines.

The overt imperial phase of the Spanish–American War represents the height of Kipling's approval of and engagement with American policy. He wrote to an American friend in August 1898:

> America is distinctly looking up ... Haven't your views on matters imperial changed in the last few months? I sit here and chuckle as I read the papers over the water. The land seems to be taking kindly to the White Man's work. Of course the boys are doing well at Santiago and elsewhere. The funny thing is to see the nation behind 'em – not understanding what America is committed to – wondering and blundering and trying to get out of her responsibilities. Remember, we've been at this little business for a matter of half a century ... It is the fate of our breed to do these things – or rather to have these things forced upon us and it is a joy and gratification beyond words to me to see you 'uns swinging into line on your side of the world and getting to business instead of heaving rocks at one another and turning out the militia for railroad strikes. Your real work will begin after peace is declared. If you don't annex the Philippines now, you'll have to do it all over again ... This has been a grand year for the White Man.[31]

As this letter makes clear, Kipling sees empire as a product of 'our breed', the 'White Man', by which he means Anglo-Saxon stock.[32] The presence of large non-British groups within the US – the Irish, 'Whose other creed is Hate [of Britain]';[33] Negroes 'unwelded into the population';[34] 'the wreckage of Eastern Europe' with their 'beady-eyed, muddy-skinned, aproned women, with handkerchiefs on their heads and Oriental bundles in their hands'[35] – meant a population unsympathetic to Anglo-Saxon ideals and aims and immune to British claims of fraternal solidarity, the appeal of one who '[b]eing of the breed … would have known the breed'.[36] Such a mongrel population would not embrace the destined work of 'our breed' or join in 'A Song of the White Man'.[37] Further, the egalitarian heritage of the US – once 'law-fearing men … changed into mere "citoyens"', especially as stimulated by the energetic labour movement of the 1890s, is the natural enemy of empire. '[The] only serious enemy to the Empire, within or without, is … Democracy'[38] because democratic principles are universal, applying to all human beings. Democrats delude themselves that universal rights, 'that written and paper constitutions can help races who have never conceived the western notion of liberty'.[39]

The expansionist movement of US policy from 1899 coincided with Kipling's closeness with Hay, Lodge and Roosevelt and represented the acme of his enthusiasm for the United States.[40] But the anticipated Anglo-Saxon imperial union of the twin powers sharing 'the earth between us as no gods have ever shared it' faltered with the outbreak of the First World War.[41] Kipling, roused to fury, regarded the initial American neutrality sentiment as apostasy. Later, in a 1917 letter to Cameron Forbes, US proconsul in the Philippines, Kipling voiced his 'sense of shock that people who talked our tongue … should, in our tongue, write and say they had no concern in the matter. One felt the sense of – horror almost … However that's ended.' The United States is in the war; 'Glory be to God'.[42]

But that American failure of Anglo-Saxon solidarity rankled. In the years following the First World War, Kipling's interest in the United States diminished to a mere low-grade resentment, a sour relishing of disappointment which Thomas Pinney even describes as '*Shadenfreude*'.[43]

The American Kipling

Despite Kipling's over-emphatic polemics about America, there is an American Kipling deeper and more interesting than the public man. The received conception of Kipling as the young Anglo-Indian bard who evolves into the English mastersinger of the British Empire and Britishness needs emendation and Americanisation. His deepest personal and literary relationships are American; and much of his most lasting work is part of American literature.

As an adult Kipling's deepest intimacies were with Americans. His closest friend and his wife were both Americans. Wolcott Balestier, charming, empathic, quick-silver, was also his sole literary collaborator. (The beloved Brattleboro house was named Naulakha partially in tribute to the Anglo-American novel Rudyard and Wolcott had written together.) Kipling's abrupt marriage to Caroline Balestier was itself a consequence of Wolcott's death. That death – like Josephine's and John's later – bound the couple together in a collaborative bond of repression: the three best beloveds who haunted all other relationships but could never themselves be openly discussed.

The American wife was only the last of a series of American girls Kipling had admired. In India he had admired and frequented the slightly older, and married, Edmonia ('Ted') Hill as muse and best friend. Later in America, Kipling visited Ted in Beaver, Pennsylvania, where her father was President of Beaver College. There he met Caroline Taylor, Ted's younger sister, and became briefly engaged to her. Whatever complaints he had about American society at large, during travels in the 1880s and 1890s he liked American women inordinately: 'I am hopelessly in love with about eight American maidens.'[44] He calls them 'the best women in the world ... above and beyond them all. They are clever, they can talk. Yes, it is said that they can think ... They are original, and regard you between the brows with unabashed eyes as a sister might look at her brother ... their freedom is large, and they do not abuse it.'[45]

While staying at Beaver,[46] Kipling claimed to have met the doubles of the wonderful March sisters of *Little Women*, each girl more charming, pretty, unaffected and sensible than the last:

> Thus it happens that she is a companion, in the fullest sense of the word of the man she weds, zealous for the interest of the firm, to be consulted in time of stress and to be called upon for help and sympathy in time of danger. Pleasant it is that one heart should beat for you; but it is better when the head above that heart has been thinking hard on your behalf and the lips, that are also very pleasant to kiss, give wise counsel.[47]

Most of all, Kipling cherished his own 'American maiden', Josephine, the child born and reared and gone to ashes in America,[48] the child whose early years he assiduously photographed and whose figure haunts the *Just So Stories* and '"They"'.

Kipling's literary intimacies are American as well. Widely and idiosyncratically read in canonical and non-canonical English literature, Kipling also owes huge debts to American writers. To Bret Harte, he owes his self-creation as the laureate of British India, consciously emulating the American's Californian sketches, stories and poems in the *Plain Tales from the Hills* as well as the soldier stories. Indeed, Kipling persuaded the editor of the *Pioneer* 'that is was unnecessary to buy stories from authors such as Bret Harte because he could fill the space himself',[49] a claim evident to any reader who ever compared Harte's 'M'Liss' or 'The Luck of Roaring Camp' with Kipling's *Soldiers Three*. To Joel Chandler Harris, depicted as the object of cultic schoolboy veneration in *Stalky & Co.*, Kipling owes key folkloric patterns and dialectic turns incorporated in the *Just So Stories*, but also a larger confidence in orchestrating dialect.[50] To Whitman he owes the largest of continental/transcontinental ambitions: to be 'born a poet who shall give the English *the* song of their own country – which is to say about half the world ... to compose the greatest song of all – The Saga of the Anglo-Saxon all around the earth'.[51] To Mark Twain, whom Kipling hero-worshipped, interviewed, emulated and recognised as a precursor, he owes the very conception of *Kim*: the Young Adult novel as national allegory. And to Mabel Mapes Dodge, editor of *St Nicholas*, which he read when very young and wrote for when very famous, he owed the comfortable experience of an Anglophile elite young American audience.

With this audience, these influences, these intimate connections, Kipling the myriad-minded becomes intermittently an American writer.[52] He is often American in his subject matter – especially in the 1898 collection *The Day's Work* (its title taken from the inscription over the mantel in Kipling's Naulakha study – 'The night cometh when no man can work'). As Andrew Hagiioannu makes clear, this volume is seriously engaged with the nature of the United States economy and particularly with the US labour movement, an engagement especially striking in the anti-union and local-colourist 'A Walking Delegate' and the pro-management '.007', in which American labour is represented as a steam engine. Kipling sometimes adopts an American subject position, for example as an expatriate American in Britain.[53] However, it is in three remarkable children's books written all or in part in the US that Kipling most fully enters into the American spirit: in *'Captains Courageous'* (1896), *Just So Stories* (1902) and *Kim* (1901).

'Captains Courageous': A Story of the Grand Banks (1896), a bicoastal novel of the North-East and the West, features two heroes and father figures – Disco Troop, a Gloucester fisherman; and Harvey Cheyne, a California multi-millionaire spanning North America and the Pacific with his rail lines and shipping lines. The millionaire's heir, the spoiled Harvey, Jr., falls overboard in the North Atlantic and is rescued by *We're Here*, Captain Troop's fishing boat. The title 'Captains Courageous' is a quotation from an Elizabethan ballad ('When captains courageous, whom death could not daunte') and hints at a transfer of heroism from the sixteenth-century Britons of the ballad to the nineteenth-century American 'captains' of the

novel:[54] the literal captain of the 'We're Here' and the metaphorical 'captain of industry'. The book depicts the giving way of an older Yankee America of small scale enterprise (the assiduously researched New England cod trade, already fading when Kipling visited Gloucester). Though the older Yankee America still retains its educational authority (the sea captain educates the magnate's son), the future is with the new global America, westering into the Pacific (the magnate co-opts the sea captain's son to serve on his Pacific fleet). '*Captains Courageous*' clearly enacts the triumph of entrepreneurial empire-building and masculine will.[55] Yet the book is also emphatically elegiac about the replacement of a local culture (the lovingly characterised New England of Disco Troop) by an imperial America (as enacted in the maniacally hurried national and international travels of Cheyne, Sr.). The complicated emotional allegiances of '*Captains Courageous*' make the book an exploration of the right direction for the USA at the end of the nineteenth century from within American culture, from one who identifies with both currents of American history.

Just So Stories (1902) is an even more emphatically American work. The first three stories were first told and re-told in Vermont and first published in *St. Nicholas* as a fifth birthday present for Josephine, the 'American daughter'.[56] The original *St. Nicholas* introduction contextualises the stories as the last of three types of American fairy story: the morning 'Blue Skalallatoot stories' (a 'Skalallatoot' is a Northwest Native American word for a forest fairy);[57] the afternoon 'stories about Orvin Sylvester Woodsey, the left-over New England fairy who did not think it well-seen to fly, and used patent labour-saving devices instead of charms'; and the bedtime stories told just-so for 'Effie', that is, Josephine, the American maiden.

As U.C. Knoepflmacher has argued,[58] the American child Josephine is the muse of *Just So Stories*: in life she was the initial recipient of the first three stories; in death she was the collaborative deuteragonist of the three Daddy–Daughter/Tegumai–Taffy stories. In these tales ('How the First Letter Was Written', 'How the Alphabet Was Made' and 'The Tabu Tale') a Neolithic father and his bumptious daughter, Taffimai Metallumai, together invent human culture – symbols, written language, law – in a Neolithic landscape that is half Surrey, half North America. (These tales feature Puget Sound Indian tribes,[59] totem poles, a beaver totem, a little girl dressed like Pocahontas in 'moccasins and deerskin cloak', letters on the bark of paper birch). Further, all the tales speak to an Anglo-American audience at the peak moment – the period of Spanish–American and Boer wars – of the assumed Anglo-Saxon special relationship and world hegemony. *Just So Stories* is set on six continents, including a Europe and North America merged into a Neolithic Never Land for Taffy and Daddy. Maps are set before the child readers, reminding them through the depiction of nineteen different shipping lines and forty-eight vessels that American hegemony and the British Empire between them command the globe. 'Look at the Atlas, please', children are enjoined in the closing poem of 'The Sing-Song of Old Man Kangaroo'. Kipling even allegorically mobilises the Republican elephant, party symbol of his friends Hay and Roosevelt, to suggest the emergence of the United States as a young, loquacious, self-assertive imperial power in the much-beloved 'Elephant's Child'.

Kim, that great Indian novel, has claims of American lineage through the line of Twain's *The Adventures of Huckleberry Finn*, source of *all* modern American literature, at least according to Hemingway. That Kipling admired Twain above all other moderns is clear. Further, the parallels between the two works are extensive: picaresque quest narratives of a redemptive river in which orphaned, marginal youths of the ruling race join an adult father figure of the subject race. Both works privilege adolescence, evade the marriage plot and resist closure, whether marital, moral, historical or formal. Most striking, in both works hybridisation is at once a linguistic, narrative and moral principle. Both works are dialectically, indeed idiolectically, diverse: Twains' multiple black and white regional Englishes parallel Kipling's multiple Englishes and englished vernaculars. Fluent to the point of mimicry in multiple dialects, the two boy protagonists themselves embody hybridity and are embroiled in it: both are of Irish stock (Kimball O'Hara, Finn as in 'Fionn') but also, some critics have insisted, of mixed race – part Indian, part black.[60] Indeed, the harsh race politics of post-Civil War America shadows *Kim*, as Paula Krebs and Tricia Lootens have discovered in a draft of 'Kim o' the Rishti' in which an armed Kim, 'in explicitly, violent racist language', exalts in 'the degradation and murder of a "Negro, wearing the Arab fez"'.[61]

Though postcolonial aesthetics have generally smiled on hybridity as a mark of the progressive and the multicultural, the hybridity of *Kim* is something of a puzzle. Certainly for Kipling himself hybridity was problematic – even *the* problematic of America. On the one hand, the young Kipling of 1889 envisioned American power as emerging from her benign mix of peoples:

Wait till the Anglo-American-German-Jew – the Man of the Future – is properly equipped. He'll have just the least little kink in his hair now and again, he'll carry the English lungs above the Teuton feet that can walk for ever, and he will wave long, thin bony Yankee hands with the big blue veins on the wrist from one end of the earth to the other. He'll be the finest writer and dramatist, 'specially dramatist, that the world as it recollects itself has ever seen. By virtue of his Jew blood – just a little, little drop – he'll be a musician and a painter too ... There is nothing known to man that he will not be, and his country will sway the world with one foot as a man tilts a see-saw plank.[62]

On the other hand, Kipling in 1921 darkly condemned the contaminations of American culture in a letter to Brander Matthews, Professor of English at Columbia University in New York:

> ... the real serious trouble with your language and literature is this. More and more it is being made and used by the *person to whom English was unknown in his infancy*. It may be more impeccable stuff than of old, produced with greater care for its tone and colour values, deeper in what is called 'thought' and 'outlook'; but fundamentally it is alien; remote, unrelated. What the immigrant from southern Europe and out of Judaea, has done to the national fabric of the US that he, and specially she, is doing to your literature. You are getting Hebraized, internationalized, cosmopolitaned.[63]

What Kipling dismisses in his later years as the weakness of American culture is his own literary strength, that hybridity, that mixture and jostle of opposing voices that he brilliantly mobilised throughout his work, above all in *Kim*. America, that source of his 'chiefest joys and sorrow', was also his persistent puzzle, representing a future that he both welcomed and feared.[64]

Notes

1 Rudyard Kipling, *From Sea to Sea: Letters of Travel, Volume 2* (New York: Doubleday & McClure, 1899), p. 120.
2 For a partial review of some of the responses see my 'How "The White Man's Burden" Lost its Scare-Quotes; or, Kipling and the New American Empire' in Caroline Rooney and Kaori Nagai (eds.), *Kipling and Beyond: Patriotism, Globalisation and Postcolonialism* (Basingstoke: Palgrave Macmillan, 2010), pp. 37–57.
3 Rudyard Kipling, *Something of Myself: For my Friends Known and Unknown* (London: Macmillan, 1937), p. 132. Literally the word 'Naulakha' means '9 lakhs' [900,000] in Hindi, and was also used as the title (misspelled 'Naulahka' by the publisher) of the Anglo-American novel Kipling co-authored with Wolcott Balestier, Caroline Balestier Kipling's older brother and Kipling's closest friend.
4 Charles Carrington, *The Life of Rudyard Kipling* (Garden City, NY: Doubleday, 1956), p. 187. Kipling's letters of the later 1890s are full of wistful references to the superiority of Brattleboro and Naulakha to stuffy England: for example, 'and we away from Naulakha with bits of the downs for Monadnock' (*The Letters of Rudyard Kipling, Volume 2, 1890–99*, ed. Thomas Pinney (Iowa City: University of Iowa Press, 1990), pp. 309–10).
5 Kipling, *Something of Myself*, p. 132.
6 The New York architect was Herbert Rutgers Marshall, a Balestier family friend. The Kiplings were much engaged in the design. See Andrew Lycett, *Rudyard Kipling* (London: Weidenfeld & Nicholson, 1999), p. 250.

7 Kipling, *Something of Myself*, p. 131; *The Letters of Rudyard Kipling, Volume 6, 1931–36*, ed. Thomas Pinney (Iowa City: University of Iowa Press, 2004), p. 431.

8 For a detailed description see the National Register Nomination Information 'Naulakha, Dummerston (Landmark Nomination)' prepared by David C. Tansey, Naulakha's Architectural historian, at www.crjc.org/heritage/Vo3–3. htm

9 Frederic F. Van de Water, *Kipling's Vermont Feud* (Rutland, VT: Academy Books, 1981), p. 27. Kipling uses the image of an ark under a capital A as an anagram for RK.

10 Tansey, 'Naulakha, Dummerston (Landmark Nomination)'.

11 The kitchen porch, however, was added by a later owner.

12 This photograph can be found among a gallery of photographs of Naulakha, now owned and administered by Landmark Trust USA, see landmarktrustusa. org/naulakha/photo-gallery.html. For additional photographs, see www.flickr. com/photos/naulakha-kipling/

13 Van de Water, *Kipling's Vermont Feud*, p. 27; Adam Nicolson, *The Hated Wife: Carrie Kipling 1862–1939* (London: Short Books, 2001), p. 40.

14 David Tansy, personal communication, 8 December 2009. I am grateful to Mr Tansy, Landmark Trust curator at Naulakha, for his patient and illuminating responses to my inquiries.

15 *The Letters of Rudyard Kipling, Volume 4, 1911–19*, ed. Thomas Pinney (Iowa City: University of Iowa Press, 1999), p. 100.

16 Kipling's most intense attention to the USA can be found in the American travel letters (*From Sea to Sea* (1889) and *From Tideway to Tideway* (1892–5)); in the works written during the American years (especially *The Naulahka*, 'Captains Courageous', *The Day's Work*); in the works begun in the United States (especially *Just So Stories*); in personal letters to American correspondents (especially to Theodore Roosevelt, Cameron Forbes and Brander Matthews); and in key short stories (especially two tales of revolutionary America in *Rewards and Fairies* and several expatriate stories of Americans in England: 'An Habitation Enforced' in *Actions and Reactions* and 'The Prophet and the Country' in *Debits and Credits*).

17 On the persisting uses of the poem, see Plotz, 'How "The White Man's Burden" Lost its Scare-Quotes'.

18 D. H. Stewart, ed., *Kipling's America: Travel Letters, 1889–1895* (Greensboro, NC: ELT Press, 2003), p. 1.

19 *The Letters of Rudyard Kipling, Volume 6*, p. 431.

20 Published in the *Pioneer* in November 1889 but not in American editions.

21 Stewart, *Kipling's America*, p. xx.

22 *Ibid.*, pp. 25–6.

23 Lycett, *Rudyard Kipling*, p. 280.

24 Kipling, *Something of Myself*, p. 120.

25 Stewart, *Kipling's America*, pp. 88–9, 93.

26 *Ibid.*, pp. 49, 8, 83.

27 Duncan Andrew Campbell, *Unlikely Allies: Britain, America and the Victorian Origins of the Special Relationship* (New York: Hambledon Continuum, 2007), p. 190.

28 Campbell, *Unlikely Allies*, p. 239.

29 Stewart, *Kipling's America*, p. 11.

30 Kipling, *Something of Myself*, p. 122.

31 *The Letters of Rudyard Kipling, Volume 2*, p. 344.

32 Indeed Kipling insists on the need to preserve Canada for the empire by limiting immigration from eastern and southern Europe and having 'men and women of our own stock, habits, language, and hopes brought in by every means possible'. Rudyard Kipling, *Letters of Travel, 1892–1913* (London: Macmillan, 1920), p. 239.

33 Kipling, *Something of Myself*, p. 116.

34 Kipling, *Letters of Travel*, pp. 34–5.

35 Kipling, *Something of Myself*, p. 117; Kipling, *Letters of Travel*, p. 185.

36 Rudyard Kipling, *A Book of Words* (London: Macmillan, 1928), p. 196.

37 Written in 1899 with both Boer and Spanish American wars in mind: 'Oh, well for the world when the White Men tread / Their highway side by side'. *Rudyard Kipling's Verse: Definitive Edition* (London: Hodder and Stoughton, 1940), p. 282.

38 *The Letters of Rudyard Kipling, Volume 3, 1900–10*, ed. Thomas Pinney (Iowa City: University of Iowa Press, 1996), p. 351; Kipling, *Letters of Travel*, p. 239.

39 *The Letters of Rudyard Kipling, Volume 2*, p. 346. For an excellent discussion of Kipling's attacks on the American labour movement, see Chapter 3, 'American Fiction: the Day's Work, US Imperialism, and the Politics of Wall Street', of Andrew Hagiioannu's *The Man Who Would Be Kipling: The Colonial Fiction and the Frontiers of Exile* (Basingstoke: Palgrave Macmillan, 2003).

40 Christopher Hitchens, *Blood, Class, and Nostalgia: Anglo-American Ironies* (New York: Farrar, Straus and Giroux, 1990), p. 28.

41 Stewart, *Kipling's America*, p. 160.

42 *The Letters of Rudyard Kipling, Volume 4*, pp. 438–9.

43 *The Letters of Rudyard Kipling, Volume 6*, p. 4.

44 Stewart, *Kipling's America*, p. 37.

45 *Ibid.*, pp. 38–9.

46 Kipling liked the name of the town in part because he had taken a liking to beavers themselves during his western travels. He later records paying a special visit to the Washington Zoo just to see the beavers. In the Taffy tales of *Just So Stories*, he chose the Beaver as the joint Daddy-Taffy family totem.

47 Stewart, *Kipling's America*, pp. 164–5.

48 The fate of Josephine's remains is uncertain. David Page has found an announcement of Josephine's cremation at Fresh Pond Crematory in the Newton Register for 16 March 1899. The disposition of the ashes, said by Carrington to have been taken to England, is, however, unknown.

49 Lycett, *Rudyard Kipling*, p. 151.

50 Kipling wrote to Harris of knowing whole pages of Uncle Remus by heart and of the craze for the Uncle Remus stories that swept 'like wild fire' through his school 'when I was about fifteen' (*The Letters of Rudyard Kipling, Volume 2*, p. 217). See the short story 'The United Idolaters' in *Debits and Credits*.

51 Stewart, *Kipling's America*, pp. 160–1.

52 The case has also been made by Nirad C. Chaudhuri for Kipling as Indian writer in 'The Finest Story about India – in English' in John Gross (ed.), *The Age of Kipling* (New York: Simon & Schuster, 1972).

53 See 'An Error in the Fourth Dimension' in *The Day's Work*, 'An Habitation Enforced', and 'A Prophet and the Country'.

54 The ballad 'Mary Ambree' is an ambiguous source, however, since the titular heroine is a woman disguised as a man who proves intrepid in battle. In the first draft of the manuscript young Harvey the protagonist was not only a boor, a cad and a spoiled brat, but depicted as an effeminate twit who wears girlish rings. Just like Mary Ambree, he's masculinised by his service.

55 See Daniel Karlin, '"*Captains Courageous*" and the American Empire', *Kipling Journal*, 251 (September 1989), pp. 11–21, and Plotz, 'How "The White Man's Burden" Lost its Scare Quotes'.

56 'How the Whale Got his Tiny Throat', 'How the Camel got his Hump' and 'How the Rhinoceros got his Skin' appeared in the December 1897, January 1898 and February 1898 issues of *St. Nicholas Magazine*. Josephine was born on 19 December 1892.

57 The term appears in Kipling's head note for 'How the Whale Got his Tiny Throat', *St. Nicholas Magazine*, 25 (December 1897), p. 89. Kipling seems to have found the term 'Skalallatoot' in Walter Shelley Phillips, *Totem Tales: Indian Stories Indian Told Gathered in the Pacific* (Chicago: Star Publishing, 1896).

58 U. C. Knoepflmacher, 'Kipling's "Just-So" Partner: The Dead Child as Collaborator and Muse', *Children's Literature*, 25 (1997), pp. 24–49.

59 Kipling's 'Tewara' is his adaptation of Phillips's 'Twana' in *Totem Tales*.

60 See Judith Plotz, 'Whose is *Kim*? Postcolonial India Rewrites Kipling's Imperial Boy', *South Asian Review*, 25:2 (2004), pp. 3–22, for the case for an Anglo-Indian Kim. For a fictional depiction of Huck as mixed race see Jon Clinch, *Finn* (New York: Random House, 2007).

61 *Rudyard Kipling's Kim*, ed. Paula Krebs and Tricia Lootens (Longman: Boston, 2010), p. 263. This racist attack on the Negro is an improbable transference to British India of the racial issues and attitudes of the Jim Crow USA.

62 Stewart, *Kipling's America*, pp. 132–3.

63 *The Letters of Rudyard Kipling, Volume 5*, p. 90.

64 *The Letters of Rudyard Kipling, Volume 4*, p. 100.

4

LAURENCE DAVIES

Science and technology: present, past and future

I

Despite the contemporary enthusiasm for sanitary reform, few Victorians wrote poems about drains. One exception was Kipling, who gave his poem the daringly unpromising title 'Municipal'. The speaker is a district commissioner who, when menaced by a stampeding elephant, took refuge in a blocked-up outfall wearing regulation 'snowy garments':

> You may hold with surface-drainage, and the sun-for-garbage cure,
> Till you've been a periwinkle shrinking coyly up a sewer.

The experience has made him 'believe in well-flushed culverts'[1] and, as a result, the death-rate in his district has gone down. Kipling's vision of empire extended to the infrastructure of railways, riverboats, bridges and sewage systems. In his prose and poetry, his fascination with technology and its consequences shows up in unexpected places, foreign, imperial and domestic. On his visit to Brazil in 1927, he sent rapturous dispatches to the ultra-conservative (and often xenophobic) *Morning Post* praising the mountain railways, the giant hydroelectric installations, and the laboratory where snakes and spiders were milked for their venom.[2] '"They"' heads towards the mystical and redemptive, but it starts by evoking the joys of motoring through rural England, and does not stint on technical details: 'I was on the point of reversing and working my way back on the second speed.'[3] The inner narrative of 'The Man Who Would Be King' goes into an archaic world beyond the North-West Frontier, but the frame-narration involves the precisely timed arrival of a long-distance train at a junction, the scanning of cables from Europe, and the management of a printing press.[4] In Kafiristan, Peachey and Daniel depend on the persuasive force of rifles, some of them outdated and nearly worn out, others brand new and fit for conquest.

In 'The Bridge-Builders' (*The Day's Work*), another story of India, we are plunged straight into the milieu of civil engineering. Girders, trusses, hoists, revetments, piers and technical drawings figure largely, as do the challenges

52

of managing a heterogeneous workforce five thousand strong. Like much else in Kipling's work, it has a topical aspect; it first appeared in 1893, six years after major bridges were completed across the Ganges, the Sutlej and the Jherum. It is also a dramatic story pitting human resourcefulness against natural forces, the tension rising as the Ganges floods. Yet for all its immediacy, Kipling achieves a narrative coup by setting this imperial drama in a context of aeons. The foreman doses the bridge's designer with opium, bringing the latter a vision of Hindu avatars who debate the bridge, the foreigners, the flood, mutability and eternity. Whatever one takes from this story, which can stand interpretations by the dozen, its conjunctions of urgency and infinite perspective frame technology with the divine and the divine with technology in a manner virtually unique to Kipling.

By contrast, 'Below the Mill Dam' begins with what is ancient (at least by English standards), as the Spirit of the Mill sings 'its nine hundred year old song' whose words come from the district's inventory in Domesday Book (*TD* 369). The audience is mixed: a pair of millstones, the waters of five watersheds and, most vocally, a witty and condescending Grey Cat given to quoting Browning, and an Old English Black Rat. It takes three whole pages for any hint of the present day to disturb the cosy atmosphere with the Black Rat's mention of 'a local ruffian' (*TD* 371), Mangles the builder, who has replaced the old and picturesque pigstys with a cube of bricks and mortar. Other incomprehensible humans have been stringing wires around the mill and connecting them to strange glass bulbs. Punctuated with more snatches of Domesday Book and plenty of medieval gossip, the narrative gradually makes the Miller's agenda clear. Some of the brooks have been rechannelled, the wheel's axle has been reinforced, the wires run from a dynamo in the new brick shed. Exposing the dust and dirt of many centuries to its glare, the electricity is switched on, but even this is a halfway stage; a bank of four turbines will soon replace the mill wheel, and the Spirit is blithely willing to be reinvented:

> 'Not like turbines? Me? My dear fellows, turbines are good for fifteen hundred revolutions a minute – and with our power we can drive 'em at full speed. Why there's nothing we couldn't grind or saw or illuminate or heat with a set of turbines! That's to say if all the Five Watersheds are agreeable.'   (*TD* 392)

All five of them acclaim the plan, but the Cat invokes Pasht, Egyptian patron of the species, to witness her devotion to old gods and ways, and the Rat has been trapped, stuffed and mounted in an exhibition case as a specimen of a dwindling breed.

Given Kipling's enthusiasm for engineering, 'Below the Mill Dam' could be described as a load-bearing structure, able to carry a convergence of

critical forces. It is a forerunner of the Puck stories and set in the same terrain. Quite without the perception of technology as magic in 'Cold Iron'
or priestcraft in 'The Knife and the Naked Chalk', or science as sorcery in
'Marklake Witches' (all in *Rewards and Fairies*, 1910), it treats of change
and resistance to change. The tone is lighter, the language wittier, more
extravagant, arguably parodic. In some readings Kipling, a modernising
Tory who admired the bustling Joseph Chamberlain, is mocking the aris-
tocratic Conservative Arthur Balfour, whose languid wit and philosophical
detachment matched those of the Cat.[5] Yet this story also acknowledges the
seductions of the past without making them into fetishes, or excuses for
nostalgia, or reasons for inaction. Kipling's sense of progress is expansive
rather than purgative; as the story goes on, the Wheel's recitations from
Domesday Book start to include the latest developments, so that 'where till
now was a stye of three hogs, Mangles, a freeman, with four villeins and two
carts of two thousand bricks, has a new small house of five yards and a half,
and one roof of iron and a floor of cement' (*TD* 381). Neither cliophobic
nor technophobic, this attitude to time (and place) is as markedly different
from the frozen ruralism of such writers as the then Poet Laureate, Alfred
Austin,[6] as it is from impatience or contempt for what has gone before. This
attitude also suggests that Kipling, in a different mode of course, sometimes
writes like a modern historian of science, intrigued by blind alleys and narrow, crooked streets as much as well-lit boulevards, and conscious that even
the most 'primitive' transition – say from stone to bronze – had its material
basis in technology.

Among other influential writers of his day, only Jules Verne and H. G.
Wells pay so much attention to machinery.[7] Verne and Wells differed on
the permissible degree of speculation in a 'scientific romance' or 'extraordinary journey',[8] but both of them, like Kipling, dwelled on the machines
themselves and their implications for society. Kipling's distinctiveness in
this regard lies in his frequent resort to personification, animism, anthropo-
morphism – no single word covers the range of implications. In '.007' (*The
Day's Work*), for example, we hear the conversations of locomotives stabled
in a roundhouse – engines designed for express, rural and suburban passenger traffic, for main-line and local freight, or for yard switching,[9] most
belonging to the company, some visiting from other lines, some equipped
with the latest Westinghouse brakes and compound cylinders, others more
old-fashioned; one, the .007 of the title, is brand new, and Homeless Kate is
a stray boxcar. Each has a distinctive manner of speech. A few human beings
speak as well; engines can hear the humans, but the humans are deaf to
what the engines say. The two societies exist in parallel, dependent on each
other but not always willing to recognise the fact. By the story's end, .007

has made such a good showing that he is initiated into the Amalgamated Brotherhood of Locomotives, a society that clearly resembles the labour unions of the human world.[10] An even more remarkable case is another story in *The Day's Work*, 'The Ship That Found Herself', which features not only talking engines, such as a bilge pump, but talking components such as a garboard strake (a long plate just above the keel) and a bow anchor. There is a long history of regarding ships as having their own personalities; in our time, many people name their cars or their computers. Yet this tendency to ascribe human characteristics rarely extends to components, nor does the animism that perceives a spirit indwelling.

II

For many contemporary readers, Kipling is at his most seductive when he embraces more than one idea or mode.[11] The stories discussed so far manage to combine sharp observations of such unglamorous objects as gears and grease guns with what the susceptible might indeed call wonder, fantasy or magic, and the sceptical, narrative bravura. They make a striking contrast with sombre narratives such as H. G. Wells's 'The Lord of the Dynamos',[12] wherein any belief in the marvelous or transcendental is the sole preserve of a mysterious 'Asiatic' who offers his unbelieving boss to the dynamo as a human sacrifice. Kipling's fiction was immune to the *Entzauberung* that Weber saw as a consequence of modernity: 'the world is disenchanted. One need no longer have recourse to magical means in order to master or implore the spirits, as did the savage, for whom such mysterious powers existed.'[13] In his essay 'The Storyteller', Walter Benjamin finds 'information', with its attendant load of explanation, 'incompatible with the spirit of storytelling'.[14] There is a great deal of information in these stories but counterweighted with much strangeness, the doings of an alternative universe where brooks talk (but do not babble), and so do waves, and steam, and scuppers. Benjamin probably did not have these examples in mind, but he did regard Kipling as 'a last refuge' of the storyteller's art.[15]

For all their playfulness, these stories of things and animals that talk have a heuristic quality to them. They speculate about materials, work, history, theology, ontology and common purpose. For the ship to find itself (or, as a philosopher might say, come into its being), all its many parts must settle in and work together, even commune with each other. In this one way, ships have an affinity with wolves: '*For the strength of the Pack is the Wolf, and the strength of the Wolf is the Pack.*'[16] Rather than oppose the mechanical to the organic, the implication is that machines are analogous to living things, and not entirely rigid. Indeed, if they are to survive for any length of time, they cannot be. Whether in the sense of making physical allowances in engineering or social terms, tolerance and tolerances are vital to survival. Thus Kipling's work takes delight in everything mechanical without endorsing a narrowly mechanistic view of the world and all that therein is.

The stories focused on technology make no apology for stretching the boundaries of literary subject matter, yet it is another feature of Kipling's multiplicity that he explores his topic as a source of metaphor and analogy as well as something to value on its literal merits. In 'Below the Mill Dam' it is evident that some aspects of the mill's environment are freer than others. The Spirit of the Mill can migrate from wheel to turbine, the Waters glory in their fluctuations. The millstones are less fortunate; they tell the Wheel 'we are not the Mills of God. We're only the Upper and the Nether Millstones. We have received no instructions to be anything else. We are actuated by power transmitted through you' (*TD* 377). In certain stories, machinery becomes the vehicle for theological conundrums. The most dramatic case is 'McAndrew's Hymn'.[17]

This monologue is a companion piece to 'The "Mary Gloster"' (*DV* 129–36). Sir Anthony Gloster is a ruthlessly self-made man who, having started as an ordinary seaman, is now the owner of a huge shipping line, foundries and shipyards. On his way up, he has cut many corners, being willing to sabotage ships for the insurance and take the credit – not to mention the income – for his dead partner's plans for a rolling mill, clearing a sixty per cent profit on naval contracts.[18] McAndrew is Chief Engineer for a shipping line, and when young served in the *Mary Gloster*. The company's board makes much of him, but he doesn't even have a pension and has never had the time to take out a patent on his differential valve gear. He finds consolation in his engines and in God. Matching the rhythm of his pistons, his monologue follows an iambic pattern, arranged in alternating four- and three-beat lines, like many well-known hymns.[19] For him, steam engines are not a substitute for the Almighty but a model of divine power and a moral lesson.

> From coupler-flange to spindle-guide I see Thy Hand, O God –
> Predestination in the stride o' yon connectin'-rod. (*DV* 120)

Robert Graves often claimed that 'the Muse accepts no footnotes'.[20] With a poem like this, his muse would be very cross. Cynics who suspect that Kipling is merely showing off, and those who consider specialised language elitist, might join the chorus. Yet these are the words of a man whose everyday life is involved with the things themselves, and their names are necessary for the orders he must give. That is one of the many differences between him and Sir Kenneth, a member of the board who is given to 'Miscallin' technicalities' (*DV* 121). The names, moreover, are not simply flung down but play a dynamic role. That plain 'stride' in the couplet above, for instance, is both a precise observation of a marine engine at work and an emblem of divine will. At other times, the prompt may be aural; when haunted by the memory of brothels and religious infidelities:

> The sins o' four an' forty year, all up an' down the seas,
> Clack an' repeat like valves half-fed. Forgie's our trespasses!
>
> (*DV* 122)

The lineage of this poem includes Browning's *Men and Women* (1855) and, more directly in its Scottish voice and frame of reference,[21] Burns's 'Holy Willie's Prayer' (1785, 1799), yet McAndrew has gone through a spiritual crisis quite unimaginable in the life of that smug hypocrite Willie Fisher. Another ancestor must be Carlyle's *Sartor Resartus* (1838), for the remedy is work and duty; McAndrew sees the Light of God shine on his engine room like carbon arc lamps. The moment of revelation comes when, off the Great Barrier Reef, he remembers a verse from Ecclesiastes exalting clarity of vision over a life of drifting; like his (literary) creator, McAndrew has been well steeped in the language of the Bible. As he discourses, however, a Kiplingesque (and thoroughly unPresbyterian) animism mingles with the biblical quotations:

> While, out o' touch o' vanity, the sweatin' thrust-block says:
> 'Not unto us the praise, or man – not unto us the praise!'   (*DV* 126)

When the arrival of the pilot boat interrupts him, he is sweeping towards a Scottish ecstasy:

> O' that warld-liftin' joy no after-fall could vex
> Ye've left a glimmer still to cheer the Man – the Arrtifex!
> *That* holds, in spite o' knock and scale, o' friction, waste an' slip,
> An' by that light – now, mark my word – we'll build the Perfect Ship.

McAndrew joins his engines and his 'purrin' dynamoes' in accepting what might easily be considered Kipling's own imperatives: 'Law, Orrder, Duty an' Restraint, Obedience, Discipline!' (*DV* 126).

Yet it would be a mistake to hear these simply as Kipling's unmediated words. Without 'knock and scale … friction, waste an' slip', there would be no call and no material for fiction. Stories like 'The Honours of War' (*A Diversity of Creatures*) hint that he knew just how irksome obedience and discipline could be. Other stories, especially those with a medical or psychological background, reveal his curiosity about heterodox science and his sympathy with heresies of all sorts. Irascible though he often was, he had ecumenical tendencies that reached rather further than a sound Calvinist like McAndrew could tolerate.

III

Maintaining a strict distinction between science and technology does not make much sense, any more than regarding scientific thought as the pre-rogative of any single group or culture. Set in the thirteenth century, 'The Eye of Allah'[22] traces a network of scientific interests linking the abbey of St Illod in England with Salerno, the great medical school in southern Italy, Cairo and Granada with its mutually tolerant population of Muslims, Jews and Christians. The second part of the story is chiefly occupied with a dinner given by the abbot: besides Thomas, who has charge of the abbey's infirmary, Abbot Stephen's guests are John of Burgos, an illuminator of manuscripts, Roger of Salerno, a surgeon, and Roger Bacon, friar, Oxford lecturer and philosopher. Roger Bacon, of course, is a historical character, according to popular legend a magician, and in academic tradition a pion-eer of the experimental method; Roger (or Rogerius), too, is historical, the author of *Practica Chirurgiae* (*The Practice of Surgery*, *c.* 1180?), an influ-ential text in the great medieval universities. But, as Kipling probably knew, Roger the surgeon died around 1195, and Roger the natural philosopher was born in 1214. Moreover, the centre of attention during after-dinner conversation is a microscope, a device first known around the beginning of the seventeenth century. Here, then, is an example of that subgenre of speculative fiction known as alternative history. In this particular case, sci-entific observation of the alien world within a drop of water depends upon the patient grinding and placing of lenses, and the recognition that this alien world is neither magical illusion nor a glimpse of Hell depends upon these processes. As Bacon puts it: 'But I – *I* can bear witness it is no Art Magic ... Nothing is it, except Art optical – wisdom after trial and experi-ment, mark you. I can prove it, and – my name weighs with men who dare think.'[23] Roger of Salerno is the pessimist here, for he has seen the lengths to which the Church will go in suppressing awkward truths. He replies: 'Find them! Five or six in all the world. That makes less then fifty pounds by weight of ashes at the stake. I have watched such men – reduced.' Kipling has an all too vivid sense of the material bases of science and their mater-ial consequences. He also has a sense of historical timing. The story ends, very swiftly, when Abbot Stephen decides to smash the lens and burn the compass frame:

> But this birth, my sons, is untimely. It will be but the mother of more death, more torture, more division, and greater darkness in this dark age. Therefore I, who know both my world and the Church, take this Choice on my conscience. Go! It is finished.[24]

One of this story's many beauties is that Stephen does not feature as a bad man, let alone a monster. He may be wrong, and a modern reader will have a visual overload of hindsight, but this is an ending that promotes argument. It is the end of a dream and the start of a debate. Stories like this one make Bertolt Brecht's admiration for Kipling all the more understandable.[25]

Since this chapter is concerned with the technological rather than speculative or experimental bands of the scientific spectrum, the treatment of a whole group of stories about heterodox science must be brusque. These are often hybrids, half uncanny, half scientific, implying some overlap or doubling. 'In the Same Boat' (*A Diversity of Creatures*) has doctors treating patients who suffer from recurrent, devastating dreams; the patients, a man and a woman, talk each other through the pangs of withdrawal from strong drugs and find the dreams to be pre-natal implants, horrid images their mothers saw in pregnancy. In 'Unprofessional' (*Limits and Renewals*), an unorthodox team of ex-servicemen – a surgeon, a physician, a pathologist and an astronomer – study the connection between metabolic health and cellular 'tides', and succeed in rescuing a cancer patient subject to suicidal impulses after a perilous relapse. Operations must be performed only when times are propitious and while practising a system of orientation much like feng shui. This story features both the only systematic account in Kipling's work of experimental procedures and a suggestion from the astronomer that what they have learned from their work is that 'it makes one – not so much think – Research is gummed up with thinking – as imagine a bit'.[26] In '"Wireless"', most of what happens takes place in two rooms of a chemist's shop. In one an early radio enthusiast is trying to receive signals on his Marconi apparatus;[27] in the other, a consumptive chemist's assistant in love with a hearty woman is watching the shop. As the evening goes on, this double of Keats begins to murmur passages from 'The Eve of St Agnes' and the 'Ode to a Nightingale' – not the finished texts but work in progress. He denies all knowledge of the poet and his poems. Meanwhile, reception in the other room is bad; when signals finally come through, they are disjointed and coming from the wrong source. 'Have you ever seen a spiritualistic séance?' the disappointed operator asks. 'It reminds me of that sometimes – odds and ends of messages coming out of nowhere – a word here and there – no good at all' (*TD* 239).

These stories have affinities with one another, but they also share motifs and themes with other stories where reference to science is fleeting or entirely absent: '"Wireless"' can be paired with '"The Finest Story in the World"' (*Many Inventions*), 'In the Same Boat' with 'The Brushwood Boy' (*The Day's Work*), and 'Unprofessional' with 'The Wish House' (*Debits and*

Credits). One could also link some of these stories with others about the healing of badly damaged people, especially those about traumatised and wounded soldiers in *Debits and Credits*. Yet the scientific background is not merely a backdrop to the psychic drama, to be raised or lowered at will. If we think as citizens of the late nineteenth and early twentieth centuries, some of the more improbable notions in these stories come back to life again. The example of Sir Oliver Lodge is instructive. A distinguished physicist, appointed to his first chair at the age of thirty and later Principal of Birmingham University, he was the second person ever to send a radio signal, the first being Tesla, and the third, Marconi. He was also attracted to the supernatural, invited the Italian medium Eusapia Palladino to Cambridge, and was President of the Society for Psychical Research in the year that Kipling published '"Wireless"'.[28] This is not to claim that Kipling was influenced by Lodge, or that Lodge equated wireless transmission with spiritualism. The better point would be that intellectual boundaries have shifted since then – and of course may shift again. In the case of Kipling's stories about the psychological effects of war, for instance, the current attention to post-traumatic stress has moved the boundaries in his favour.

IV

Three stories propose versions of the near future. 'The Army of a Dream' is a vision of a new social compact rather than new hardware. In one exception, the narrator is surprised by the small bore of the latest rifle, but reassured when told that the bullets 'expand a bit when they arrive' (*TD* 294).[29] The real improvements, though, are in the organisation of the armed forces, their morale and their standing in society. Almost all men volunteer for a military unit (and lose the right to vote if they do not); the men are so well drilled that they can carry out any manoeuvre astonishingly quickly by the standards of 1904, the year of the story's serial in the *Morning Post*.[30] Another contrast with the present (the years immediately after the Second Anglo-Boer War) is the absence of red tape and a diminution of snobbery. Although not a work of science fiction, this 'dream' is closely related to the future war novels which appeared in large numbers and many countries between the Franco-Prussian War and First World War. These novels usually advanced some military or social agenda; the harbinger was *The Battle of Dorking* (1871), in which the Royal Engineers save the day: its author, George Chesney, had served in the Bengal Engineers and became an energetic proponent of army reform in India and at home.

The lack of interest in technology notwithstanding, 'The Army of a Dream' had an influence on science fiction. Robert Heinlein's *Starship*

Troopers (1959) borrows many of its military and political features from Kipling. This influence, though, is slight in comparison with that of the two stories about flight: 'With the Night Mail' (*Actions and Reactions*) and 'As Easy as A.B.C.' (*A Diversity of Creatures*), especially the former.[31] This is a *jeu d'esprit* framed as a magazine article describing a flight from London to Quebec City in a G[eneral] P[ost] O[ffice] mail dirigible. The article is accompanied by spoof advertisements and official notices all relevant to aviation; these paratexts, as narratologists would call them, are clever parodies of the editorial comments, book reviews, gossip columns, official notices and advertisements of Kipling's own time, but they also help tell the story of the future debate over the rival merits of dirigibles and aeroplanes, and flesh out the culture of a whole future society. The year in book form is 2000; in the *McClure's* serial (November 1905), it is 2025, and the story is printed as if it were an article in that magazine.[32] For information on the advantages of dirigibles, Kipling probably drew on articles by and about the Brazilian 'sportsman of the air' Alberto Santos Dumont, who had won many prizes for his exploits in the skies over Paris.[33]

Kipling was by no means the first to write fiction about flying, and several near-contemporaries were intrigued by the political possibilities,[34] among them Jules Verne (*Robur-le-conquérant*, 1886), Sir Julius Vogel (*Anno Domini 2000, or Woman's Destiny*, 1889), Lady Florence Douglas Dixie (*Gloriana*, 1890), George Griffith Jones (*The Angel of the Revolution*, 1893) and, most notably, H. G. Wells, whose *When the Sleeper Wakes* (1899) actually includes a tribute to Kipling.[35] These works feature struggles over the future of the world. In 'With the Night Mail', the problem has been resolved. The Earth is at peace under the supreme international authority of the Aerial Board of Control, or A.B.C, whose primary duty is to smooth the to and fro of passenger- and cargo-carrying dirigibles. As long as traffic (always a resonant word for Kipling) is not disturbed, harmony prevails. This is a global culture at its confident height. On the transatlantic journey, the journalist learns a great deal about the motive power of the Fleury ray, sees freighters from every part of the globe and a hospital dirigible taking TB patients up for clear cold air, and experiences a dangerous electrical storm, but the only human turbulence is caused by the occasional private flyer breaking the speed limit or failing to observe navigational beacons.

Set sixty-five years further into the future, 'As Easy as A.B.C.' is a more oblique story, and for all the emphasis on laughter as a purgative, a darker one with a dystopian subtext. By 2065 public gatherings have been prohibited as an intrusion on personal space. Illegal assemblies have appeared in small-town Illinois and in Chicago itself, where groups have been chanting 'McDonough's Song' and demanding the right to vote. The song is actually directed against any form of excessive power: 'Holy State or Holy King – / Or Holy People's Will', but is considered too inflammatory to permit.[36] The rebels have also uncovered a statue known as 'The Nigger in Flames', a clear allusion to lynching as a manifestation of populist will, and a forbidden sight. The rebels are to be disciplined by a punitive raid by airships of the A.B.C. Thus power is exercised to subdue those who sing songs opposing power. There are no bombs, but a blinding and deafening display – shock and awe in all its arrogant glory. No one is killed, but the machines that have made the world happy and at peace are capable of mass intimidation. Even one of the four representatives of the A. B. C. is horrified by what is taking place: '"No!" cried Dragomiroff ... "I do not know all that you can do, but be kind! I ask you to be a little kind to them below! This is horrible – horrible!"'[37] All ends apparently happily as the protestors are taken off to London to perform their queer electoral rituals before audiences in a music hall. But ridicule in this story is not quite as satisfactory a solution as it is in another story in *A Diversity of Creatures*, 'The Village That Voted the Earth Was Flat'. Kipling himself despised the 'solemn pump and incontinent peedle of Democracy',[38] but the Board's position is all too contradictory. This is social entropy at work. As science fiction, these two stories are thought experiments, contributions to debates about the future of aviation and nationality, the power of science and technology to shape the world, the role of technocrats, and the stability of cultural and political institutions. Taken in postcolonial terms, they reflect the hopes and anxieties, the ambiguities and contradictions of imperial power in all its manifestations, from admiration of the work of empire to a fear of decadence, from the romance of global travel and the exhilaration of flying high to the punitive raid.

Notes

1 First published in the *Civil and Military Gazette*, 9 May 1887, as 'The D.C.'s Story'; with fewer of the Anglo-Indian expressions, collected in the third edition of *Departmental Ditties* (1888), and quoted here from *Rudyard Kipling's Verse: Definitive Edition* (London: Hodder and Stoughton, 1940), pp. 20–1. Further references in the text as *DV*.

2 His letters appeared in the *Morning Post* between 29 November and 30 December 1927; they were collected in the Sussex Edition, and have also appeared in a slim volume, Rudyard Kipling, *Brazilian Sketches*, ed. Paul E. Waters (Bromley, Kent: P. E. Waters, 1989).

3 Rudyard Kipling, *Traffics and Discoveries* (London: Macmillan, 1904), p. 304. Further references in the text as *TD*. 'Steam Tactics', another story in the collection, pits steam against petrol-powered cars.

4 In Rudyard Kipling, *The Phantom Rickshaw* (1887).

5 For the political context, see Angus Wilson, *The Strange Ride of Rudyard Kipling* (London: Secker & Warburg, 1977), p. 232, and Andrew Lycett, *Rudyard Kipling*

(London: Weidenfeld & Nicolson, 1999), pp. 348–9. When he wrote the story, Kipling was about to install a turbine-driven generator in the watermill at Bateman's (Lycett, pp. 347–8).

6 The notion that the English countryside was and should be timeless and unchanging persisted: as late as 1924, Kipling's cousin Stanley Baldwin was lauding the horse-drawn plough in a speech to the Royal Society of St George. Stanley Baldwin, *On England: And Other Addresses* (London: Allan, 1926), p. 7.

7 Other contemporaries had the knowledge, but, whether for reasons of decorum or concern about readership, tended to keep all but the generalities out of their work. Zola knew about mining and railway operation, Conrad about marine engines, Willa Cather about bridge-building; Henry James had enough grasp of 'McAndrew's Hymn' to translate it at sight into 'vigorous idiomatic French' (Mrs Humphry Ward, *A Writer's Recollections* (3rd edn London: Collins, 1919), p. 326). The exception was the American magazine story, especially at *McClure's* under Willa Cather's editorship, and the *Metropolitan* under Carl Hovey's, but most of the writers concerned are now forgotten and the technical references are often casual.

8 Verne was famously scornful, for example, about Wells's 'Cavorite', the gravity-resistant mineral that enables the voyage of *The First Men in the Moon*. R. H. Sherard, 'Jules Verne Re-Visited', *T. P.'s Weekly* (London) (9 October 1903), p. 589.

9 The story grew out of lengthy chats with the stationmaster at Brattleboro, Vermont, and was first published in *Scribner's Magazine*, so Kipling makes a point of using American terms, such as 'freight' rather than 'goods', 'switching' rather than 'shunting'. For a detailed discussion of the technical background, see the notes on the story in the *New Readers' Guide* on the Kipling Society's website at www.kipling.org.uk/rg_007_notes.htm

10 Commentators usually note the resemblance to Masonic practice, but the primary reference here must be to the oldest of the railway unions, the Brotherhood of Locomotive Engineers, founded as the Brotherhood of the Footplate in 1863 and renamed in 1864.

11 As opposed, for instance, to the relentlessly monocular perspective of such poems as '"Cleared"' or 'Ulster', *DV*, pp. 227–30, 232–3.

12 Collected in H. G. Wells, *The Stolen Bacillus and Other Incidents* (1895).

13 Max Weber, *Essays in Sociology*, trans. and ed. H. H. Gerth and C. Wright Mills (London: Routledge, 1948), p. 139, from 'Wissenschaft als Beruf' (1919). By *Entzauberung*, Weber meant not so much disillusionment as a lack of sympathy with the magical.

14 Walter Benjamin, *Illuminations*, trans. Harry Zohn (New York: Schocken, 1968), p. 91.

15 *Ibid.*, pp. 101–2.

16 Rudyard Kipling, 'The Law of the Jungle', *DV*, p. 558.

17 Collected in *The Seven Seas* (1897); *DV*, pp. 120–7.

18 'And I'm no fool to finish if a man'll give me a hint. / (I remember his widow was angry.) So I saw what his drawings meant, / And I started the six-inch rollers, and it paid me sixty per cent' (*DV*, p. 132). Whether 'six-inch' refers to the diameter of the rolls (puny, even by the standards of the 1870s) or the thickness of the armour plating they produced, Sir Anthony has made an immense profit

from shoddy work. The moral differences between Gloster and McAndrew are much greater than P. J. Keating suggests in his *Kipling the Poet* (London: Secker & Warburg, 1994), pp. 108–10.

19 Each pair of lines, however, is printed as one long line, rhyming in couplets. Making a quite different rhythmic effect, Sir Anthony speaks in anapaests.

20 See for instance his lecture '"These Be Your Gods, O Israel"' in *The Crowning Privilege* (London: Cassell, 1955). For those whose muse is less strict, the *New Readers' Guide* on the Kipling Society website has excellent notes on the technicalities www.kipling.org.uk/rg_mcandrew_notes.htm

21 A Glaswegian voice, as suggested by rhyming 'seas' with 'trespasses'.

22 Rudyard Kipling, *Debits and Credits* (London: Macmillan, 1926).

23 *Ibid.*, p. 391.

24 *Ibid.*, p. 394.

25 Brecht raises many similar issues in his *Life of Galileo* – the aims and outcomes of scientific research, the virtues of speaking out and the virtues of staying silent, the kinship of science and technology.

26 Rudyard Kipling, *Limits and Renewals* (London: Macmillan, 1932), p. 281.

27 The story appeared in *Scribner's Magazine* in August 1902, eight months after the first transmission across the Atlantic. This enthusiast, however, is waiting for a signal from Poole, just forty miles away.

28 For more details of Sir Oliver Lodge's career, see his entry in the *Oxford Dictionary of National Biography*.

29 The bore is .256, whereas the bore of Kipling's day was .303. He is scoring a political point here against humanitarians and internationalists: the signatories of the Hague Convention of 1899 had renounced the use of expanding bullets in wars between sovereign nations.

30 By endorsing efficiency, Kipling prefigures the ideas set out in Frederick Winslow Taylor's *The Principles of Scientific Management* (1911) but does not share the latter's authoritarianism. Whereas Taylor expects the worst from his factory workers, Kipling trusts in the good will and intelligence of his citizen soldiers.

31 For details of that influence, see Fred Lerner's essay 'A Master of Our Art: Rudyard Kipling Considered as a Science Fiction Writer' at www.kipling.org.uk/rg_scifi.htm

32 The British serial (*Windsor Magazine*, December 1905) gives the date as 'October, A.D. 2147' and omits the spoof advertisements.

33 Dumont's article 'The Future of Aerial Navigation', *The London Magazine*, 14 (June 1905), pp. 499–507, is particularly close in technical detail to Kipling's story.

34 Among earlier relevant texts are Book Three of Swift's *Gulliver's Travels* (1726; fuller text 1735) and the vision of the future at the end of Tennyson's 'Locksley Hall' (1842).

35 When the Sleeper begins to explore the future London, he comes across what he thinks is a library (but is really a collection of videotapes); the only titles named are 'The Heart of Darkness', 'The Madonna of the Future' and 'The Man Who Would Be King'. Like Kipling, Wells dwells on the popular culture of the future, but his version is far more sombre. Another likely intertext is

Wells's *A Modern Utopia* (1905): his Samurai in many ways resemble members of the A.B.C.

36 Rudyard Kipling, *A Diversity of Creatures* (London: Macmillan, 1917), p. 44.
37 *Ibid.*, p. 12.
38 Letter to Andrew Macphail, 5 December 1911, in *The Letters of Rudyard Kipling, Volume 4, 1911–19*, ed. Thomas Pinney (Basingstoke: Macmillan, 1999), p. 74.

5

KAORI NAGAI

Kipling and gender

'Unfortunately, everybody must be either a man or a woman' according to Dick Heldar, the hero of *The Light That Failed* (1891), who goes on to tell Maisie, his childhood sweetheart, that she is not a woman.[1] Maisie, now a young artist, craves the professional recognition reserved only for men, and, to Dick's horror, chooses a same-sex companionship over marriage, which she senses would compromise her independence. In many ways, Maisie embodies the fin-de-siècle figure of 'the New Woman', which gave expression to feminist ideals and aspirations, but also to society's fears and anxiety about the budding women's movement and its threat to conventional values.[2] There is a strong sense in Kipling's world that men and women live in separate spheres and should abide by different laws, and that women, as J. M. S. Tompkins argued, 'should not attempt to play a man's part in a man's world'.[3] This makes Maisie, who seeks to be liberated from her traditional gender roles, problematic for Dick, who wants to marry her, and for Kipling, who wishes to put her back in her place; for both, she is neither a man nor a woman.

Female gender transgression like Maisie's poses a significant threat to Kipling's predominantly male world of colonisers, which is supported by, and is defined against, the marginal 'feminine' presence. For instance, 'the little mother' of the Infant, a character in *Stalky & Co.*, feeds her son's guests to satisfaction and then leaves. She sets the scene for the imperial boys' reunion, and the staging of Stalky's colonial adventures, with her parting remark: 'You boys want to talk, so I shall say good-night now.'[4] The woman is assigned the roles of lovingly bestowing blessings and recognition on acts of male bonding ('You boys'), and consolidating them by her withdrawal ('I shall say good-night'). The colonial Others are made to play a similar role, sometimes as the smiling faces which welcome the White Man's rule (for instance, the women in *Kim*), and sometimes as threats to colonial authority, characterised as effeminate and/or castrating and therefore dangerous. 'The untamable hostility of the natural world', as Jan Montefiore puts it, also figures in Kipling's world as feminine and maternal, something which 'it is a man's part to outwit to endure'.[5] The vision of the eternal battle between Man and Mother Nature elevates the colonial Mission to mythic heights, rendering it never-ending, as can be seen in 'The Bridge-Builders' in *The Day's Work*, in which the Civil Engineers struggle to harness the power of Nature embodied as Mother Gunga. Moreover, 'the feminine' is called upon to give expression to the White Man's own anxieties and ambivalences, which are depicted as the signs of effeminacy, or the return of the feminine hitherto repressed. As Zohreh T. Sullivan rightly points out, 'gender' in Kipling is so overriding that it makes 'race' almost redundant: 'The colonizer needs no native Other on whom to project threat: it lies within the self or it is gendered in terms of female otherness and the metaphysical world.'[6] In other words, 'the feminine' in Kipling's world suffers an even more fundamental subjugation to white men than the racial other. The biggest offence committed by Maisie, Dick's 'companion in bondage' in his childhood,[7] is not her gender crossing, but her refusal to live out the role which Kipling assigns to all women.

According to the woman from Kulu, an old native widow in *Kim* (1901), 'there are but two sorts of women in [this world] – those who take the strength out of a man and those who put it back. Once I was that one, and now I am this.'[8] Of course, as Sandra Kemp argues, this is 'a markedly misogynist reduction of women to stereotypes' on Kipling's part, seeing women as either 'Virgin or Vampire',[9] but nevertheless a useful framework to start with. Some of Kipling's female characters are depicted as life-givers and men's dependable helpmates. In 'The Daughter of the Regiment' in *Plain Tales from the Hills,* for instance, when cholera breaks out in an Irish regiment in India, a colour-sergeant's wife heroically takes charge of the situation by mobilising all the regimental women as nurses. These women value and share the best qualities and ideals of their male counterparts. This is probably why the eponymous heroine of 'William the Conqueror' in *The Day's Work*, who follows her brother to Southern India to aid him with famine relief, is given a boy's name as her nickname. William 'conquers' not just an Indian famine, but also the heart of her brother's colleague, through the love and understanding which she demonstrates during the difficult time of the famine. Some women, on the other hand, pose a serious threat to men's lives and their manliness. In *The Light That Failed* and 'The Man Who Would be King' (1888), the male protagonists are symbolically castrated at the hands of women. Dick, after his ill-fated encounters with Maisie, her red-haired companion and Bessie the model, goes blind and loses his potency as a professional painter. Similarly Daniel Dravot, who successfully passes as a god among natives, dramatically falls from power when his bride bites him, drawing blood, which proves that he is a mere human. Both men subsequently die.[10] Female influence is shown to be all the more destructive because it disrupts male homosocial bonding, which is for Kipling the foundation of the colonial enterprise. It is no accident that in the final scenes of the two stories we find the dead male protagonist being attended by his faithful male companion, highlighting at once the female power irreparably to destroy the strongest of brotherhoods, and men's devotion to each other and to the ideal which once united them.

More importantly, however, these two types of women are two sides of the same coin; as the woman from Kulu puts it, 'Once I was that one, and now I am this.' Either way, they are part of a man through the exchange of love and vitality (some 'take the strength out of a man' and some 'put it back'). Indeed, there is hardly a woman in Kipling's world who does not, in some way or other, accept her role as the man's 'companion in bondage', which makes Maisie a rare exception. There is Kate Sheriff, an American girl, in *The Naulahka* (1892; co-written with Wolcott Balestier), who likewise chooses her 'calling' over marriage: she goes to the East to 'better the condition of the women of India'.[11] However, the enormity of the task and her fruitless efforts – 'against thousands of years of traditions, and training, and habits of life'[12] – cruelly crush her spirit, and in the end she falls into the arms of her suitor Nick, agreeing to marry him. This novel of the successful 'taming of the shrew' contains an astute criticism of, and valuable insight into, men's need for female companions. As Kate says to Nick, in one of her countless rejections of his marriage proposals:

> But what is it you really want? ... You want me to round out your life; you want me to complete your other ambitions. Isn't that so? Tell me honestly, Nick; isn't that so? ... Marriage means that – to be absorbed into another's life: to live your own, not as your own but another's. It is a good life. It is a woman's life. I can like it; I can believe in it. But I can't see myself in it. A woman gives the whole of herself in marriage – in all happy marriages. I haven't the whole of myself to give. It belongs to something else. And I couldn't offer you a part; it is all the best men give to women, but from a woman it would do no man any good.[13]

She points out that the companionship between a man and a woman is by no means equal: a woman is a man's supplement to complete his life as a helper of his ambitions. Moreover, a woman is expected to give 'the whole of herself' and lose herself in her man, while a man only gives a part of himself back and keeps the other parts intact.

Kate's view on marriage encapsulates a pattern in Kipling's representation of male–female companionship. There is a curious relationship between part and whole: a woman, represented as 'a whole', becomes a part of the man, while a man is only a part, which needs to be supplemented by a woman to be 'a whole', always lacking in something, divided, fragmented and often broken. This does not limit itself to a marriage relationship; for instance, in 'The Woman in his Life' in *Limits and Renewals*, a 'woman' who becomes a part of John Marden's life and heals his post-war trauma is a female Aberdeen terrier called Dinah. The mother–son relationship, the most prevalent in Kipling's fictions, also falls into this pattern. As Kipling's poem 'Mother o' Mine', which he used as a dedication to *The Light That Failed*, expresses, a mother's love, prayers and tears always 'follow' her son, and this is what makes him 'whole'.[14] The repetition of 'O' in the refrain visually shows ('*Mother o' mine, O mother o' mine!*') the wholeness of the maternal love and that of the mother–son union, as well as the opening of a gap, or a lack, in himself, which the male child calls upon his mother to fill in. There is something essentially egoistical about Kipling's attitude to women – the egoism of a spoiled and needy child, who needs to keep all the maternal care and attention for himself. Leonard Shengold, in his analysis of Kipling's semi-autobiographical story 'Baa Baa, Black Sheep' (1888), characterises Punch's foster mother, Aunty Rosa, as a phallic mother who 'threatened Rudyard's masculinity'.[15] Arguably, however, Punch's deep hatred of her comes from the fact that she is unable to bond with Punch as *his* mother (whether good or bad), as she already has a son of her own, Harry, which makes Punch 'the extra boy about the house'.[16] If, as Shengold suggests, Harry is Aunty Rosa's 'phallic extension',[17] the threat to Punch's masculinity comes from his not being able to take his place as her phallus.

Kipling's women are usually round and lifelike characters, whom he treats as psychological entities. Each of them is made to embody the wholeness of a woman to be given to a man as a gift. On the other hand, Kipling's child-hero, who craves undivided female attention, refuses to give the whole of himself to a woman, even to his 'real' mother. As Randall Jarrell observed, Kipling's world is full of surrogate parents – 'wild animals turn out to be the abandoned Mowgli's real father and mother, a heathen Lama turns out to be the orphaned Kim's real father'[18] – while the biological parents are characteristically absent. The proliferation of surrogate mothers presupposes the lack of a Real Mother, and even Punch's own mother is made to play the role of a mother surrogate, by substituting his ayah and foster mother. In this way, Punch can enjoy the company of his devoted ayah and Indian servant *and* of his parents, without any conflict of loyalty – an ideal arrangement for the coloniser who thereby becomes the 'real' child of as many colonised nations as possible.

Women and desire

Kipling is the author of a famous anti-suffragist poem, 'The Female of the Species' (1911), with its memorable refrain: 'For the female of the species is more deadly than the male'.[19] The gist of the poem is that Woman is created 'more deadly' than Man to protect her children and ensure the perpetuation of her species. Shortly after it appeared Kipling wrote to Edward Bok, the editor of the American women's magazine, the *Ladies' Home Journal*:

> the driving force of the suffrage agitation comes (a) from the surplus who, consciously or unconsciously want a man and don't care a curse for politics (b) from the women without power to hold or charm the man they've got. In fact a regular female Cave of Adullam.
>
> *Summa. You* [Americans] won't treat women as companions of men in your new civilization. *We*, in our old civilization, treat 'em maybe too much as companions but there ain't enough men to go around. In both lands arises the cry for 'comradeship'. Your women *do* need being treated more as comrades. Ours (the surplus) want something else.[20]

In this gloss on the Woman Question, the suffragettes' desire for freedom is construed as originating in their secret yearning for men. The expression 'Cave of Adullam', designating a group of political dissidents, here sounds almost vaginal, as Kipling hints at suffragettes' sexual frustration. What makes this passage even more 'sexist' is his apparent belief in men's power to appease women by offering themselves as their companions. 'The attention and companionship of the man'[21] is the tried and tested art of mastering women, which Kipling, as the representative of the old civilisation, recommends to the Young America as a remedy for the raging Suffrage movement – even though, he has to admit, the system is faltering in England as a consequence of the chronic shortage of marriageable men due to emigration and loss of life on the imperial frontier. This has given rise to 'the surplus' that now 'wants something else'.

In Kipling's works, women figure as desiring subjects. His female characters are often depicted as being driven by their desire for their chosen man; this is characterised as something akin to Magic, which often manifests itself as the woman's spoken words or command. 'The Cat That Walked By Himself' from the *Just So Stories* is a beautiful example of this, in which the Woman appears as a sorceress whose Magic tames the wild Man and all the animals she needs for her household. Her spoken wishes are magic words which shape her world; even a He-Cat, 'the wildest of all the wild animals',[22] uses his cunning to ensure that he is snared by her magic, being seduced by the warmth and comfort of her Cave. Miss Sichliffe, in 'The Dog Hervey' in *A Diversity of Creatures*, one of the most uncomely of Kipling's heroines, who, with her pair of pince-nez, looks 'like a camel',[23] is undoubtedly another sorceress, who works some kind of magic by creating uncanny puzzles – where she becomes just such a puzzle herself – that bemuse the narrator and the reader alike, eventually leading her to the reunion with the one man in her life who ever cared for her. Even though she, like her dog, is inscrutable, we are left with the impression of the depth of her desire, when she expresses to the narrator her mysterious wish that he should know her real name and age: 'her face worked like glass behind driven flame'.[24]

Kipling, in his letter to Bok quoted above, mentions a surplus of unmarried women as the cause of Women's Suffrage. However, such women would not be a problem, as long as they preoccupy themselves in bestowing the magic of love and companionship on the men they desire. In fact, the deep attachment of the middle-aged single woman to her nephew, her illegitimate son or a younger man is a recurrent theme in Kipling's later stories (for instance, 'Mary Postgate' in *A Diversity of Creatures* and 'The Gardener' in *Debits and Credits*). What is truly unsettling for Kipling is that which male company fails to harness in women and which thereby escapes man's control: the true 'surplus', the big *O* of the Adullamite Cave, the side of women which wants 'something else' – the mouth which does not speak of him, or consent to fill his void.

Kipling has been highly praised for his sympathetic treatment of women in his late fictions,[25] but comparisons between some of his earlier and later stories reveal recurring patterns. Take, for instance, 'The Education of Otis Yeere' (first published in 1888 and later collected in *Wee Willie Winkie and Other Stories*) and 'The Wish House' (1924) in *Debits and Credits*. In both stories, the feminine sphere is represented in the form of the conversation between two women, the main topic of which is, of course, the men in their lives. 'The Education of Otis Yeere' is the story of Mrs Lucy Hauksbee, who makes appearances in a number of Kipling's early Indian stories. She is a witty and mischievous 'grass widow', who enjoys her social and flirtatious life in Simla, while her husband is away toiling in the plains. She has a unique talent of manipulating men, which she uses for her own amusement as well as to save the Raj: 'if Mrs Hauksbee gave the order, the whole Great Indian Administration would stand on its head'.[26] In this story, however, Mrs Hauksbee, confiding to her bosom friend Mrs Mallowe, shows her vulnerable side. Despite her 'half-a-dozen attachés' and the significant control she exercises over the Indian Government, she has not yet found fulfilment in her heart-felt desire: 'I want to be a Power before I die' (*WWW* 6). She thus decides to try Mrs Mallowe's suggestion that she be a Power and Influence: take a man under her wing – 'be his guide, philosopher, and friend' (*WWW* 15) – and mentor him into achieving success. The scheme fails when her chosen man, Otis Yeere, spoils her plan by falling in love with her, but the story interestingly reveals what Kipling wants women to want: women desire neither fame nor political power, but a spiritual and intellectual influence ('Now, understand that there must be no flirtation') over one man; they want to take complete control of him and his life, and, as it were, write Him according to their wishes ('Do exactly what I tell you, profit by my instruction and counsels, and all will yet be well' (*WWW* 15)).

In 'The Education of Otis Yeere', the two women meet in Mrs Mallowe's house, 'The Foundry' (*WWW* 4) – suggestively so named because it is where they scheme to mould the raw material of a man into an artwork. The House as a magical space, which binds, shapes and creates Man according to Woman's spoken words, is also the central device of 'The Wish House'. This story has the same theme of ageing as the earlier one – 'Has it ever struck you, dear, that I'm getting old?'(*WWW* 6) – where it becomes a matter of urgency for Mrs Hauksbee to make her life meaningful by becoming a Power before she dies. In 'The Wish House', two elderly women, Mrs Ashcroft and Mrs Fettley, look back upon their lives, and we learn that the former, slowly dying from cancer, painfully clings to her belief that she has been secretly in control of the life of her man and 'master', Harry Mockler.[27] The Wish House is an abandoned house in a London street, in which lives 'a Token' – 'a wraith of the dead or, worse still, of the living' (*DC* 126) – which grants one's wish to take over somebody else's suffering for love. Mrs Ashcroft tells Mrs Fettley how she wished 'the Wish House' to 'take everythin' bad that's in store for [her] man, 'Arry Mockler, for love's sake' (*DC* 131). Harry is a much younger man, with whom Mrs Ashcroft, after her husband's death, had a brief relationship and fell fatally in love. After Harry breaks up with her, by paying back 'every penny' he had owed her (*DC* 123), 'the Wish House' becomes the only way for her to keep him and remain a significant influence in his life by incurring his debts. The pain of her cancer has become a sure sign that the magic is working: ''E got 'is good from me 'thout knowin' – for years and years' (*DC* 135).

Both 'The Education of Otis Yeere' and 'The Wish House' depict women's desire to take control over a man by becoming a secret spiritual influence. The former ends in utter failure, and we are not very sure of the success of the latter either, as Mrs Ashcroft's story is purely based on coincidences and the strength of her belief. Towards the end of the story, she herself asks Mrs Fettley for reassurance of the truthfulness of her own story: 'I was wonderin' … But the pain *do* count, don't ye think, Liz? The pain do count to keep 'Arry where I want 'im. Say it can't be wasted, like' (*DC* 137). The last image of Mrs Ashcroft is her lips as she repeats the same question – a fitting ending to the story, as her life was bound by the wishes uttered by her lips – which Mrs Fettley kisses as she leaves the house (*DC* 138). Kipling would not give his female characters the satisfaction of having control over their man – provided, that is, that he is enough of a man in the first place. (In "'Yoked with an Unbeliever'" in *Plain Tales from the Hills*, a Hill-girl Dunmaya manages to make 'a decent man' out of her English husband, but he is a weak character, who is deemed by the narrator to be 'no use' as a coloniser.)[28] Instead, Kipling casts them in the role of surrogate mothers. Mrs Ashcroft, though her attachment to Harry is no doubt driven by her obsession and sexual desire, is forced to compete for his love with his mother, to whom "E slipped off 'ere back 'ome' after he left her (*DC* 123). 'The Wish House' is a story of the two houses: on the one hand, Harry's Mother's House, in which she, as 'a watch-dog' (*DC* 124), keeps a close eye on her boy and keeps him away from other women, and on the other hand, the Wish House, through which Mrs Ashcroft, his 'other mother', forces upon Harry a spiritual relationship based on the economy of pain. It is perhaps more than convention that leads Kipling to refer to his female characters in both stories by their (absent) husbands' surnames (Mrs Hauksbee, Mrs Ashcroft, etc.); these surnames represent the Law of the surrogate home, preventing women from becoming real mothers of their surrogate children.

Kipling's women, however, are allowed to take all, in death. Another uncanny similarity can be seen between 'By Word of Mouth' (1887, collected in *Plain Tales from the Hills*) and 'A Madonna of the Trenches' (1924, in *Debits and Credits*), both of which tell of a man's rendezvous with a female apparition, which comes to claim his life and his eternal companionship. In the former story, Dumoise, a Civil Surgeon in India, receives a message from his dead wife via his Indian servant, who has seen her ghost lifting 'the veil of her bonnet' to say: 'Ram Dass, give my *salaams* to the *Sahib*, and tell him that I shall meet him next month at Nuddea.'[29] Immediately after this, Dumoise is ordered to go to Nuddea to attend an outbreak of cholera. He goes there and dies. The title, 'By Word of Mouth', beautifully captures the feminine essence – imperishable even after death – as spoken wishes directed at men, which pierce through, and annihilate for a moment, multifarious veils and distance, which separate men and women, as well as life and death. It is significant that she chooses to speak to Dumoise's servant, rather than giving him her message in person. The British rule in the colonial space has granted white women the power as *Memsahibs* over native servants, and it is with this absolute authority, which should never be disobeyed, that she also commands her husband. Kipling thereby characterises the Indian household, together with the Raj, as dictated by, and at the mercy of, the female power; she not only has power over her house, servants and husband, but also becomes one with the ravaging power of nature in India, which takes life as she pleases.

In 'A Madonna of the Trenches', the image of countless cholera victims in India is substituted by that of corpses in the trenches of the Great War, which 'creak in the frost' (*DC* 242), and into this scene of mass destruction of life, a female apparition arrives again to take away the life of her chosen man. In this story, Bella Armine, who is dying of cancer, sends a message to her lover, John Godsoe, who is fighting in France, informing him of the likely date of her death and telling him that she is 'dyin' to see him as soon as possible after that date' (*DC* 250). On that fixed date, Bella dies and visits Godsoe as a ghost, and he commits suicide to accompany her. This plot is almost identical to 'By Word of Mouth', though it is further complicated by the illicit nature of the characters' relationship: both of them are married to others. Bella entrusts her message to her nephew, a young private, Clem Strangwick, who knows nothing about her affair with Godsoe. She first orally dictates it to Clem, in the manner of 'By Word of Mouth', but then decides to write it down, saying that he has 'a head like a sieve' (*DC* 251). Writing as coded messages, substituting her desiring mouth and Godsoe's receptive ears – and not unlike Kipling's late style in general – becomes an oblique way in which the two lovers communicate with each other: while at the Front, Godsoe, an old family friend of the Strangwicks, writes letters to Clem's mother with news of her son, and Bella, her sister, always reads the letters aloud to her, as her eyesight is failing. Their meeting in the trenches is thus a powerful moment in which all the texts and pretexts which kept them apart collapse, as Bella's apparition 'answer[s] to [Godsoe's] spoken word' (*DC* 256).

'A Madonna of the Trenches' is set in a Masonic Lodge some years after the War. Clem appears as an ex-soldier suffering from a nervous breakdown, who recounts to his Medical Officer and the narrator the circumstance of Godsoe's suicide. The horror of witnessing Bella's ghost turns out to be the main cause of his mental condition, though it is not so much the supernatural as the discovery of the extramarital relationship which had psychologically shattered him. The shock of finding powerful desire and sexuality in Bella, whom he calls Aunty Ar*mine* (my emphasis) –'she nearer fifty than forty an' me own Aunt!' (*DC* 256) – affected his view of women and the nature of female companionship and prompted him to break off his engagement with his fiancée. There is also the strong sense of betrayal by two of the most trusted people in his life: Godsoe, whom he always called Uncle John, was his father figure from childhood, and, as for Bella, he believed 'I was always her favourite' (*DC* 251), as she did not have a child of her own. The wartime trauma thus coincides with the collapse of the ego of the surrogate child, who took for granted that he was the centre of every household he visited, only to find out that he had been an instrument of somebody else's love.

Feminine writing

Max Beerbohm, in his theatre review of *The Light That Failed*, an adaptation of the novel by a female playwright, 'George Fleming', attacks Kipling's representation of male characters, in particular, his over-idealisation of manliness and manhood, which he sees as a sign of effeminacy. Kipling's male characters are 'portrayed in an essentially feminine manner, and from an essentially feminine point of view', and he even goes so far as provokingly to say that 'Rudyard Kipling' could be 'a lady's pseudonym', or 'the veil of a feminine identity'.[30] Beerbohm's article has been mentioned by critics in support of their view that Kipling is in touch with his 'feminine side', and that he is sympathetic and insightful in his treatment of his female characters. As Sandra Kemp puts it, 'Max Beerbohm's famous attack ... is curiously suggestive. It is not often noted how frequently Kipling assumes a woman's voice, and, especially in the late stories, the way he privileges distinctly "feminine" sensibilities.'[31] Both Beerbohm and Kemp characterise Kipling's work as a kind of *écriture féminine*: for the former, this is at the core of his imperialism and, for the latter, it is what makes his writing a potent criticism of imperialist ideologies, including his own.

U. C. Knoepflmacher, in his analysis of the mother figure in Kipling's fictions, argues that Kipling's resourcefulness and creativity depend upon 'the continuing feminine attachments':[32] Kipling, in his role as 'a mother's son', 'releases and gains for himself the femininity his stereotypical male rivals were unable to free'.[33] The mother figure, then, plays a similar role to what Freud calls creative writers' 'day-dreaming', which allows them to recapture the joy and creativity of childhood.[34] Kipling, in this sense, is a daydreamer par excellence. According to Freud, a grown-up man cannot 'give up a pleasure he has once experienced' as a child, and, instead of renouncing it, he forms 'a substitute or surrogate' of that pleasure in the form of day-dreaming. Kipling's fictional world, built upon the pleasure of edenic childhood in India, gives rise to the proliferation of 'surrogate' mothers, at once the recognition of, and compensation for, what he irretrievably lost.

It is then interesting to compare 'the feminine' as a source of Kipling's creativity with what he called his 'Daemon', a supernatural power which takes possession of him and forces him to write his masterpieces like *Kim* and *The Jungle Books*. His 'Daemon' is something outside him, which visits him from time to time to take control of his pen,[35] and whose command to him is absolute: 'When your Daemon is in charge, do not try to think consciously. Drift, wait and obey.'[36] In stories like '"Wireless"' and '"The Finest Story in the World"', this supernatural power uses a most ordinary and untalented character as a literary medium, and is referred to as gender-neutral – 'It came by itself';[37] 'There's something coming through from somewhere.'[38] In *Something of Myself*, however, Kipling refers to his Daemon as the masculine 'he', suggesting that this is another form of feminine writing, which transforms Kipling into 'a woman', a passive and receptive instrument for higher messages. Not unlike the Woman in 'The Cat That Walked By Himself', who makes her house cosy to entice her Man, Kipling also has to learn the art of snaring his Daemon: he takes care to make his Daemon's abode, his pen, conducive to his arrival by using the 'blackest' ink, and he avoids '[a]ll "blue-blacks" [which] were an abomination to my Daemon'.[39] If day-dreaming is, to use Freud's phrase, the working of 'His Majesty the Ego',[40] Kipling's Daemon is connected with the unconscious and night-time dreaming. The woman's desire for her man is a double-edged sword: it helps his day-dreaming but is detrimental to his Daemon, because she is the power which nurtures the Man and his Ego. It is interesting that, in '"The Finest Story in the World"', the young man can receive the memories of his past incarnations, as long as 'no woman has thought about him'.[41] But 'the love of woman' eventually 'kills [his] remembrance'.[42]

There is one woman artist in Kipling's world who is allowed access to both forms of female writing, day-dreaming and night-time dreaming, just like Kipling the male artist – till the fatal day when she meets her lover. Miriam, in 'The Brushwood Boy', lives alone with her widowed mother, with no father to suppress her creativity. She enjoys the privileges and parental attention which many of Kipling's child-heroes enjoy: not only is she the only child in her own house, but also 'a regular pet'[43] and object of admiration of the neighbouring home, in which she takes the place of its only son, Georgie, who is absent, serving in India. She composes music and also writes lyrics to her songs, and her inspiration comes from her dreams, in which she has many adventures with her dream-Muse, her 'Brushwood Boy'. When George comes back from India, however, it turns out that he is her dream-boy who has shared the same dream-world since they were children. When the realisation comes, it is no coincidence that she sobbed 'as [Georgie] had seen *a man* sob under the touch of the bullet' (*DW* 401, my emphasis). It was a moment when a free girl, who has enjoyed a man's freedom, loses the source of her inspiration and creativity, which has now been transformed into the proof that she is destined to be this man's companion. Considering that Georgie dreamed of her frequently while in India, her dreams, without her knowing, have supported the colonial world, as every English maiden's dreams should do. In the end, Miriam falls into Georgie's arms in ecstasy, having found her 'Brushwood Boy'. However, will she be able to write her songs again, now that her sources of creativity have been snatched away from her? Georgie takes back from her his rightful place as the only child of the household, and, though she does not know it, she has been reduced to one of many women who love and adore him. In this story, motherly figures abound. These include his own mother who 'blessed him and kissed him on the mouth' (*DW* 389–90), and Mrs Zuleika, an old lady whom he met on the P&O liner and who professed a 'motherly' interest in his welfare (*DW* 384). The latter makes an appearance in Miriam's dream, suggesting that any woman whom Georgie takes a liking to can enter into their dream-world. The Brushwood Girl will give him all but the Brushwood Boy will only give her a part, and this is why when he reassures Miriam that she is the only woman in his life, he is, according to Kipling, committing 'though he knew it not … black perjury' (*DW* 405).

However, it would also be fair to say that Kipling's representations of women, no matter how 'misogynistic' and appropriative they might be, are based on a deep understanding of the limitations and social constraints which they were up against. Women were confined in domesticity to the role of companion, with little freedom to explore the world on their own. If Kipling equates women with desire, it is because they are not given 'the power or the insight', above all 'the training', to achieve their goal, but are allowed to have '[o]nly the desire'.[44] Kipling's poem 'The Mother's Son', in which a madman sees the tortured image of himself in the mirror – 'They laid on My Mother's Son / More than a man could bear'[45] – is often referred to as the expression of Kipling's divided and broken self. This poem, however, should be seen as the picture of women as the Man's Mirror, not even allowed self-expression. Such a mirror is already present in *The Light That Failed*, in the shape of Dick's masterpiece, 'Melancolia'. To draw a female head as 'Melancolia' is initially Maisie's project, in which she aspires to portray herself as a struggling woman artist.[46] Dick, in deciding to paint a 'better' version of 'Melancolia', reinterprets the subject as the Man's suffering: 'So will every man who has any sorrow of his own … He shall see his trouble there.'[47] Kipling thereby depicts the ways in which a man turns a woman's dreams, ideas and emotions into his artistic inspiration, and reduces her to his companion in bondage, a female gaze which returns his gaze, without his seeing anything of her. We should congratulate Maisie for her lucky escape, and also Kipling for letting Bessie destroy the picture, and thereby break the mirror of 'His Mother's Son'.

Notes

1 Rudyard Kipling, *The Light That Failed* (London: Macmillan, 1900), p. 108.
2 For the fin-de-siècle discourse of the New Woman, see, for instance, Sally Ledger, *The New Woman: Fiction and Feminism at the Fin-de-siècle* (Manchester University Press, 1997).

3 J. M. S. Tompkins, *The Art of Rudyard Kipling* (London: Methuen, 1959), p. 163.
4 Rudyard Kipling, *Stalky & Co.* (London: Macmillan, 1899), p. 248.
5 Jan Montefiore, *Rudyard Kipling* (Tavistock: Northcote House, 2007), p. 67.
6 Zohreh T. Sullivan, *Narratives of Empire* (Cambridge University Press, 1993), p. 70.
7 Kipling, *The Light That Failed*, p. 3.
8 Rudyard Kipling, *Kim* (London: Macmillan, 1901), p. 394.
9 Sandra Kemp, 'Kipling's Women', in Angus Ross (ed.), *Kipling 86* (Brighton: University of Sussex Library, 1987), pp. 30–6, p. 30.
10 In this chapter, I will discuss the standard version of *The Light That Failed*, published in March 1891 by Macmillan, which ends with the tragic death of Dick, rather than the *Lippincott's Monthly Magazine* version of *The Light That Failed* (January 1891), which ends with a reunion between Dick and Maisie. This is not only because Kipling described the Macmillan version as 'originally conceived by the writer', but also, as I argue in this chapter, because it is a unique text in Kipling's oeuvre, as the heroine manages to escape the hero's control.
11 Rudyard Kipling and Wolcott Balestier, *The Naulahka: A Story of West and East* (London: Macmillan, 1901), p. 2.
12 *Ibid.*, p. 257.
13 *Ibid.*, pp. 260–1.
14 Kipling, *The Light That Failed*, np.
15 Leonard Shengold, 'An Attempt at Soul Murder: Rudyard Kipling's Early Life and Work', in Harold Orel (ed.), *Critical Essays on Rudyard Kipling* (Boston, MA: G. K. Hall, 1989), pp. 105–13, p. 109.
16 Rudyard Kipling, 'Baa Baa, Black Sheep', in *Wee Willie Winkie, Under the Deodars, The Phantom Rickshaw and Other Stories* (London: Macmillan, 1901), p. 282. Subsequent references in the text as *WWW*.
17 Shengold, 'An Attempt at Soul Murder', p. 109.
18 Randall Jarrell, 'On Preparing to Read Kipling', in Elliot L. Gilbert (ed.), *Kipling and the Critics* (London: Peter Owen, 1965), pp. 133–49, p. 148.
19 *Rudyard Kipling's Verse: Definitive Edition* (London: Hodder and Stoughton, 1940), p. 367.
20 Kipling's letter to Edward Bok, dated 4 December 1911. *The Letters of Rudyard Kipling, Volume 4, 1911–19* (Basingstoke: Macmillan, 1990), pp. 70–1. The poem, originally published in the *Morning Post* of 20 October 1911, was reprinted in the November issue of the *Ladies' Home Journal*.
21 *The Letters of Rudyard Kipling, Volume 4*, p. 70.
22 Rudyard Kipling, *Just So Stories* (London: Macmillan, 1903), p. 175.
23 Rudyard Kipling, *A Diversity of Creatures* (London: Macmillan, 1917), p. 131.
24 *Ibid.*, p. 144.
25 For instance, see Kemp, 'Kipling's Women'.
26 Rudyard Kipling, 'Kidnapped', *Plain Tales from the Hills* (London: Macmillan, 1900), p. 133.
27 Rudyard Kipling, *Debits and Credits* (London: Macmillan, 1926), p. 122. Subsequent references in the text as *DC*.
28 Kipling, '"Yoked with an Unbeliever"', in *Plain Tales from the Hills*, pp. 41, 39.
29 Kipling, 'By Word of Mouth', in *Plain Tales from the Hills*, pp. 321–2.

30 Max Beerbohm, 'Kipling's Entire', *Around Theatres* (London: Rupert Hart-Davis, 1953), pp. 245–9, p. 245, p. 247.

31 Sandra Kemp, *Kipling's Hidden Narratives* (Oxford: Basil Blackwell, 1988), p. 8.

32 U. C. Knoepflmacher, 'Female Power and Male Self-Assertion: Kipling and the Maternal', *Children's Literature*, 20 (1992), pp. 15–35, p. 28.

33 *Ibid.*, p. 31.

34 Sigmund Freud, 'Creative Writers and Day-Dreaming', in Peter Gay (ed.), *The Freud Reader* (London: Vintage, 1995), pp. 436–43, p. 437.

35 Rudyard Kipling, *Something of Myself* (London: Macmillan, 1937), p. 208.

36 *Ibid.*, p. 210.

37 Rudyard Kipling, '"The Finest Story in the World"', in *Many Inventions* (London: Macmillan, 1899), p. 99.

38 Rudyard Kipling, '"Wireless"', in *Traffics and Discoveries* (London: Macmillan, 1904), p. 229.

39 Kipling, *Something of Myself*, p. 230.

40 Freud, 'Creative Writers and Day-Dreaming', p. 441.

41 Kipling, *Many Inventions*, p. 124.

42 *Ibid.*, p. 135.

43 Rudyard Kipling, *The Day's Work* (London: Macmillan, 1901), p. 392. Subsequent references in the text as *DW*.

44 Kipling, *The Light That Failed*, p. 152.

45 Rudyard Kipling, *Limits and Renewals* (London: Macmillan, 1932), p. 151.

46 Kipling, *The Light That Failed*, pp. 149–50.

47 *Ibid.*, p. 184.

6

DAVID BRADSHAW

Kipling and war

'If Kipling were with us today,' L. C. Dunsterville (Stalky's original) told the 1,600 members of the Kipling Society just after the start of the Second World War, 'he would doubtless give the nation a message of faith in our righteous cause, and courage to meet our inevitable losses and hardships leading to ultimate victory.'[1] What Dunsterville didn't mention is that Kipling might reasonably have scrawled 'I told you so' across his message,[2] because in the years leading up to his death in 1936 he had been as indefatigable in urging his fellow countrymen to prepare more effectively for the looming showdown with Hitler as he had been consistently critical, in the decades before the First World War, of Britain's grossly inadequate planning for that cataclysm. As the interwar years drew on, however, fewer and fewer people were willing to listen to Kipling, and having been in his pre-1918 heyday 'the most widely read and influential writer on war in the English-speaking world',[3] he found himself all too often whistling in the wind. 'As the pacifist revulsion against the first World War intensified in the early 1930s,' Frank Field has observed, 'as the flood of autobiographies and memoirs denouncing war now poured from the presses … the views of an unregenerate imperialist, Francophile and Germanophobe like Kipling carried little weight. Many believed that Nazism was a product of the harshness of the Versailles settlement that Kipling had denounced for its softness.'[4]

When Kipling arrived at the United Services College at the age of twelve he entered a school where 'some seventy-five per cent of us … hoped to follow their fathers in the Army',[5] and in 'Ave Imperatrix!', a poem of 1882, he sent greetings to Queen Victoria 'from those / Whose fathers faced the Sepoy hordes, / Or served you in the Russian snows, / And, dying, left their sons their swords'.[6] In the event, poor eyesight would prevent Kipling from joining the army, but as a young writer he was anxious to link the martial values inculcated at a school like his own (and the considerably grander public schools) not just with the fearless Stalky, whose resourceful derring-do as a soldier is recounted, for instance, in the final chapter of *Stalky & Co.*

(1899), but also with the no less plucky but rather more mortal kind of officer described in 'Arithmetic on the Frontier' (1886):

> A scrimmage in a Border Station –
> A canter down some dark defile –
> Two thousand pounds of education
>   Drops to a ten-rupee jezail –
> The Crammer's boast, the Squadron's pride,
> Shot like a rabbit in a ride! (103)

Nor was it only gallant subalterns and their superiors whom Kipling celebrated in his early writings. He regarded both the officers and the rank-and-file regulars engaged in Britain's seemingly incessant imperial wars and border skirmishes as unjustly denigrated or ignored by those at home, and in a number of poems and stories from this time, such as 'Ford O' Kabul River' (1890) and 'The Lost Legion' (1892), he set out both to entertain and to inform his readers about a body of men whose 'lives are as hard as their own muscles, and the papers never say anything about them' (94).

The soldiers through whom Kipling first made his name were not his courageous frontier officers, 'Cheltenham and Haileybury and Marlborough chaps' (122), but his resilient, salt-of-the-earth privates like Mulvaney, Ortheris and Learoyd (who are first introduced in 'Three Musketeers' (1887) and who reappear in a number of the *Plain Tales from the Hills* (1888) and some of the stories of *Soldiers Three* (1888)), alongside the equally plain-talking 'Tommy' (1890) and the other personae who speak their minds in *Barrack-Room Ballads* (1892). By conveying in his own version of the regular soldier's vernacular what a Tommy had to put up with both in peace and in war, Kipling's poems and stories of army life had a considerable impact on popular prejudices about the military, while in a story like 'The Taking of Lungtungpen' (1887) and in a poem such as 'The Widow's Party' (1890), he brought home to his audience that although a soldier's life might occasionally flare into action it 'was not all beer and skittles', to borrow a phrase Kipling himself had used in 'The Drums of the Fore and Aft' (1889). This last story revolves around an act of cowardice, and while another account of a military reversal, the poem '"Fuzzy-Wuzzy"', is an unsettling read nowadays, the speaker's respect for the Sudanese tribesmen who 'broke a British square!' remains as sincere as it is distasteful.[7] 'That Day' (1895) is another poem focused on a military calamity, and David Gilmour makes an important distinction when he remarks:

> The charge that Kipling's view of war was romantic can be judged by comparing him with figures such as Macaulay [or] Tennyson ... Mulvaney and his friends are not heroes ... In Kipling's work there is no Roman leaping into the

Tiber after holding a bridge against an entire army, no undismayed man riding into 'the jaws of death' … Kipling's soldiers have human proportions.[8]

Indeed, even when Kipling might have been bullish, he was often far from gung-ho. 'Recessional', for example, was written to celebrate Queen Victoria's Diamond Jubilee (1897), but it seems far more palpably concerned with the possible dissolution of the Empire than with its permanence, with the vulnerability of Britain's 'far-flung battle-line' rather than the enduring might of her armed services. And while it begins by proclaiming Britain's 'Dominion over palm and pine', it soon presents us with rather less imperious images of her over-stretched forces and her fading global clout:

> Far-called, our navies melt away;
> On dune and headland sinks the fire:
> Lo, all our pomp of yesterday
> Is one with Nineveh and Tyre![9]

'Hymn before Action' (1896) was written in an equally anxious mood, and in a number of other late Victorian poems and prose works Kipling agonises over what he saw as Britain's chronic unreadiness for the inevitable war with Germany, while the events of the Second Anglo-Boer War (1899–1902) gave him even greater cause to believe that Stalky's day was over, and that when the 'really … big row' (122) broke out it would bear no resemblance at all to a 'scrimmage in a Border Station'.

The Boer War began disastrously. Ladysmith, Mafeking and Kimberley were soon invested and the British army was defeated three times in quick succession. Things improved only slowly, and by the conclusion of the conflict, a little of which he had witnessed at first hand, Kipling knew that nothing less than a root-and-branch overhaul of the nation's military, bureaucratic, educational and social infrastructures was essential if Britain was to avoid a similar humiliation in future. His admonitory mood finds expression in 'Stellenbosh', 'Two Kopjes', 'Ubique', 'Boots', 'Piet' and 'Chant-Pagan', poems collected in *The Five Nations* (1903) and all focused on such pressing concerns as military incompetence, poor equipment and social division. As Daniel Karlin notes, however, unlike the *Barrack-Room Ballads*, these Boer War poems are 'marked by an impulse to make speeches in the voices of soldiers, rather than voicing soldiers' speech'.[10]

Similarly, the Boer War stories Kipling collected in *Traffics and Discoveries* (1904) – 'A Sahibs' War' (1901), 'The Captive' (1902), 'The Comprehension of Private Copper' (1902) and 'The Army of a Dream' (1904) – are not only critical of British military conduct in South Africa but also engage with the issues that dominated domestic coverage of this discomfiting conflict and its recriminatory aftermath, such as eugenics.

In 'The Comprehension of Private Copper', for example, the Transvaal 'renegid' who holds Copper at gunpoint taunts him with a common charge: '*We* know and you know it now. Your Army – it is the laughing-stock of the Continent' (188). He goes on to characterise the British working classes as 'diseased, lying, drinking white stuff', having previously told Copper he is 'an ignorant diseased beast like the rest of your people' (184). But just when Copper's (and Britain's) degradation is at its most shameful, the quick-witted Tommy, who has only been feigning injury, lands his fist 'to a hair on the chin-point' of his captor and knocks him out (188). Copper may well be dysgenically undersized and ill-educated, this tale suggests, but his steely British nerve is still more than a match for anything his bovine and dull-witted Boer adversary can muster.

Similarly, Laughton O. Zigler, the detained American gun runner in 'The Captive', tells the sentry looking after him that the British army is being run by 'an effete aristocracy' (198), while 'A Sahibs' War' shows experienced Sikh and Pathan soldiers doing their job with ruthless efficiency (albeit unofficially) while the British high command make a complete hash of things. In 'The Way that he Took' and 'The Outsider' top brass incompetence is again exposed; 'The Army of a Dream' is a more clunking propaganda exercise on the same theme, while in a poem called 'The Islanders' (1902) Kipling makes the case for compulsory military service and attacks Britain's dangerously peaceable enchantment with 'flannelled fools at the wicket or the muddied oafs at the goals'.[11]

It is often alleged that Kipling glorified war and occasionally he did, but an interview published at the end of 1913, in which he declared that there was 'no more romance or glamour' in war, reflects his more considered standpoint:

> I have seen very, very little fighting in India ... But I did see war in South Africa. I said to myself before I went out, 'I'll see the dash and get the rattling inspiration of it. I'll see charges, and thin red lines, and hear hoarse commands and stand silent and thrilled in that dread hush before the battle.'
>
> But what a disillusion! ... Nobody galloped up on a lathered horse and fell unconscious after handing the general the long-waited dispatch. The general himself bestrode no charger, but sat in a comfortable camp-chair beside a neatly spread tea-table. You heard a few tick-ticks and somebody handed him a slip ... and he read it and drank his tea and said, 'Um-m-m, good. Workin' out just as I thought. Wire Binks to bring up that battery' ...
>
> And all this method and precision and application of modern efficiency ideas makes the carnage that follows all the more ghastly ... the dreadful dead men and the shrieking wounded men ... seem to you like innocent bystanders who have got in the way of some great civil-engineering scheme and been torn and blown up.[12]

Like many of Kipling's comments on war in the years leading up to 1914, these words would prove all too prescient. Many generals, like the one in 'The Captive', may have convinced themselves that the Boer War was 'a first-class dress-parade for Armageddon' (212), but Kipling knew that the approaching war with Germany would unleash a type of armed conflict most senior officers had not even dreamed of, never mind rehearsed.

He marked the beginning of the Great War with a poem called '"For All We Have and Are"':

> For all we have and are,
> For all our children's fate,
> Stand up and take the war.
> The Hun is at the gate!
> Our world has passed away,
> In wantonness o'erthrown.
> There is nothing left to-day
> But steel and fire and stone![13]

It was aimed at steadying the nation's nerve, while *The New Army in Training* (1915) was intended to boost recruitment. Other works of national uplift followed, such as *France at War* (1915), which included Kipling's account of his August 1915 visit to the Front, *The Fringes of the Fleet* (1915), *Sea Warfare* (1916) and a series of articles about the Italian Front called *The War in the Mountains* (1917). All of these publications and many of the speeches he gave at this time touch or dwell on the vileness of the 'Hun', and German barbarity was to remain one of Kipling's most unshakeable obsessions. It braces a poem called 'The Outlaws' (1914), for instance, and it underpins '"Swept and Garnished"', a short story of 1915 in which an obsessively tidy yet temporarily delirious German woman, Frau Ebermann, is convinced that her Berlin apartment has been occupied by five dirty, gaunt and bedraggled Belgian orphans: as they wander about her orderly bedroom pawing her fittings and ornaments, she looks on indignantly from her sickbed. German atrocities in Belgium were widely reported in the British press at the time and one of these five children seems to have been seriously injured, but these prying and probing youngsters have not been cowed; with their 'little explosive giggles' (230) they carry out a kind of fidgety, sticky-fingered reprisal for the murder of their parents and the devastation of their home, their livestock and their country. They have entered Frau Ebermann's flat without her permission and soiled her floor with their blood just as the German army (including Frau Ebermann's soldier son) entered neutral Belgium uninvited and both killed civilians and deported them to Germany.

The most extraordinary war story Kipling ever wrote is 'Mary Postgate' (1915), the macabre tale of how a spare, gawky and self-effacing lady's companion finds ecstatic fulfilment in cruelty and hatred. Not long after the beginning of the war, Wynn Fowler, the nephew of Mary's employer, is killed while training with the Flying Corps, and Mary is delegated to burn his belongings in his aunt's 'destructor' (242) at the bottom of her garden. However, that Mary is not quite the mousy cipher she appears to be is first hinted at when she sets out to buy paraffin for the incinerator and she '*lunge*[s] into the blind wet' (243, my emphasis) more in the manner of a bayonet-thrusting infantryman than a retiring and 'ladylike' helpmate. On reaching the local village, Mary is speaking to a nurse when they hear what sounds like 'a gun' (244), but which Mary is convinced is a bomb. German air raids on England had begun in December 1914, the month in which the story is set, and Mary is certain that young Edna Gerritt (who is killed in this incident) has been slain by a bomb dropped from a German plane, though why the Gerritts' rickety stable, the roof of which is destroyed in the incident, as opposed to a more significant building more likely to be housing the enemy, should be the target of a planned air assault – or even the hasty jettisoning of a warplane's payload – is one of the tale's many unanswered questions. But it is not one that crosses Mary's mind as she walks home denouncing the Germans as 'bloody pagans' (245). The local doctor (who is also a special constable) overtakes Mary in his car and tells her that Edna most probably died as a result of the collapse of the stable roof, which has 'been dangerous for a long time' (245), rather than a bomb, and the gun-like explosion she heard may well have been the snapping of its rotten beam. He cannot be sure, he says (and we cannot be sure of his motive in saying so), but he does not want Mary to 'stir people up' before the full facts have been established. But it is too late. Mary is stirred up beyond recall, and the paraffin she sprinkles on the 'pyre' when she returns to the destructor is nothing less than 'sacrificial oil' (246). Moreover, it is strongly implied that her boots, which she also places in the furnace, are stained with Edna Gerritt's blood – 'what *have* you got on your boots?', Miss Fowler asks Mary when she returns home from the village. Mary carries her boots to the destructor wrapped in sheets of newspaper that would no doubt have contained reports of German 'horrors' (248) of the kind she has read out to Miss Fowler, so it is quite likely that accounts of Hunnish barbarity will soon help kindle Edna's innocent blood and Wynn's adolescent effects in what is poised to be no less than a symbolic cremation of British youth.

Suddenly, by the light of the 'pyre', Mary sees an airman with 'closely cropped' (246) hair who, she presumes, must have fallen from the plane that dropped the 'bomb': she has 'no doubt as to his nationality' (247). He is 'sitting very stiffly' at the foot of a tree and while he can just about speak, roll his head and pick at 'the dead … leaves' on the ground around him, he seems to be otherwise paralysed. Mary resists all the airman's pleas for medical assistance, returning to the house only to collect the 'huge revolver with flat-nosed bullets' (247) that she and Miss Fowler have acquired in case of German invasion and that Mary has been trained to use. In fact, the airman could hardly have jumped or fallen into a more hostile environment. Despite appearances, Miss Fowler's house is a kind of semi-militarised zone, where Mary is accustomed to listening 'unflinchingly' to her employer's racy stories with her 'trained mind' (235) and is 'deadly methodical' (242) in all she does, while Miss Fowler, soon after the start of the war, 'gazetted' (a verb usually confined to the notification of military appointments) her odd job man's daughter to the post of housemaid and promoted his wife 'to the *rank* of cook' (237; emphasis added). After Wynn's death neither Mary nor Miss Fowler allows herself to cry and all Mary can say is that it is 'a great pity [Wynn] didn't die in action after he had killed somebody' (239). If she *had* finished off the airman with the revolver, however, Mary would have committed a war crime as well as murder, because dum-dum bullets had been outlawed by the Hague Convention of 1899.

The question of whether this French-speaking airman is really a German aviator or a French flyer, perhaps seriously disoriented or, more likely, stationed at the same nearby 'training centre' (237) where Wynn was based and who has suffered an accident similar to his – or, indeed, is a confused Englishman from the same airfield (he wears, after all, 'a uniform something like Wynn's' (246) and Mary thinks the plane she hears before the explosion is 'one of ours' (244), and tells herself that she 'could almost hear the beat of [Wynn's] propellers' (243) on her way to the village), who in his agony and bewilderment imagines he has fallen to earth in France – grows more compelling as the tale progresses. But Mary's mind is set against such possibilities and she looks on impassively as the airman slowly dies. And whether he is German, French or English, her barking out of orders in English and repeating in approximate German that she has seen the dead child can only have increased both the airman's terror and despair. Moreover, Kipling's setting of the final scene suggests possible readings to which Mary is completely blind. For example, if we, like Mary, are tempted to construe the airman's use of a 't' instead of a 'd' – 'Laty! Laty! Laty!'; 'Toctor!' (246, 247) – as firm evidence of his German nationality, we should also note, contrariwise, that his final resting place is located, highly significantly, within a 'laurel shrubbery' and beneath 'three oaks' (242), which between them create a 'sanctuary' (246) filled with heroic and patriotic associations, while the aviator's stirring of dead leaves, an age-old topos for those who have died in battle, only strengthens the possibility that 'It' may not be a sub-human foe at all. But the oblivious Mary only 'lunges' at her fire ever more busily with her poker, 'her underlip caught up by one faded canine, brows knit and nostrils wide' (248). At the end of the story, she leans contentedly on her poker and listens, 'while an increasing rapture laid hold on her', for the airman's predictable death throes. When she hears them, she smiles.

The tension between Mary's hate-filled blinkeredness and the reader's accelerating unease with her interpretation of the events to which she is party is masterly. She clearly does wrong in withholding assistance from the airman, but we do not find out whether she has stood by as one of Britain's enemies has died a horrible death, or one of her sons or allies; or, indeed, whether 'Mary is assuredly the victim of a hallucination and ... the airman never existed outside of her own mind.'[14] Assuming that he is not phantasmal, Mary's 'secret thrill' (249) in the shrubbery has been interpreted as 'unmistakably sexual'[15] and even 'orgasmic',[16] but such audacious readings seem at best overdetermined and, paradoxically, serve only to make tame both the protagonist and her tale. Mary's feelings for Wynn quiver between a kind of quasi-maternal affection and an abject, spinsterish crush, but it is hard to see why either emotion might climax in such an unequivocally carnal fashion. No: Mary's ecstasy in the shrubbery betokens something more deeply atavistic and disturbing.

When 'Mary Postgate' was reprinted in *A Diversity of Creatures* (1917) it was followed by a poem called 'The Beginnings' ('It was not part of their blood, / It came to them very late / With long arrears to make good, / When the English began to hate')[17] and this coupling is highly significant. Before setting eyes on 'the ripped and shredded body' (244) of Edna Gerritt, hating had (probably) not been 'part of [the] blood' (235) of Mary Postgate; if not 'late', hating has come to her in middle age, and it is the sheer malignancy of Mary's loathing that makes the tale all the more chilling. And while her vindictiveness towards the 'German' lies square with Kipling's tendency to regard 'the Hun' as bestial, it is simply too facile to propose that Mary merely embodies her creator's Germanophobia. When Wynn was alive, Mary was 'his butt and his slave' (236) and she has been uncommonly exposed to death (her father, mother, aunt and cousin a while ago, and Wynn and Edna in the recent and immediate past) throughout her life, so these factors alone might help to explain why she responds with such callous detachment to the airman's groans and whimpering: she may have heard them too often before and become emotionally deaf to such cries. But the key point, surely, is that this shocking tale cannot be reduced, neutered or normalised: timid and 'colourless' (235), Mary Postgate transcends the limitations of her 'craven' (247) existence in a paroxysm of hate, not an orgasm of pleasure, and her sadistic 'rapture' blows to smithereens both the sleepy innocence of the 'Home Front' and the moral superiority which many in Britain then felt was theirs by gift of God. Old-maidish Mary may '*look* more or less like a human being' (237) to begin with, but as she stokes the destructor's flames she regresses to something more ogreish, her nostrils flared, her mind narrowed. By the end of this story, the 'monstrosity' (246) that was supposed to be uniquely German has been gruesomely domesticated: coiled tight within the rich ambiguity of 'Mary Postgate' is its ineffaceable obscenity. The pagan and the Christian have been fused in the destructor's flames.

In the same month that 'Mary Postgate' first appeared in print, the war dealt Kipling a terrible personal blow. John, his only son, had twice been declared unfit for military service owing to his extremely poor eyesight, but Kipling exploited his connections to obtain a commission for him in the Irish Guards. 'There is no chance John will survive unless he is so maimed from a wound as to be unfit to fight,' his mother told a correspondent in October 1914, the month after John reported for duty with the regiment. 'We know it and he does. We all know it, but we must give and do what we can and live on the shadow of a hope that our boy will be the one to escape.'[18] He wasn't. After basic training and being kept back at the regimental depot until he had turned eighteen, John Kipling arrived at the Front in August 1915. He was lost in action on 27 September during the Battle of Loos and his remains have never been found. 'It was a short life,' Kipling told Dunsterville on 12 November. 'I'm sorry that all the years work ended in that one afternoon but – lots of people are in our position and it's something to have bred a man. The wife is standing it wonderfully tho' she of course clings to the bare hope of his being a prisoner. I've seen what shells can do and I don't.'[19] Kipling would never really emerge from the 'dark defile' of his guilt-stricken grief for John, and in a speech he gave in December 1915, during the dedication of a school rifle range in memory of an ex-pupil of about John's age who had also been killed in action, Kipling's mind and heart must have been crowded with his own sorrow when he told the assembled boys that George Cecil, the alumnus concerned, 'was one of that original army in France which was sacrificed almost to a man, in order that England might gain time to create those armies which, till then, she had not thought necessary.'[20] Further on in his address Kipling placed Cecil, tenderly, 'among the first of that company of young dead who live without change in the hearts of those who love them'.[21]

His profound sense of bereavement almost certainly explains why Kipling showed no inclination to portray the fighting in Flanders as he had previously depicted warfare in Afghanistan, the Sudan (for example, Chapter 2 of *The Light That Failed* (1891)) and South Africa. Yet his anguish does seep out in a number of poems that have since become iconic, and above all in 'My Boy Jack', where the device of a distressed mother desperate for news of her seaman son wholly fails to conceal, and the broad-brush seascape setting entirely fails to engulf, the raw torment of Kipling's mourning:

> 'Have you news of my boy Jack?'
> *Not this tide.*
> 'When d'you think that he'll come back?'
> *Not with this wind blowing and this tide.*
>
> 'Has any one else had word of him?'
> *Not this tide.*
> *For what is sunk will hardly swim,*
> *Not with this wind blowing, and this tide.*
>
> 'Oh, dear, what comfort can I find?'
> *None this tide,*
> *Nor any tide,*
> *Except he did not shame his kind –*
> *Not even with that wind blowing, and that tide ...*[22]

Similarly, 'A Recantation' (1917) draws on John's love of the music hall and concerns an artiste named Lyde who has earlier that day learned of the death of her son at the Front yet who insists on going ahead with her performance:

> Ere certain Fate had touched a heart
> By fifty years made cold,
> I judged thee, Lyde, and thy art
> O'erblown and over-bold.
>
> But he – but he, of whom bereft
> I suffer vacant days –
> He on his shield not meanly left –
> He cherished all thy lays ...
>
> Never more rampant rose the Hall
> At thy audacious line
> Than when the news came in from Gaul
> Thy son had – followed mine.   (276–7)

The speaker's faltering discomposure contrasts all too glaringly with the professional equanimity of Lyde, while in the third stanza of a poem from the same year, 'The Children', we read:

> They believed us and perished for it. Our statecraft, our
>   learning
> Delivered them bound to the Pit and alive to the burning
> Whither they mirthfully hastened as jostling for honour –
> Not since her birth has our Earth seen such worth loosed upon her.[23]

Once again, Kipling's words take on a self-lacerating edge when we recall that his son was killed in an area of the Loos battlefield called 'Chalk Pit Wood', while even the verb 'loosed' seems to reach back with poignant specificity to the terrible bloodbath in which John met his end. The last stanza of 'The Children' envisages a hideously unstable landscape that only intensifies our sense that Kipling may well have had in mind his son, the ghastly circumstances of his death and his unrecovered remains when he penned it:

> The flesh we had nursed from the first in all cleanness was given
> To corruption unveiled and assailed by the malice of Heaven –
> By the heart-shaking jests of Decay where it lolled on the wires –
> To be blanched or gay-painted by fumes – to be cindered by fires –
> To be senselessly tossed and retossed in stale mutilation
> From crater to crater. For this we shall take expiation.
> *But who shall return us our children?*[24]

As Daniel Karlin observes, Kipling's corpse 'takes on a "heart-shaking" parodic life, "lolling" and "gay-painted", as though it were still a child fond of idleness and dressing up. In a final pun it is "senselessly tossed", both because it is, itself, without sensation, and because its fate is beyond reason.'[25] And if 'Justice' (1918) reveals that Kipling's loathing of the Hun did not diminish in the wake of John's death, in 'Gethsemane' (1919), Karlin argues persuasively, 'Kipling's art reaches beyond its author's grasp, implying the fellowship his hating soul repudiated. This greatest of all Kipling's poems of the War casts a German, because a human, shadow.'[26]

Someone we do not hear from in Kipling's First World War verse is the son of Tommy Atkins. As Kipling noted in the Introduction to his two-volume history of *The Irish Guards in the Great War* (1923), a work of painstaking 'expiation' that took him five years to complete, 'the old Regular Army of England', like John, 'passed away in the mud of Flanders in less than a year':

> In training, morale, endurance, courage and devotion the Earth did not hold
> its like, but it possessed neither the numbers, guns, nor equipment necessary
> for the type of war that overtook it. The fact of its unpreparedness has been
> extolled as proof of the purity of its country's ideals, which must be great con-
> solation to all concerned.[27]

The *History* is a meticulous work of remembrance, yet Kipling's bitter sense of loss cannot help but ooze out of even its most densely detailed recesses. His pain is audible, for example, both in the irony of 'great consolation' above and in the following excerpt from the *History*'s account of the catastrophic Battle of Loos:

[It] does not seem to have occurred to anyone … that direct Infantry attacks, after ninety-minute bombardments, on works begotten out of a generation of thought and prevision, scientifically built up by immense labour and applied science, and developed against all contingencies through nine months, are not likely to find a fortunate issue.[28]

In his Introduction, Kipling mentions the 'many, almost children, of whom no record remains. They came out from [their depots] with the constantly renewed drafts, lived the span of a Second Lieutenant's life and were spent.'[29] Second Lieutenant, of course, was John's rank when he was 'spent'.

His son's missing remains were surely instrumental in Kipling's decision to join the Imperial (now Commonwealth) War Graves Commission in 1917. He outlined the scope of the Commission's work in *The Graves of the Fallen* (1919) and observed in a section headed 'Memorials to the Missing' that '[t]his matter is naturally of the deepest concern to the relatives of those whose bodies have never been recovered or identified, or whose graves, once made, have been destroyed by later battles'.[30] When the War Graves project was debated in Parliament, with powerful factions doing their best to oppose both the secularity of the proposed cemeteries and the Commission's guiding principle of equality of treatment regardless of rank, a letter from Kipling was read out: 'Our boy was missing at Loos. The ground is of course battered and mined past all hope of any trace being recovered. I wish some of the people who are making this trouble realised how more than fortunate they are to have a name on a headstone in a known place.'[31] It was Kipling who chose the inscription for each cemetery's Stone of Remembrance – 'Their Name Liveth for Evermore' – and the formula that was to appear on the headstones of all those whose identities had died with them ('Known Unto God'), though when Samuel Hynes recalls the words which occur five verses before 'their name liveth for evermore' in Ecclesiasticus – 'And some there be, which have no memorial; who are perished, as though they had never been; and are become as though they had never been born' – he cannot 'help think-ing of Kipling's only son … missing at Loos, his body never found'.[32]

During his visits to the Commission's cemeteries Kipling witnessed the confusion and distress of the bereaved as they struggled to find the graves of loved ones. Partly as a result of his efforts, proper local enquiry offices were established from 1920, and Helen Turrell makes use of such a facility in 'The Gardener', one of Kipling's most powerful war stories. Michael Turrell's bat-talion were suddenly 'hurled out' of England in 1915 'to help make good the wastage of Loos' (313) and not long afterwards, 'a shell-splinter dropping out of a wet dawn killed him at once' (314). As with John Kipling, no word of Michael arrives, but in time (unlike the Kiplings) Helen receives 'an offi-cial intimation … to the effect that the body of Lieutenant Michael Turrell had been found, identified, and re-interred in Hagenzeele Third Military Cemetery' (325). Helen soon finds herself in 'a world full of exultant or broken relatives, now strong in the certainty that there was an altar upon earth where they might lay their love' (315) and in the care of a mysterious gardener, probably Christ, who shows her 'where [her] son lies' (320). Once again, connections between Kipling's post-1915 war writings and his personal tragedy unavoidably suggest themselves. 'Helen's inner distress is mirrored in the surreal quality of her perceptions', Sandra Kemp comments astutely, 'which are at once disturbed and psychologically acute: the village of Hagenzeele becomes "a razed city full of whirling lime-dust and blown papers"; the Military Cemetery a "waist-high wilderness of weeds, stricken dead, rushing at her" ... However ... this disorientation marks the beginning of the process of healing',[33] just as Kipling's work for the War Graves Commission provided at least some solace for him as he made his way through the stony 'wilderness' of his grief.

One of Kipling's most peculiar war stories, 'A Madonna of the Trenches' (1924), has clear affinities with his earlier tales of the eerie and the inexplicable, such as "They" and 'Mrs Bathurst'. David Cannadine has described how 'the combat zone might remain littered for weeks with bodies ... New trenches might be dug through them; parapets might be made of them; even bodies decently buried might come to the surface again',[34] and this tale highlights how dreadfully present the dead were for those who continued to occupy the ground on which their comrades or adversaries had met their ends. We learn that when Stanwick, for instance, whose 'nerves' are now shot, was a runner in the trenches he got used to living cheek by jowl with 'the frozen dead who creak in the frost' (296). Yet 'A Madonna of the Trenches' is not just about the ubiquity of the fallen: it goes on to explore the idea that death may not necessarily be terminal. Kipling publicly disavowed spiritualism, but it is hard to resist linking his unrelieved yearning for news of John's remains with Auntie Armine's posthumous rendezvous with Sergeant Godsoe in this story, a meeting that gives hope that the creaking of corpses need not betray their carrion lifelessness but, more heart-rendingly, their ongoing animation.

'This is the midnight – let no star / Delude us – dawn is very far', Kipling begins one of his last poems, 'The Storm Cone' (1932); 'This is the tempest long foretold – / Slow to make head but sure to hold';[35] and in 'An Undefended Island', an address of May 1935, he loaded 'all the despair of thirty years' unacknowledged foresight'[36] into his account of how Britain had yet again failed to prepare properly for war with Germany. He died in January 1936, and the Nazis re-occupied the Rhineland only a few months later. Kipling might well have felt vindicated by this development, had he still been alive, but in view of all the miseries of war he had experienced since 1915, we can be certain that he would not have felt smug.

Notes

1 L. C. Dunsterville, 'The Kipling Society and the War', *Kipling Journal*, 51 (October 1939), pp. 6–9. Quote from p. 6.

2 Kipling used this phrase in a letter of August 1914. See Lord Birkenhead, *Rudyard Kipling* (London: Weidenfeld & Nicolson, 1978), p. 258.

3 Andrew Rutherford, Introduction to his edited collection, Rudyard Kipling, *War Stories and Poems* (1990; Oxford University Press, 2009), pp. xii–xxv. Quote from p. xii. Subsequent references to this volume are in brackets in the text.

4 Frank Field, *British and French Writers of the First World War: Comparative Studies in Cultural History* (Cambridge University Press, 1991), p. 173.

5 Rudyard Kipling, *Something of Myself: For my Friends Known and Unknown* (London: Macmillan, 1937), p. 22.

6 *Rudyard Kipling's Verse: Definitive Edition* (London: Hodder and Stoughton, 1940), p. 169.

7 *Ibid.*, p. 401.

8 David Gilmour, *The Long Recessional: The Imperial Life of Rudyard Kipling* (London: Pimlico, 2003), pp. 47–8.

9 *Rudyard Kipling's Verse*, pp. 328–9.

10 Daniel Karlin, 'From Dark Defile to Gethsemane: Rudyard Kipling's War Poetry', in Tim Kendall (ed.), *The Oxford Handbook of British and Irish War Poetry* (Oxford University Press, 2007), pp. 51–69. Quote from p. 64.

11 *Rudyard Kipling's Verse*, p. 302.

12 Harold Orel, ed. *Kipling: Interviews and Recollections*, 2 vols. (London: Macmillan, 1983), vol. II, pp. 323–4.

13 *Rudyard Kipling's Verse*, p. 329.

14 Norman Page, 'What Happens in "Mary Postgate"?', *English Literature in Transition*, 29:1 (1986), pp. 41–7. Quote from p. 44.

15 Jan Montefiore, *Rudyard Kipling* (Tavistock: Northcote House, 2007), p. 152.

16 Bernard Bergonzi, 'Kipling and the First World War', in John Gross (ed.), *Rudyard Kipling: The Man, his Work and his World* (London: Weidenfeld & Nicolson, 1972), pp. 136–41. Quote from p. 138.

17 Rudyard Kipling, *A Diversity of Creatures* (1917; London: Macmillan, 1918), p. 442.

18 Quoted in Gilmour, *The Long Recessional*, p. 257.

19 *The Letters of Rudyard Kipling, Volume 4, 1911–19*, ed. Thomas Pinney (Basingstoke: Palgrave Macmillan, 1999), p. 345.

20 Rudyard Kipling, 'The War and the Schools', in *A Book of Words: Selections from Speeches and Addresses Delivered between 1906 and 1927* (London: Macmillan, 1928), pp. 123–7. Quote from p. 123.

21 Kipling, 'The War and the Schools', p. 124.

22 *Rudyard Kipling's Verse*, p. 216.

23 *Ibid.*, p. 522.

24 *Ibid.*, p. 523.

25 Karlin, 'From Dark Defile to Gethsemane', p. 53.

26 *Ibid.*, p. 69.

27 Rudyard Kipling, *The Irish Guards in the Great War, Volume 1, The First Battalion* (London: Macmillan, 1923), p. vii.

28 Rudyard Kipling, *The Irish Guards in the Great War, Volume 2, The Second Battalion and Appendices* (London: Macmillan, 1923), p. 15.

29 Kipling, *The Irish Guards in the Great War, Volume 1*, p. viii.

30 [Rudyard Kipling], *The Graves of the Fallen* (London: His Majesty's Stationery Office, (1919)), p. 12.

31 Quoted in Philip Longworth, *The Unending Vigil: A History of the Commonwealth War Graves Commission 1917–67* (London: Constable, 1967), p. 52.

32 Samuel Hynes, *A War Imagined: The First World War and English Culture* (London: Pimlico, 1990), p. 271.

33 Sandra Kemp, *Kipling's Hidden Narratives* (Oxford: Basil Blackwell, 1988), p. 121.

34 David Cannadine, 'War and Death, Grief and Mourning in Modern Britain', in Joachim Whaley (ed.), *Mirrors of Mortality: Studies in the Social History of Death* (London: Europa Publications, 1981), pp. 187–242. Quote from p. 204.

35 *Rudyard Kipling's Verse*, p. 824.

36 Birkenhead, *Rudyard Kipling*, p. 348.

7

JAN MONTEFIORE

Kipling as a children's writer and the *Jungle Books*

> My Daemon was with me in the *Jungle Books*, *Kim* and both Puck books.
> —Rudyard Kipling
> Complicity in Empire marks, more or less, all the Mowgli stories.
> —John McBratney[1]

Tales for children

Rudyard Kipling is famous as a storyteller for children, some of whom fell in love with his stories and grew up to be authorities on Kipling. Roger Lancelyn Green became a Kipling enthusiast as a schoolboy 'playing Jungle'; Harry Ricketts heard 'my mother read me the *Just So Stories*'; Daniel Karlin re-read the *Jungle Books* 'dozens of times' between the ages of eight and twelve; and Joyce Tompkins thrilled to 'a sense of something wild and deep and old [that] infected me as I listened'.[2] I too read Kipling as a child, taking my first conscious delight in word-play from the *Just So Stories* and later relishing the rhetoric of the *Jungle Books*. Yet few children in the twenty-first century know more of Kipling than the Disney cartoon of Mowgli, Baloo and Bagheera, unless they happen to hear the *Just So Stories* read aloud by an adult enthusiast or to join the Cub Scouts.[3] This is not because Kipling's stories are too difficult and 'literary' to appeal to children acclimatised to TV and computer games, for children who wouldn't read the *Jungle Books* listen to them with great pleasure (though I have yet to meet a contemporary child who liked the Puck books).

Kipling is neglected as a children's writer because his reputation for imperialist racism and more recently, for warmongering,[4] makes him unpopular with the adult teachers, librarians, critics of children's literature and parents who purchase children's books, and influence their production and consumption in the twenty-first century. With the shining exception of Judith Plotz, editor of the special Kipling issue of *Children's Literature* (1992), who combines informed enthusiasm for Kipling with a postcolonial 'take' on his work, most recent critics of children's literature rarely accord Kipling more than a passing mention unless they choose to focus specifically on 'Empire' writing, like Joseph Bristow's *Empire Boys* (1991) or Daphne Kutzer's *Empire's Children* (2002), which respectively allot Kipling one chapter.[5] The *Jungle Books* are unmentioned in Aidan Chambers's *Booktalk* (1982), Styles, Bearne and Watson's *After Alice* (1992) or Peter Hollindale's *Signs of Childness in Children's Books* (1997); they get one sentence in Humphrey Carpenter's *Secret Gardens*, and one paragraph in Alison Lurie's *Don't Tell the Grown-Ups* (1990). And nothing in Perry Nodelman's magisterial *The Hidden Adult* (2008).[6]

The reason for this relative critical neglect cannot, however, simply be Kipling's imperialist views. True, the liberals Lurie and Carpenter are clearly put off by Kipling's well-publicised commitment to law and order, but many contemporary critics of children's literature are much preoccupied with these, especially in relation to empire and its ideologies which get a central emphasis in Nodelman's book. In 2009, the journal *Children's Literature* featured an article on 'British Imperialism and American Multiculturalism' and the *Children's Literature Association Quarterly* one on 'The Post-Mutiny Imperial Boy Hero'.[7] Imperialism is an important focus for critics of children's literature, and Kipling was unquestionably an imperialist whose views not only coloured but in some respects inspired his writings for children. John McClure argued in 1981 that the Mowgli stories amount to 'a fable of imperial education and rule, with Mowgli behaving towards the beasts as the British do to the Indians ... To be above yet to belong, to be obeyed as a god and loved as a brother, this is Kipling's dream for the imperial ruler, a dream that Mowgli achieves.'[8] This, I think, overstates its case since, as I argue below, Mowgli is only 'Master of the Jungle' by name; but one need not concur completely with McClure's judgement to agree that Mowgli's position in the Jungle does in some measure correspond to the European imperialist's daydream of lording it among 'the natives'. Moreover, the first written 'Mowgli' tale 'In the Rukh', published in *Many Inventions*,[9] shows the grown-up Mowgli as a minor wood-god turned game warden for the British, a career choice giving obvious ammunition to the postcolonial critics McClure and McBratney, who lay heavy stress on this story, which Kipling's admirers dismiss as poor or even uncanonical work. J. I. M. Stewart mocked the Mowgli of 'In the Rukh' as 'a cross between a Wordsworthian child of nature and a Boy Scout. He walks out of the story at the other end in the company of a nice girl and with the intention of settling down. He knows all the answers – just as the uninspired Kipling did.'[10] When Daniel Karlin edited the *Jungle Books* for Penguin Classics, he omitted this tale as nothing more than 'a half-baked anticipation' of the true Mowgli.[11]

Earlier readers of Kipling's writings for children saw the *Jungle Books* more simply, as a charmed world to which politics were irrelevant. Roger Lancelyn Green argued that the *Jungle Books* give access to 'universal' resonances that last a lifetime. To the child who reads them

> the lasting joy, and one making itself felt at a deeper level than mere excitement or entertainment, is the immediate identification of himself [*sic*] with Mowgli. For Mowgli's adventures are both of the body and the spirit ... We must each read our own environment and aspect of the Great Predicament into his adventures. In whatever outward form it comes to each of us the inward experience is the same as Mowgli's, with the emphasis on different facets perhaps, but the whole recognisably universal.[12]

This passage unintentionally demonstrates how claims for Kipling's 'universality' are liable to rest on assumptions of privilege in terms of class and gender. Lancelyn Green's argument assumes that everyone – or perhaps every boy – has inhabited a 'Jungle' of childhood, at once wild and secure, in which he learns the Law by which he will live when he leaves it, as he must if he is to become an adult (this, I take it, is the 'Great Predicament' – being both 'of the Jungle and *not* of the Jungle' (*SJB* 86)). But Mowgli is so obviously exceptional in his beauty, intelligence and strength, as well as his experiences of adoption by animals and his freedom from the curses of Adam (he never has to work) and of Babel (he converses equally readily with men and animals), that his story can be 'universal' only in the sense that he invites identification as the ideal boy everybody would like to be – as when Oswald Bastable in E. Nesbit's *The Would-Be-Goods* announces, 'We'll play Jungle Book and I shall be Mowgli.'[13]

But this raises another question: who are the children for whom Kipling wrote the *Jungle Books*? One answer might be 'His own', since Kipling wrote all his children's books except for the late *Land and Sea Tales for Scouts and Guides* while he was father to a young family. The first three *Just So Stories* originated as bedtime stories for his eldest daughter Josephine, born in 1892 at his house 'Naulakha' in Brattleboro, Vermont, where the *Jungle Book* stories and '*Captains Courageous*' were also written and *Kim* begun. The high-spirited stories of *Stalky & Co.* were begun after the birth of John Kipling in 1897 and appeared as a book in 1899, after the death of Josephine, while *Puck of Pook's Hill* and *Rewards and Fairies* feature Kipling's own children Elsie and John as 'Una' and 'Dan'. But since Kipling's own children were not remotely of an age to enjoy the *Jungle Books* at the time of writing, still less *Stalky & Co.*, another answer might be 'himself' – or at least what his admirer Rosemary Sutcliff called 'the small unlived pocket of childhood in [him]self'.[14] The fact that Kipling wrote the stories of Mowgli's abandonment, fostering, exile and revenge when his first child was a baby suggests that becoming a father put him in creative touch with his own childhood, enabling him to turn his lost Bombay paradise and his wretched years in the 'House of Desolation' at Southsea into a triumphant fable of exile and adoption. In this reading, Kipling's parents are subliminally held guilty (the toddler Mowgli is abandoned to the tiger) and displaced into animal and 'native' protectors (Father and Mother Wolf, the mentors Bagheera, Baloo, Akela and Kaa, and the woman Messua to whom he will finally return). As Randall Jarrell, Kipling's most percipient reader, wrote:

> To Kipling the world is a dark forest full of families: so that when your father and mother leave you in the forest to die, the wolves that come to eat you are always Father Wolf and Mother Wolf, your real father and mother, and you are always – as not even the little wolves ever quite are – their real son. The family Romance, the two families of the Hero, have so predominant a place in no other writer. Kipling never said a word or thought a thought against his parents, 'both so entirely comprehending that except in trivial matters we had hardly need of words'; few writers have made authority so tender, beautiful and final – have had us miserable mortals serve better masters; *but* Kipling's Daemon kept bringing Kipling stories in which wild animals turn out to be the abandoned Mowgli's real father and mother, a heathen Lama turns out to be the orphaned Kim's real father – and Kipling wrote down the stories and read them to his father and mother.[15]

Yet this still doesn't tell us about the actual or implied child readers of Kipling's stories. Certainly these books had eager buyers, at least until the 1950s and 1960s, for from their first publication the *Jungle Books* were an instant success with reviewers and the public. Lancelyn Green claims that as soon as they appeared 'children seized upon them and began to "play Jungle" even as we have done ever since', citing as evidence E. Nesbit's fictional 'Bastable' children who are all Kipling enthusiasts. But his only real-life example is Major Cotterill, who in his Edwardian boyhood belonged to a 'secret society called the Prowl' whose members wrote asking for the names of Mowgli's three younger 'lair-brothers' (Kipling wrote back to tell them, but unfortunately they failed to keep his answer).[16] He also cites Robert Baden-Powell using the *Jungle Books* as the theme of his immensely popular *Wolf Cub's Handbook* in 1916, acknowledging his debt to Kipling 'who has done so much to put the right spirit into our rising young manhood'.[17] But although the popularity of the Wolf Cubs proved Baden-Powell right about Kipling's appeal to youth, it was he who 'seized upon' Kipling's *Jungle Books* as suitable for enthusing children.

According to Jacqueline Rose's influential book *The Case of Peter Pan*, the question of Kipling's child readers is irrelevant. For Rose, the reader for whom children's books are written is never, even in books addressed to named children, a real young person but an *ideal* child invented or fanta-sised by the adult writer. The issue is not 'what the child wants, but ... what the adult desires – desires in the very act of construing the child as the object of its speech. Children's fiction draws in the child, it secures, places and names the child.'[18] The adult desires to 'frame' the child as innocent, in the senses both of being asexual (much of Rose's intricate argument deals with adults' need to occlude childhood sexuality so as to keep their own uncon-scious conflicts about sexual identity safely repressed) and of possessing a primordial simplicity of experience and language. The logic of her argument is that 'what most defines children's literature is its existence as a force to shape and control children – to make them into the children – and eventu-ally, presumably, the adults – that adult [writers] want them to be'.[19] And the way in which children's literature 'secures' children is deeply complicit with imperialist ideology, for 'children's fiction has a long-established set of links with the colonialism which identified the new world with the infantile state of man'.[20]

Such literature represents a form of colonisation, by constructing its read-ers as at once primordially free of restraint and as disciplined adults in the making – an argument elaborated authoritatively by Perry Nodelman in *The Hidden Adult*, which argues that stories for children work by setting up conflicting values for the implied child reader. On the one hand, children's literature celebrates the wildness and spontaneity of childhood (which is why Lurie idealises it as 'subversive' and Carpenter as a magical 'secret gar-den'); on the other hand, it insists on the bourgeois adult values of self-control, symbolised in a characteristic 'home-and-away' movement towards adventure and back to safety. The child-hero learns a lesson about the wis-dom of adult values – but never completely, for the wildness of childhood will always need to be disciplined by another book. The adults who write these fantasies can thus sentimentalise about childhood (including their own), while endorsing children's always incomplete subjection to the rule of law and order. John McBratney's suggestion that 'it is doubtful whether Kipling's public commitment to empire would have been so strong had not his private "Daemon" allowed him the respite of such Mowglis in the glade' would thus make Kipling the most representative of children's writers.[21]

The problem with such arguments for a reader of Kipling is that, despite their obvious relevance, they don't quite explain the strength and subtlety of his appeal. Certainly there is both wildness and discipline in the *Jungle Books*; certainly the versified 'Law of the Jungle' taught to the Wolf-Pack sets a distinctly public school value on cleanliness and self-control: 'Wash daily from nose-tip to tail-tip; drink deeply but never too deep.'[22] The elab-orate provisions for dividing a carcass, including the mother's 'Lair-Right' to 'One haunch of each kill for her litter', 'Cub-Right', 'Pack-Right' and 'Cave-Right' (*SJB* 30), have a less schoolmasterly sound, yet they too assume subjection to a Law which limits the primitive instincts of greed and aggression. In addition, Kipling addresses us with reasonable-sounding sermons, as when he explains how after new cubs have been inspected at the Pack's monthly Council 'no excuse is accepted if a grown wolf of the Pack kills one of them. The punishment is death where the murderer can be found; and if you think for a minute you will see that this must be so.'[23] That seemingly informal phrase 'if you think for a minute' subtly pulls a young reader into accepting its wisdom about wolf behaviour – and by implication, about the justice and necessity of capital punishment for infanticide. Taking our intelligence and assent for granted, Kipling's rhetoric flatteringly constructs us as thoughtful, judicious and if need be ruthless, as befits future officers of the Empire. This fantasy position can easily be occupied by those excluded from this imperial destiny by sex or class – hence presumably the 'universal' appeal of the Law as 'part of the "Tao" – the basic knowledge of Good and Evil, of Right and Wrong conduct implanted in Mankind'.[24]

For as Lancelyn Green saw – and this is the strength of his account of Kipling – the great appeal of the *Jungle Books* is that their readers can enter a realm of wonder and untrammelled wildness which is nonetheless secure. They offer children the delights of entering and possessing the primordial forest, knowing the 'Jungle People' out of the jurisdiction of the 'Man-Pack', as Mowgli contemptuously calls human villagers, *and* of boundaries securely drawn by the 'Jungle Law', ultimately ratified by the distantly powerful justice of 'the English at Khanhiwara' (*SJB* 70–1, 80–3). Thus Mowgli's adventures with the monkeys in 'Kaa's Hunting' turn out well, thanks to his own courage and presence of mind and, even more, to his mentors' tough, loving discipline. Baloo beats into him the 'Master-Words' which he needs to be safe ('Better he should be bruised all over by me who love him than that he should come to harm by ignorance' (*JB* 47–8)), and after risking his own and Bagheera's lives to rescue the boy, agrees reluctantly ('He is very little') that 'He has done mischief, and blows must be dealt now' (*JB* 27). Mowgli himself prefers corporal punishment to the tedium of the monkeys' aimless play: 'Baloo will surely beat me, but that is better than chasing silly rose-leaves with the Bandar-Log' (*JB* 70). No wonder these books were approved as long as the British Empire lasted by British parents and teachers; no wonder, either, that its demise has left them somewhat unfashionable.[25]

Kipling's 'Puck' books are similarly loaded with old-fashioned teaching about the virtues of patriotism and public service. *Puck of Pook's Hill* begins with the Norman conqueror Sir Richard falling in love with England and its customs, continues with the soldier Parnesius heroically defending the

Great Wall and the *Pax Romana* against the Picts and their 'Winged Hat' allies, and culminates with 'Magna Carta' transforming the Barons' militarism into English justice in 'The Treasure and the Law' ('The Sword gave the Treasure, and the Treasure gave the Law'), followed as coda by the intensely patriotic 'Children's Song', which in the 1960s we used to sing as a hymn at school assembly before Remembrance Sunday:

> *Land of our Birth, we pledge to Thee*
> *Our love and toil in years to be,*
> *When we are grown and take our place*
> *As men and women with our race.*[26]

The companion volume *Rewards and Fairies* takes as its theme the hard choices summed up in the book's leitmotif, 'What else could I have done?' This question is first put by the Boy accepting his harsh destiny in 'Cold Iron'; next, in 'Gloriana', the children meet Queen Elizabeth I, who after relating how in order to stake England's claim to the colony Virginia she lured her young knights on a deadly quest, asks Dan, 'D'you think they were right to go … D'you think she was right to send them?'[27] He replies 'after thinking it over' that he doesn't see what else they or she could have done (Una is less forgiving).[28] In 'The Knife and the Naked Chalk', the children meet a Bronze Age shepherd who saves his people from the terror of wolves at the cost of a blinded eye and his chance of human happiness: 'And yet, what else could I have done?' In 'Brother Square-Toes', they hear of President George Washington refusing to take his unprepared country to war 'though every city in the Union burn me in effigy … What else can I do?' A Saxon bishop advises the pagan Meon to keep faith with his own gods in 'The Conversion of St Wilfred', adding, 'I don't see even now what else I could have said,' just as Meon's boatmen in the story's accompanying poem keep faith by going out in a storm to find him because 'a man must stand by his master'. In 'A Doctor of Medicine', Nicholas Culpeper the trained physician risks his life because 'the plague was here. What else could I have done?' while in Armada year the shipbuilder Simon answers his country's and his friend Drake's need by giving him a ship and most of the contents of his own shipyard: 'What else could I ha' done? *I* knew what he'd need most.'[29] The heroes of all these stories are the great and lesser men who keep faith and act for the public good, whatever it may cost. The Puck books thus imply a more complex and considered version, directed at an older child, of the *Jungle Book*'s guidance to young readers: 'You will see if you think for a minute that this must be so' (*JB* 16).

You don't need to invoke Jacqueline Rose on the adult's dream of the child's innocence or Perry Nodelman's theory of children's literature colonising its readers' minds with a double fantasy of the child as both noble savage and embryo good citizen, to see that the *Jungle Books* and the Puck tales give their readers a vicarious experience of adventure both as freedom and as service to a just State (or, anyway, a State assumed to be just). Hence presumably the lack of interest they hold for contemporary critics, apart from the school stories in *Stalky & Co.*, in which the overt anti-authoritarianism of the boys destined to be army officers for once offers interpreters of Kipling a paradox on which to exercise hermeneutic skills.[30]

Man and beast in the jungle

Ideological and/or imperialist readings of Kipling's *Jungle Books* are, then, not wrong; they just don't quite do the books justice. To concentrate too heavily on these aspects of the *Jungle Books* is to risk oversimplifying them as much as Joseph Bristow did *Kim* when he equated that book's meaning with Baden-Powell's unsubtle interpretation of it in *Scouting for Boys*.[31] Such readings tend to ignore the verbal pleasure (which children can feel if not necessarily articulate) of the stories' constantly shifting registers, Kipling's seductively clear storytelling voice alternating with the splendour and/or archaism of his human and animal speakers. More crucially, they don't allow for the complexity and subtlety of the relation which the stories set up between the worlds of the animals or 'Jungle People' and of the humans who live apart from and are feared by them. The relation of humans and animals is, of course, the theme of non-Mowgli stories also: as symbiosis in 'Rikki-Tiki-Tavi' where the mongoose defends both his English masters and his friends the weaver-birds from the predatory cobras, or as predation in 'The White Seal' where Kotick searches for a place where seals can be safe from human killers, or in 'The Undertakers' where the crocodile recalls a gluttonous lifetime of preying on Indian villagers. But despite Kipling's empathy with the animals, these stories do not explore the terrain of identification with and difference between man and beast, both key issues in the Mowgli stories. These relationships are both explored and embodied by the hybrid hero; named by Mother Wolf after the frog, an amphibious and vulnerable creature, Mowgli belongs to the worlds of humans and animals whom in the end he must leave because 'Man goes to Man at the last' (*SJB* 80).

Of course, the fact that this prophecy is spoken by an animal also indicates how humanised Kipling's animals are, almost in the manner of the classic 'beast-fable'. Their 'Jungle Law' is no neo-Darwinian law of the survival of the fittest, but an elaborate civil and criminal code which 'never orders anything without a reason' (*JB* 7), and is 'as perfect as time and custom can make it' (*SJB* 3). Apart from the unruly monkeys or *Bandar-log*, the animals inhabit a society governed by law under Hathi, the 'Master of the Jungle' (*SJB* 16), who trumpets the 'Water Truce' in 'How Fear Came'. The animals understand not only law but exchange when Mowgli's acceptance by the Wolf-Pack is paid for by Bagheera's gift of a bull: 'The cub can be bought for a price. It is the Law' (*JB* 21). The wolves themselves discover the hard way how much they need the Law; at the end of 'Tiger! Tiger!' the masterless members of the former Pack cry, 'Lead us again, O Akela ... for we be sick of this lawlessness, and we would be the Free People once more.' Although Bagheera contemptuously denies them – 'Ye fought for freedom, and it is yours. Eat it, O Wolves' (*JB* 121) – by the penultimate Mowgli story 'Red Dog', the Seeonee Pack is reconstituted under 'Phao, son of Phaona, who fought his way to the leadership of the Pack, according to the Jungle Law' (*SJB* 223), with Akela as his adviser.

The Jungle Beasts possess not only a Law but a lively oral culture, in which wisdom is passed on through storytelling. When in 'How Fear Came' the Jungle People want to know what Shere Khan means by his 'right' to kill man, Hathi's explanation begins 'It is an old tale, a tale older than the Jungle' (*SJB* 16), describing how all animals lived in peace until the First Tiger first brought death to the world and then taught Man to kill. (Bagheera, however, sounds a note of scepticism about Hathi's tale of 'Tha, the First of the Elephants' creating the world, whispering to an amused Mowgli that it 'has not lost fat in the telling' (*SJB* 18).) 'How Fear Came' is a myth about the origin of death and evil strongly resembling the Judeo-Christian story of the Fall; but other stories told by animals hold practical counsel. Mowgli's plan to destroy the village that threw him out in 'Letting in the Jungle' is inspired by the tale he has heard from the hunter Buldeo, otherwise a liar, of Hathi's 'Sack of the Fields of Bhurtpore', a story confirmed by Hathi himself (*SJB* 90–2). When in 'Red Dog' Mowgli asks Kaa the python for advice on how he and wolves can even the odds against the innumerable invading dhole, Kaa tells him the story of the hunted buck who jumped a gorge into the river, rousing the wild bees to destroy his pursuers. These stories told by the animals are true, unlike the 'wonderful tales of gods and men and ghosts' (*JB* 47) which humans tell each other. That sounds attractive, except that the humans turn out to be far too easily seduced by tall stories. '"True, true; that must be the truth," said the greybeards, nodding together' (*JB* 97) when Buldeo insists that Shere Khan the tiger limps because he is really the ghost of a lame moneylender. A band of charcoal-burners are just as easily taken in by Buldeo's story of 'how he himself had really killed Shere Khan; and how Mowgli had turned into a wolf, and fought with him all the afternoon, and changed into a boy again, and bewitched Buldeo's rifle' (*SJB* 69–70). Only Mowgli the former Jungle-dweller perceives from the start that

Buldeo's stories are 'cobwebs and moonshine' (*JB* 98). Matters get worse when Buldeo dazzles the villagers with a farrago of self-serving lies about Mowgli as a 'Wolf-Demon' and his adoptive mother Messua as a witch, a situation briefly summarised by Mowgli: 'They are all sitting around Buldeo, who is saying that which did not happen'(*SJB* 80). Mowgli here sounds very like one of Swift's Houyhnhms in *Gulliver's Travels* (1726, 1735), the horses who 'have no word in their Language for Lying or Falsehood', instead using the periphrasis *'saying the thing which is not'*.[32] As in Swift's fable, the point is made that cruelty and lying are purely human vices, and Buldeo's story is all too readily accepted by the credulous villagers who turn into a lynch-mob bent on torture and murder: 'Nay, beat them first! Torches! More torches! Buldeo, heat the gun-barrels!' (*SJB* 87).

Once the man-eating tiger Shere Khan and his toady Tabaqui the jackal are dead, the 'Jungle People' may appear more human than the humans in their obedience to the Jungle Law, and even in their command of language. They excel in rhetoric and truthful storytelling, whereas the villagers' stories are at best 'cobwebs and moonshine'. Yet although the animals speak and have their own society, they never become simply humans in disguise. From the first sentence of 'Mowgli's Brothers', where Father Wolf 'woke up from his day's rest, scratched himself, yawned and spread out his paws one after the other to get rid of the sleepy feeling in their tips' (*JB* 3), the stories are located in an animal world. True, Mowgli's friends and enemies in the Jungle are given individual names and personalities: Shere Khan is a bully and a thug, Baloo is a schoolmaster, Tabaqui is a sneak and a toady, Bagheera is worldly wise – yet they also remain animals. As Daniel Karlin eloquently says: 'There is something *other*, something recalcitrantly estranged from human experience, in the silky violence of Bagheera, the silence and lordship of Hathi, and the cold, ageless, fathomless wisdom of Kaa.'[33] So Hathi the herbivore recalls the scent of blood with revulsion: 'My tusks were red at the Sack of the Fields of Bhurtpore, and I would not wake that smell again' (*SJB* 94). And in one of Kipling's best comic moments, when Baloo discovers that the 'Man-cub' has been abducted by the monkeys, he roars with ursine hyperbole, 'Put dead bats on my head! Give me black bones to eat! Roll me into the hives of the wild honey-bees that I may be stung to death, for I am the most miserable of bears! *Arrulala! Wahooa!*' (*JB* 58). Yet though Kipling's animals speak quite as well as men, they still think like beasts, not humans. When Kaa the python searches his memory, saying 'What is, has been. What will be is no more than a forgotten year striking backward' (*SJB* 233), his phrasing may echo Ecclesiastes – 'The thing that hath been, it is that which shall be'[34] – but he speaks as a snake who thinks of time 'striking backward'.

The firmly drawn boundary between animals and humans often discredits the humans, especially if they are Indian, by contrast with the 'Free People' of the Jungle who fear their traps and rifles. (The distant English rulers who 'do not suffer people to burn or beat each other without witnesses' (*SJB* 81) are made to sound much more benign.) This boundary appears in the humans' and animals' very different attitudes to fire and food – although there is a certain amount of censorship about this issue. We are frequently told that Mowgli, his wolf-brothers and his friend Bagheera the panther kill and eat, but we don't see them hunting game, still less taking their meals – and with reason: it would be difficult to think of the Wolf-Pack as admirable 'Free People' if we saw them actually cracking bones and chewing raw flesh. Mentioning cookery would likewise betray the raw savagery of the wolves, making Mowgli's position as inhabitant of both human and wolf worlds impossible. Also, cookery uses fire, which is terrible to animals, though it doesn't scare Mowgli, who recalls 'how, before I was a wolf, I lay beside the Red Flower and it was warm and pleasant' (*JB* 35). Holding his stolen fire-pot, he sees the red glow as a hungry living creature: '"This thing will die if I do not give it things to eat", and he dropped twigs and dried bark on the red stuff' (*JB* 33). His status as 'Man' is affirmed both by his possession of fire, which will divide him utterly from the beasts he has grown up with who 'live in deadly fear of it' (*JB* 31), and by his use of metaphor as cognitive tool which enables him to keep his fire going. The difference between Mowgli's figure of speech and those of Kaa and Baloo quoted above, is that Mowgli's metaphor, unlike theirs, does more than represent external reality in terms drawn from his own experience; it is also a means of *mastering* reality.

Fire, plus his own courage and intelligence, enable Mowgli to singe and mock Shere Khan and the treacherous Wolf-Pack – after which he leaves the Jungle 'to meet those mysterious things that are called men' (*JB* 41). When he returns after nearly being lynched by the villagers, he brings a knife with him but not fire, which he shuns until 'The Spring Running', where the sight of a distant cooking-fire which he recognises as 'the Red Flower – the Red Flower that I lay beside before – before I came even to the first Seeonee Pack!' (*SJB* 281) – draws him back to Messua his human mother, and through her to adult life. On his first abortive return to human society, Mowgli has difficulty adapting to human ways: 'First he had to wear a cloth around him, which annoyed him horribly; and then he had to learn about money, which he did not in the least understand, and about plough-ing, of which he did not see the use ('Tiger! Tiger!' (*JB* 95)). Changing his diet would surely be even more difficult; but since we never see Mowgli at his meals, we don't hear anything about it. Since caste matters a great deal to the villagers, they are clearly Hindus whose diet would consist of the grains and vegetables they grow themselves, plus milk and butter from their herd of cattle and buffalo. But Mowgli doesn't seemingly miss his meat diet while he's in the village, nor does he acquire a taste for cooked food from his stay there. When he rejoins the Jungle he clearly goes back, though this isn't dwelt on, to eating raw meat.[35]

One food, however, crosses the divide between humanity and the Jungle: milk, which is natural yet not 'wild'. Milk comes from a mother suckling her child, or from a domestic animal, like the 'long drink of milk' which Messua gives Mowgli when she first receives him as her lost son: 'He has the very look of my boy' (*JB* 90). Her ready acceptance ensures Mowgli's re-entry into human society; and she never grumbles or doubts Mowgli when her neighbours later try to lynch her for being his adoptive mother, unlike her husband complaining, 'Look! I bleed' (*SJB* 77). Mother Wolf's experience of adoptive mother-love at first sight is even more closely linked to giving Mowgli milk: '"How little! How naked – and how bold!" said Mother Wolf softly. The baby was pushing his way between the cubs to get close to the warm hide. "*Ahai!* He is taking his meal with the others"'(*JB* 10). Both adoptive mothers are responsible for bringing Mowgli into their own worlds;[36] for although the Wolf-Pack and the Indian village are each ruled by males, it is mothers who give the hero his identity as an animal ('Mowgli the Frog I will call thee' (*JB* 15)) and as a human ('I gave thee milk, Nathoo ... because thou wast my son whom the tiger took, and because I loved thee very dearly' (*SJB* 77)). Mother Wolf will fight to the death for him against Shere Khan and, if need be, against her own Pack (*JB* 12, 20). Much later, she calls 'the woman who gave thee milk' the only human she would not kill: 'Yes, I would have spared her alone' (*SJB* 63). Later she looks at Messua and realises that this woman represents Mowgli's future: 'I gave thee thy first milk: but Bagheera speaks truth: Man goes to Man at the last' (*SJB* 80). It is fitting that Messua should greet Mowgli's reappearance in 'The Spring Running' by 'bustling among the cooking-pots ... "I will make a fire, and thou shalt drink warm milk."' After the milk has put him to sleep, she gives him a meal, described in detail for the first and last time in the Mowgli stories: 'a few coarse cakes baked over the smoky fire, some rice and a lump of sour preserved tamarinds – just enough to go on with till he could get to his evening kill' (*SJB* 286–7). Mowgli has not yet said farewell to the Jungle; and we know from 'In the Rukh' that he will not become a ploughman.

It is not surprising that Mowgli should hate the idea of rejoining the human race, 'deeply as he loathed them, their talk, their cruelty and their cowardice' (*SJB* 90). Yet as all the Jungle People are well aware, he is not one of themselves but a 'man's cub'. 'Mowgli's Brothers', the first story in *The Jungle Book*, turns on adoption followed by expulsion and exile to 'those mysterious things that are called men' (*JB* 41). Even as a boy, Mowgli can stare the wolves down, which they come to resent as much as his human dexterity; as Bagheera tells him, they perversely hate him 'because thou hast pulled out thorns from their feet – because thou art a man' (*JB* 30). The animals who love him are equally well aware of his humanity; Mother Wolf wonders who else 'could boast of a man's cub among her children' (*JB* 18), and when he leaves the Jungle she tells him to 'Come back soon, little naked son of mine; for listen, child of man, I loved thee better than ever I loved my cubs' (*JB* 41).

Mowgli's humanity makes him both more lovable and more formidable than any of the beasts. As a child in 'Kaa's Hunting' his intelligence saves him from the *Bandar-Log*, and enables him in 'Tiger! Tiger!', when he is older and more formidable, to plot the death of Shere Khan under the hooves of cattle driven by his wolf-brothers, whom he uses as sheepdogs. He masterminds the destruction of the village by the 'Eaters of Grass' and the elephants in 'Letting in the Jungle'; and in 'Red Dog' his resource and daring, aided by Kaa's wisdom, lure the invaders into the deadly trap that enables the wolves' hard-won victory. By the last story 'The Spring Running', we learn that 'The Jungle People who used to fear him for his wits now feared him for his strength, and when he moved quietly on his own affairs the mere whisper of his coming cleared the wood-paths', and whatever his mood, his unchanging gaze 'like a stone in wet or dry weather' can always subdue the animals (*SJB* 264).

John McClure equates Mowgli's cold gaze with the conventional 'White Man' mastering hapless natives; but although Mowgli claims to be 'Master of the Jungle' he actually behaves less like an imperial ruler than a prince (*SJB* 267). He never shows a kingly authority comparable to Hathi's majestic dismissal of Shere Khan from the communal drinking-place in 'How Fear Came': 'Go, then. The river is to drink, and not to defile ... Clean or unclean, get to thy lair, Shere Khan!' (*SJB* 15). For all Mowgli's power to out-stare the animals, he cannot take his own mastery for granted in 'Red Dog', where he needs all his eloquence to persuade the Wolf-Pack to stand and fight the invading dhole. And he sulks like a spoilt child in 'The Spring Running' because he is ignored by his animal friends in their spring fever, which he cannot simply share with them because beautiful as the Jungle is, it holds no mate for him. When he defiantly left the Wolf-Pack, the boy Mowgli was seized by mortal grief, recognised by Bagheera: 'Those are only tears such as men use. Now I know that indeed thou art a man' (*JB* 40); in the 'Time of New Talk' he is left to prove this truth on his own pulses. At first he believes again that he is dying, and is prey to adolescent self-pity: 'He was so sorry for himself that he nearly wept ... miserable as he was, Mowgli felt happy that he was so miserable, if you can understand that upside-down sort of happiness' (*SJB* 278). None of the animals who bid him their moving fare-wells at the end of the story are subject to such complexities of feeling, for these constitute the difficult privilege of being human. As Mowgli sang in his earlier psalm of triumph and mourning:

> As Mang flies between the beasts and the birds, so fly I between the village
> and the Jungle. Why?
> I dance on the hide of Shere Khan, but my heart is very heavy. My mouth is
> cut and wounded with the stones from the village, but my heart is very
> light because I have come back to the Jungle. Why?   (*JB* 123–4)

Mowgli's 'Why?' is answered, not by himself but by the narrative. By cross-ing the threshold of the wolf's lair as a toddler, he – and through identifi-cation, we as readers – gained entry to a realm of otherness, wildness and adventure in which to realise the human capacities whose full development would ineluctably drive him beyond it.[37] For all the apparently human qual-ities of the 'Jungle People', Mowgli is finally defined by his difference from them. Kipling's writing for children was undoubtedly fired by the pieties of empire and by the imperialist fantasy of mastering otherness, but its lasting achievement was the creation of the Jungle which readers could enter in imagination to discover the meanings both of wildness and of humanity.

Notes

1 Rudyard Kipling, *Something of Myself: for my Friends Known and Unknown* (London: Macmillan, 1937), p. 210; John McBratney, 'Imperial Subjects, Imperial Space in Kipling's *Jungle Book*', *Victorian Studies*, 35 (1992), p. 290.

2 Roger Lancelyn Green, *Kipling and the Children* (London: Elek Books, 1975), p. 123; Harry Ricketts, *The Unforgiving Minute: A Life of Rudyard Kipling* (London: Chatto & Windus, 1999), p. xii; Daniel Karlin, Introduction to Rudyard Kipling, *The Jungle Books* (London: Penguin, 1987), p. 7; J. M. S. Tompkins, *The Art of Rudyard Kipling* (1959; London: Methuen, 1965), p. 56.

3 Because the 'Cub Scouts' ('Wolf Cubs' until 1967) drew their inspiration from the *Jungle Books*, 'Mowgli's Brothers' is still read to new recruits, and adult leaders of the 'Pack' still take the names 'Akela', 'Bagheera', 'Hathi' and 'Baloo'. The *Jungle Books*, however, now play a much smaller part than formerly in Cub rules and activities.

4 David Haig's stage play *My Boy Jack* (London: Nick Hern Books, 1997), shown on British television in November 2007 and subsequently made available as a DVD, has done much to enforce public perceptions of Kipling as a jingo patriot.

5 Joseph Bristow, *Empire Boys: Adventures in a Man's World* (London: HarperCollins, 1991); Daphne Kutzer, *Empire's Children: Empire and Imperialism in Classic British Children's Books* (New York: Garland, 2000).

6 Aidan Chambers, *Booktalk: Occasional Writing on Literature and Children* (London: Bodley Head, 1982); Humphrey Carpenter, *Secret Gardens: A Study*

of the Golden Age in Children's Literature (London: Allen and Unwin, 1985), p. 15; Alison Lurie, *Don't Tell the Grown-Ups: Subversive Children's Literature* (London: Bloomsbury 1990), pp. 10–11; Morag Styles, Eve Bearne and Victor Watson, eds., *After Alice: Exploring Children's Literature* (London: Cassell, 1992); Peter Hollindale, *Signs of Childness in Children's Books* (Stroud: Thimble, 1997); Perry Nodelman, *The Hidden Adult: Defining Children's Literature* (Baltimore: Johns Hopkins University Press, 2008). See also John McBratney, *Imperial Subjects, Imperial Spaces: Rudyard Kipling's Fiction of the Native-Born* (Columbus: Ohio State University Press, 2002). Sue Walsh's *Kipling's Children's Literature: Language, Identity, and Constructions of Childhood* (Farnham: Ashgate, 2010), whose principal focus is the *Just So Stories*, appeared since I wrote this essay.

7 See Rosemary Managoly George, 'British Imperialism and American Multiculturalism: The Americanization of Burnett's *A Little Princess*', *Children's Literature*, 37 (2009), pp. 137–66; Supraya Goswami, 'The Post-Mutiny Imperial Boy Hero: Bridging Cultural Divides in Sara Jean Duncan's *The History of Sonny Sahib*', *Children's Literature Association Quarterly*, 34:1 (Spring 2009), pp. 38–50.

8 John McClure, *Kipling and Conrad: The Colonial Fiction* (Cambridge, MA: Harvard University Press, 1981), p. 60; see also McBratney, 'Imperial Subjects, Imperial Space in Kipling's *Jungle Book*', pp. 288–90.

9 See Green's discussion of the textual history of 'In the Rukh' in his *Kipling and the Children*, pp. 109–11.

10 J. I. M. Stewart, *Rudyard Kipling* (London: Gollancz, 1966), p. 116.

11 Karlin, Introduction to Kipling, *The Jungle Books* (1987), p. 13. W. W. Robson's Oxford World's Classics edition (1988) compromises by printing 'In the Rukh' as an appendix.

12 Green, *Kipling and the Children*, p. 119.

13 E. Nesbit, *The Would-Be-Goods: Being the Further Adventures of the Treasure Seekers* (London: T. Fisher Unwin, 1901), p. 5.

14 Rosemary Sutcliff, quoted in Hollindale, *Signs of Childness in Children's Books*, p. 75.

15 Randall Jarrell, 'On Preparing to Read Kipling', in *Kipling, Auden & Co.* (Manchester: Carcanet, 1982), p. 325. The Kipling quote is from *Something of Myself*, p. 89.

16 Green, *Kipling and the Children*, p. 123.

17 *Ibid.*; Hugh Brogan, *Mowgli's Sons: Kipling and Baden-Powell's Scouts* (London: Jonathan Cape, 1987), p. 43.

18 Jacqueline Rose, *The Case of Peter Pan: The Impossibility of Children's Fiction* (London: Macmillan 1984), p. 2.

19 Nodelman, *The Hidden Adult*, p. 162.

20 Rose, *The Case of Peter Pan*, p. 50.

21 McBratney, 'Imperial Subjects, Imperial Space in Kipling's *Jungle Book*', p. 290.

22 Rudyard Kipling, *The Second Jungle Book* (1895; London: Macmillan, 1951), p. 29. Subsequent references in the text as *SJB*.

23 Rudyard Kipling, *The Jungle Book* (1894; London: Macmillan, 1951), p. 16. Subsequent references in the text as *JB*.

24 Green, *Kipling and the Children*, p. 119.

25 Bristow, *Empire Boys*, pp. 158–60.
26 Rudyard Kipling, *Puck of Pook's Hill* (1906; London: Macmillan, 1954), pp. 303, 305.
27 Rudyard Kipling, *Rewards and Fairies* (1910; London: Macmillan, 1952), pp. 23, 49–50.
28 Paul March-Russell points out Una's questioning role in his essay '*Rewards and Fairies* and the Neo-Romantic Debt', *Kipling Journal*, 82 (April 2007), pp. 6–16.
29 Kipling, *Rewards and Fairies*, pp. 139, 171, 236, 244, 262, 298.
30 Nodelman, *The Hidden Adult*, pp. 274–5; Hollindale, *Signs of Childness in Children's Books*, p. 75.
31 Bristow, *Empire Boys*, pp. 158–60.
32 Jonathan Swift, *Gulliver's Travels and Selected Writings*, ed. John Hayward (London: Nonesuch Press, 1968), p. 229.
33 Daniel Karlin, Introduction to Kipling, *Jungle Books* (1987), p. 23.
34 Ecclesiastes 1.9.
35 Charles Allen pointed out to me that William Henry Sleeman's *An Account of Wolves Nurturing Children in their Dens* (Plymouth: Jenkin Thomas, 1852), one of Kipling's printed sources, describes wolf-boys as only eating raw flesh. Those who did start eating cooked food might stay in human society; those who didn't went back to the wild.
36 Kipling's invocation of the mother in his best children's writing has been noticed both by U. C. Knoepflmacher in his fine essay 'Female Power and Male Self-Assertion: Kipling and the maternal', *Children's Literature*, Kipling issue edited by Judith Plotz, 20 (1992), pp. 15–35, and more recently by Charles Allen in *Kipling Sahib: India and the Making of Rudyard Kipling* (London: Little, Brown, 2007), pp. 361–2.
37 Sue Walsh analyses the relation between human and animal, arguing for Mowgli's 'unstable' identity, at some length in her chapter 'Translating "Animal" or Reading the "Other" in Kipling's "Mowgli" Stories', in *Kipling's Children's Literature*, pp. 51–70.

8

HARRY RICKETTS

'Nine and sixty ways': Kipling, ventriloquist poet

'The ambiguous status of Kipling's poetry', observes Jan Montefiore in her 2007 critical study *Rudyard Kipling*, 'is aptly summed up by Dan Jacobson's exasperated tribute to "Kipling, a poet I cannot abide yet cannot stop reading".'[1] This sentence might stand as an epigraph for any discussion of Kipling's poetry.

Jacobson's remark was made in the *Times Literary Supplement* in 2005. A century earlier in 1904, a cartoon by Max Beerbohm was fuelled by a similar combination of extremes. (This was in the immediate aftermath of the Boer War, during which Kipling had 'come out' as the undisputed bard of empire and literary spokesperson for imperial values.) In the cartoon, a diminutive, check-suited Kipling, kicking up his heels and blowing on a toy trumpet, hangs on the arm of a tall, languid Britannia. The two have swapped hats: he wears her war helmet, she his bowler. She leans away, seemingly unimpressed by his pipsqueak imperial trumpetings. The caption, mimicking the cockney idiom of his soldier ballads, reads: 'Mr Rudyard Kipling takes a bloomin' day aht on the blasted 'eath, along with Britannia, 'is gurl.' Only someone well versed in Kipling's work could have put the knife in so wittily.[2]

Beerbohm's cartoon and Jacobson's comment point to one aspect of Kipling's poetry on which everybody seems to agree: its sheer memorability. The *Oxford Dictionary of Quotations* (1964) includes eighty extracts from his poems (out of an overall total of ninety-eight Kipling items), while the more recent *Oxford Dictionary of Twentieth-Century Quotations* (1998) finds room for twenty-seven (out of a total of thirty-six).

Writing in 1942, George Orwell, an admirer of Kipling but with strong reservations, commented on how quickly his lines had become part of the general, quasi-anonymous phrase-pool.[3] A shortlist of his more adhesive lines might include: 'He travels the fastest who travels alone'; 'Oh, East is East, and West is West, and never the twain shall meet'; 'You're a better man than I am, Gunga Din!'; 'And what should they know of England who only England know?'; 'Or lesser breeds without the Law'; 'Take up the White Man's burden'; 'With the flannelled fools at the wicket or the muddied oafs at the goals'; 'And – which is more – you'll be a Man, my son!'; 'For the female of the species is more deadly than the male'; 'And the Glory of the Garden it shall not pass away!'. Which is not to forget 'those two imposters' from 'If–', beloved of sportswriters, 'Triumph and Disaster'. Nor that on 9/11, the day of the destruction of the World Trade Towers in New York in 2001, it was Kipling's 'The Storm Cone' (1932) that gave at least one commentator the necessary words: 'This is the midnight – let no star / Delude us – dawn is very far.'⁴

Orwell himself enjoyed pointing out that Kipling was so memorable, so apt, that he was even quoted unconsciously by those of radically different political views: 'Nothing could exceed the contempt of the (left-wing) *New Statesman*, for instance, for Kipling, but how many times during the Munich period did the *New Statesman* find itself quoting that phrase about paying the Dane-geld?'⁵ 'Paying the Dane-geld' comes from a poem about Danish invasions of England in the tenth and eleventh centuries. The poem's moral is that 'if once you have paid him the Dane-geld / You never get rid of the Dane' (*DV* 713). Kipling had long been predicting war with Germany and writing 'Dane-geld' in 1911, was undoubtedly also warning against German military aggression. By the 1930s, 'paying the Dane-geld' (meaning 'to pay protection money') had become a stock expression.

So deeply imprinted did certain lines of Kipling's become that when Evelyn Waugh wants to render officer talk in his Second World War trilogy *The Sword of Honour*, he has his characters break into quotations from Kipling: '"A woman's only a woman but a good cigar is a smoke," said the major'; '"The captains and the Kings depart," said de Souza.'⁶ Anthony Powell's Captain Gwatkin in *The Valley of Bones* even tries (unsuccessfully) to model his military and moral conduct on that of Kipling's Roman centurion in *Puck of Pook's Hill*, with special reference to 'A Song to Mithras': 'Mithras, also a soldier, keep us pure till the dawn!' (*DV* 523). On a more populist level, a 1995 national poll voted Kipling's 'If–' the United Kingdom's favourite poem, and three years later a voice-over reading of the same poem to an extended sequence of highlights wrapped up the BBC's coverage of the Football World Cup:

> If you can fill the unforgiving minute
>   With sixty seconds' worth of distance run,
>   Yours is the Earth and everything that's in it,
>   And – which is more – you'll be a Man, my son!   (*DV* 577)

*

Kipling's qualities as a poet, including his memorability, can in part be attributed to his early experiences (the Indian childhood, persecuted years in Southsea, schooldays at Westward Ho!), and also to early influences and audience. Kipling's mother's sister Georgie was married to the Pre-Raphaelite painter Edward Burne-Jones, and Kipling grew up steeped in (among others) William Morris, Algernon Swinburne and Robert Browning. His imagination and literary expectations were shaped thus by aestheticism, empire-training and the idea of words as verbal defence and controllable space – an unusual combination. He found himself in print early too, his mother to his annoyance privately publishing *Schoolboy Lyrics* in 1881.

Four early poems anticipate Kipling's future directions as a poet. 'Credat Judaeus' (meaning roughly 'Tell it to the marines') imagines three couples (upper-, middle- and lower-class), each asserting that their love is unique. In a final ironic twist, the narrator just as confidently claims the uniqueness of his own passion: 'For Love that is real was given to me!'[7] The more obviously Browningesque 'Overheard' eavesdrops on a young prostitute telling her story ('Failed, lost money, undone') to a potential client (*EV* 94). 'Donec Gratus Eram' ('While I was dear (to thee)'), handed in as a homework exercise, translates Horace *Odes*, III, ix, with the lovers' tiff and reconciliation rendered in broad Devonshire. These three poems with their confident deployment of voice and social register foreshadow the ventriloquism of Kipling's later work. 'Ave Imperatrix!', written after an assassination attempt on Queen Victoria in March 1882, sounded a different note, looking forward to the later empire hymns: 'Such greeting as should come from those / Whose fathers faced the Sepoy hordes' (*DV* 169).

At nearly seventeen, Kipling returned to India to work as a journalist. During the next six years, in addition to gruelling journalistic assignments, he published seven collections of short stories and two volumes of poems – although these volumes did not remotely cover the several hundred poems he wrote over that time. (These poems mostly remained uncollected and unavailable until Andrew Rutherford's meticulously annotated 1986 edition of Kipling's early verse.) Much of this poetry was occasional light verse. His primary audience was civilian and military Anglo-India (the British in India called themselves Anglo-Indians). Kipling perfectly matched the taste of this audience with *Echoes* (1884), lively parodies of nineteenth-century poets from Wordsworth to Whitman, co-written with his sister, and *Departmental Ditties* (1886), a volume of equally lively light verse. Parody and light verse allowed Kipling – an outsider attracted to the in-group – to take potshots at both mainstream literary culture and his Anglo-Indian world under cover of a self-protective irony.

'Jane Smith', one of the best parodies in *Echoes*, sends up the unintentional banality and bathos of some of Wordsworth's lyrical ballads. 'The Flight of the Bucket' retells the nursery rhyme of Jack and Jill in the manner

of Robert Browning. *Departmental Ditties* is full of characters with prepos-
terous-sounding names: Ahasueras Jenkins, Delilah Aberyswith, Boanerges
Blitzen, Mehitabel Lee. However, the perennial Anglo-Indian subjects are serious enough: local scandals, love, loneliness, longing for 'Home'. In 'Public
Waste', '*the Little Tin Gods on the Mountain Side*' (the bigwigs in Simla)
snobbishly cheat Exeter Battleby Tring out of his rightful promotion (*DV*
14). 'The Story of Uriah' gives a local spin to the Old Testament episode in
which King David sends Bathsheba's husband Uriah to his death in battle:

> And, when the Last Great Bugle Call
>   Adown the Hurnai throbs,
> And the last grim joke is entered
>   In the big black Book of Jobs,
> And Quetta graveyards give again
>   Their victims to the air,
> I shouldn't like to be the man
>   Who sent Jack Barrett there.   (*DV* 10)

*

Within a year of leaving India in March 1889, Kipling had conquered literary London. His meteoric success was due to the novelty of his subject matter (in effect, he created India as a literary subject for the English-speaking
world) and his immediate style. It was his poems quite as much as his short
stories which made his reputation, nationally and soon worldwide. 'The
Ballad of East and West' (1889), an early favourite, told a tale of derring-do
on the North-West Indian frontier. The opening line – '*Oh, East is East, and
West is West, and never the twain shall meet*' – quickly became famous (later
infamous) as the encapsulation of irreconcilable racial difference. Ironically,
Kipling's slogan-like quotability obscured the real point. Which was to set
up the irreconcilable and then reconcile it – if under admittedly exceptional
circumstances:

> *Oh, East is East, and West is West, and never the twain shall meet,*
> *Till Earth and Sky stand presently at God's great Judgment Seat;*
> *But there is neither East nor West, Border, nor Breed, nor Birth,*
> *When two strong men stand face to face, though they come from the ends of*
>   *the earth!*   (*DV* 234)

The 'two strong men' who 'stand face to face' and bond after a frenetic
horse-chase 'up and over the Tongue of Jagai' are the brigand-chief Kamal
and the Colonel's son, heroic spirits from the officer class (*DV* 235).
However, the series of barrack-room ballads which Kipling started to
publish in the *Scots Observer* in February 1890 gave a voice to 'Tommy
Atkins' (the average British private soldier). The ballads describe aspects

of the Tommies' often harsh and despised life in the phonetically rendered cockney that Beerbohm was to take off in his cartoon. 'Danny Deever', the first of the ballads, chillingly records the reactions of veterans and new recruits, on parade to witness the hanging of a fellow soldier for shooting a comrade:

> 'What's that so black agin the sun?' said Files-on-Parade.
> 'It's Danny fightin' 'ard for life,' the Colour-Sergeant said.
> 'What's that that whimpers over'ead?' said Files-on-Parade.
> 'It's Danny's soul that's passin' now,' the Colour-Sergeant said.
>   For they're done with Danny Deever, you can 'ear the quickstep play,
>   The Regiment's in column, an' they're marchin' us away;
>   Ho! the young recruits are shakin', an' they'll want their beer to-day,
>   After hangin' Danny Deever in the mornin'!   (DV 398)

'Mandalay' shows a returned soldier yearning for the old life 'somewheres east of Suez' and the Burmese girl he has left behind (DV 420). 'Tommy' hits back at civilian indifference and complacency: 'Yes, makin' mock o' uniforms that guard you while you sleep / Is cheaper than them uniforms, an' they're starvation cheap' (DV 399). 'Gunga Din' tells how a regimental water carrier gives his life for a wounded trooper.

When it appeared, 'Gunga Din' resonated rather differently from the way it does now. What struck, and moved, its first readers was the soldier-narrator's unsentimental tribute to Gunga Din's selfless courage, summed up in the admiring last line: 'You're a better man than I am, Gunga Din!' (DV 408). What tends to stand out now is the terms in which that admiration is expressed: not only the masculinist loading of that final line, but also the assumptions underpinning lines like 'An' for all 'is dirty 'ide / 'E was white, clear white, inside', which implicitly reinforce the imperial gold standard of 'being white' (DV 407). By contrast, the subversive aspect of 'The Widow at Windsor' may now be more detectable than it was at the time. Here jaunty imperial swagger is undercut by parenthetical lines whose self-rhyme spells out the human cost:

> Walk wide o' the Widow at Windsor,
>   For 'alf o' Creation she owns:
> We 'ave bought 'er the same with the sword an' the flame,
>   An' we've salted it down with our bones.
>   (Poor beggars! – it's blue with our bones!)   (DV 414)

These poems, indebted to contemporary music hall as well as to traditional and broadside ballads, were soon set to music and became regular recitation pieces. Popular with the soldiers for whom they spoke, the poems (though there were complaints about coarseness and vulgarity) also secured a highbrow readership. Lionel Johnson praised 'their unforced vigour and unexaggerated truth'; Edmund Gosse commended 'the rollicking storm of the verses', their 'genuine humour' and underlying 'melancholy'.[8]

The publication in early 1892 of *Barrack-Room Ballads & Other Verses* cemented Kipling's poetic reputation throughout the English-speaking world. That year, now married, he settled in Vermont where he lived for the next four years. His fifth volume of poems, *The Seven Seas*, appeared shortly after his return to England in 1896. Kipling might playfully refer to the collection as 'The cccccc's', but the globalising title gave the key.[9] This was a volume specifically aimed, as the American critic W. D. Howells noted, at 'the Larger England', the emerging Empire nations, who are duly saluted in 'The Song of the Cities', a fifteen-quatrain round trip of the British Empire from Bombay to Auckland.[10] 'The Song of the Dead' provides this audience with an upsurge of imperial Romanticism and capital-ised mystical justification: 'Came the Whisper, came the Vision, came the Power with the Need, / Till the Soul that is not man's soul was lent us to lead' (*DV* 172).

The message was both exorcistic and practical: '*Clear the land of evil, drive the road and bridge the ford*' (*DV* 170). 'McAndrew's Hymn', about a Glaswegian engineer, portrays the kind of doer who kept the wheels of empire turning. However, being a Browningesque monologue, the poem also allows the speaker an interior world of some intricacy and his own 'natural' theology, 'alone wi' God an' these / My engines' (*DV* 121). 'Song', 'Hymn' – titles and manner strongly evoke the oral tradition, and Kipling is at times plainly casting himself as the tribal bard of 'Greater Britain'. Yet 'In the Neolithic Age' affirms an altogether wider and longer perspective and asserts both cultural difference and artistic freedom:

> Here's my wisdom for your use, as I learned it when the moose
> And the reindeer roamed where Paris roars to-night: –
> '*There are nine and sixty ways of constructing tribal lays,*
> '*And-every-single-one-of-them-is-right!*' (*DV* 343)

Henry James thought the collection 'all prose trumpets and castanets' though 'full of the most insidious art'.[11] Howells heard something beyond the imperialist mantra. He heard the humanist dimension which animates American poems like 'Pan in Vermont' (1893).[12] Celebrating the arrival of the New England spring, Kipling imagines Pan as a slightly dodgy, travelling seed-salesman:

> Hub-deep in slush Apollo's car swings north along the Zod
> -iac. Good lack, the Spring is back, and Pan is on the road!
> (*DV* 356)

Here line-break and internal rhyme perfectly enact the sense as 'Apollo's car' skids, swerves and bumps before righting itself and carrying on.

By the time *The Five Nations* was published in 1903, the Boer War had taken place, and the empire-tooting Kipling of Beerbohm's cartoon was to the fore. The collection contains a number of memorable 'service songs', drawing on Kipling's participation in the war as a volunteer journalist. 'Riding in, in the rain', the refrain of one 'service song', 'Lichtenberg', includes 'its own swallow of emotion', as Craig Raine has acutely commented.[13] The volume remains most notable, however, for three poems still widely quoted as evidence of Kipling's general outlook and views.

'Recessional' was written in response to Queen Victoria's Diamond Jubilee in 1897. Kipling, alarmed by the national mood of arrogance and boasting that accompanied the Jubilee, intended the poem, he later claimed, as 'a *nuzzur-wattu* (an averter of the Evil Eye)' – the tribal bard trying to deflect the gods' punishment.[14] There is, however, as Elliot L. Gilbert pointed out, a 'discrepancy between the announced and the implicit subject of the poem'.[15] While the poem calls for national humility ('An humble and a contrite heart') and pleads for divine forgiveness and suspension of judgement ('Judge of the Nations, spare us yet'), it does not itself sound either humble or merciful (*DV* 328–9). Quite the reverse. It assumes a special status for the English ('Thy People, Lord!'), implicitly thrills to imperial rule ('Beneath whose awful Hand we hold / Dominion over palm and pine') and judges others ('Or lesser breeds without the Law') (*DV* 328–9). Such disjunctions now seem self-evident, yet when the poem appeared in *The Times* it appealed to liberals and conservatives alike and became for several decades a popular hymn.

'The White Man's Burden' provoked strong opposition from the first. Kipling began the poem as another Jubilee ode, a call to a reluctant Britannia to accept her full imperial responsibilities, but put it aside for 'Recessional'. The imminent ceding of the Philippine Islands to America in February 1899 encouraged Kipling to resurrect the poem which (again) appeared in *The Times*. Now subtitled '(The United States and the Philippine Islands)', 'The White Man's Burden' had turned into an invitation to America to join the Imperial club. The 'burden' (colonisation) is presented as the ultimate test of national maturity/virility ('Comes now, to search your manhood') – also as an obligation, unsought, self-sacrificing and thankless: 'Watch Sloth and heathen Folly / Bring all your hope to nought'; 'The blame of those ye better: / The hate of those ye guard' (*DV* 324). The colonised are seen as 'Half devil and half child', and the colonial enterprise as entirely disinterested: 'To seek another's profit, / And work another's gain' (*DV* 323). The poem and its empire-freighted assumptions were immediately challenged. Henry

Labouchère's angry parody 'The Brown Man's Burden', published the same month in *Truth*, spelt out the discounted mercenary motive: 'Pile up the brown man's burden / To gratify your greed'.[16] This huge moral blank in Kipling's imperial vision was later highlighted by Orwell and, more recently, by postcolonial critics such as Rajeev S. Patke: 'Kipling promoted a view of Western imperialism that downplayed its exploitative intent'.[17] In 2002 Craig Raine offered a revisionist reading, arguing that the final line ('The judgment of your peers!') made it 'clear that, in the end, the judgement of the colonised on the colonisers will be the judgement of equals'.[18]

'The Islanders' also gained great notoriety in its day. The poem attacked English insularity and self-satisfaction in swingeing terms, particularly that of the Tory Old Guard: 'Arid, aloof, incurious, unthinking, unthanking, gelt [gelded]' (*DV* 304). If the Old Guard hoped to preserve its privileged existence ('Ancient, effortless, ordered, cycle on cycle set'), it needed, according to Kipling, to pay more attention to military training than to sport: 'Then ye returned to your trinkets; then ye contented your souls / With the flannelled fools at the wicket or the muddied oafs at the goals' (*DV* 303, 302). Angus Wilson vividly caught the poem's overall effect: Kipling 'takes each sacred cow of the clubs and senior common rooms and slaughters it messily before its worshippers' eyes'.[19]

During the decade following the publication of *The Five Nations*, Kipling's standing plummeted in English liberal and literary circles though his sales remained prodigious. By July 1914, it had become commonplace to dismiss his poetry as 'terribly tub-thumping stuff', as a nervous Siegfried Sassoon did to Rupert Brooke – only for Brooke to speak up for Kipling's 'Cities and Thrones and Powers': 'There aren't many better modern poems than that, you know.'[20] By 1919, T. S. Eliot could dub Kipling 'a laureate without laurels', not 'anathema' in serious literary circles, 'merely not discussed'.[21] This was in a review of *The Years Between*. The collection contained plenty of examples ('"For All We Have and Are"', 'Ulster', 'The Covenant', 'The Holy War') to exemplify Eliot's point that Kipling's was 'a poetry of oratory', persuading 'not by reason, but by emphatic sound'.[22] Eliot summarised Kipling's 'true formula': 'its touch of the newspapers, of Billy Sunday, and the Revised Version filtered through Rabbi Zeal-of-the-Land Busy'.[23]

Eliot's review, however, virtually ignored the poems written in response to the First World War. These include a number of elegies for Kipling's son John, killed at Loos in 1915. In 'My Boy Jack' and 'Nativity' Kipling channels his grief through that of two grieving mothers, who reach out for consolation. 'A Recantation' is more direct: 'he, of whom bereft / I suffer vacant days' (*DV* 369). So too are 'A Son' and 'Common Form' from 'Epitaphs of the War', a sequence modelled on the classical Greek Anthology and commemorating a wide range of casualties and combatants. 'A Son' is bleakly stoical: 'My son was killed while laughing at some jest. I would I knew / What it was, and it might serve me in a time when jests are few' (*DV* 387). 'Common Form' goes further: 'If any question why we died, / Tell them, because our fathers lied' (*DV* 390). Here, speaking for the betrayed dead, Kipling simultaneously reiterates his earlier attacks on the Conservative and Liberal Old Guard, glances at the anti-war poetry starting to surface during 1917 and 1918, and implicitly includes himself among the lying fathers.

*

When Kipling died in 1936, he had published no further volumes of poems. The popular but incomplete *Definitive Edition* appeared in 1940, followed by T. S. Eliot's *A Choice of Kipling's Verse* (1941). Eliot's highly influential introductory essay set the terms of discussion on Kipling's poetry for the next fifty years.

Eliot's main proposition is that Kipling is not a poet at all but a writer of verse. Kipling had claimed much the same in 1889: 'I am not a poet and never shall be,' he told Caroline Taylor, ' – but only a writer who varies fiction with verse.'[24] But whereas Kipling's comment is equivocal (defeated? modest? anti-aesthete?), Eliot insists that Kipling's very distinctiveness lies in his not trying to write poetry but sometimes producing it nonetheless: 'Kipling does write poetry, but that is not what he is setting out to do.'[25] Here Eliot is specifically evaluating Kipling the ballad-writer; yet, ironically, when he discusses a specific example, 'Danny Deever', his analysis suggests powerful poetic qualities at work:

> The regular recurrence of the same end-words, which gain immensely by imperfect rhyme (*parade* and *said*) gives the feeling of marching feet and the movement of men in disciplined formation – in a unity of movement which enhances the horror of the occasion and the sickness which seizes the men as individuals; and the slightly quickened pace of the final lines marks the change in movement and in music.[26]

As though persuaded by his own explication, Eliot eventually concedes that 'Danny Deever' is 'a barrack-room ballad which somehow attains the intensity of poetry'.[27]

Elsewhere Eliot claims that while 'introduc[ing] remarkable variations of his own ... as a poet [Kipling] does not revolutionize'. Crucially, for Eliot, Kipling fails the cardinal test: 'What fundamentally differentiates his "verse" from "poetry" is the subordination of musical interest.'[28] Having rescued Kipling from poetry, Eliot grants him variety, virtuosity, craftsmanship, passionate invective, and praises his epigrams and hymns. Eliot briskly refutes the idea that Kipling was a Fascist, argues for '"the development [in his work] of the imperial imagination into the historical imagination"' and heralds him as 'the inventor of a mixed form' of prose and verse.[29] He was, Eliot concludes, a 'great', probably 'unique' verse-writer, 'a writer impossible wholly to understand and quite impossible to belittle'.[30]

Eliot's version of Kipling has proved extremely durable. Ian Hamilton was still recycling it in 2002 in *Against Oblivion*: 'it was this ability to reach for the verse-tap ... that made Kipling such a stunningly effective public-poet, or verse-writer'.[31] Kipling leads Hamilton's cavalcade of well-known twentieth-century poets (along with Frost, Pound, Plath) threatened by the literary dark.

Eliot's introductory essay had other consequences. His promotion of Kipling as 'the inventor of a mixed form' ('a poem and a story together') helped in the 1950s and 1960s to open up new readings by critics like J. M. S. Tompkins and C. A. Bodelsen.[32] These readings explored the ways in which, from *Traffics and Discoveries* (1904) onwards, story and bracketing poem(s) might shine a light on each other. For instance, 'The Return of the Children' (poem) imagines Heaven as a vast orphanage, full of forlorn children, who thanks to Mary's intercession are permitted to return home. The considerably more cryptic story '"They"' imagines a remote country house, full of the ghosts of dead children in which a visitor is permitted a single, brief reunion with his dead daughter.

Links between poem(s) and story are often more intricate (as between the stories themselves in the later collections). In *Debits and Credits* (1926), 'The Survival' (itself from an imaginary fifth book of Horace's *Odes*) ponders the ironies of literary survival: 'Mere flutes that breathe at eve, / Mere seaweed on the shore'.[33] The succeeding story, 'The Janeites', shows (among other things) how a love of Jane Austen's novels bonded a disparate group of combatants in the trenches and, temporarily, helped them to survive. Sometimes the connections reach out more widely. 'A Friend of the Family' (again from *Debits and Credits*) demonstrates antipodean unconventionality: an Australian ex-soldier fakes a German air raid in order to help a dead English comrade's persecuted family. The accompanying poem, 'We and They', reflects on cultural difference and 'otherness' in terms very different from those of, say, 'The White Man's Burden':

> All good people agree,
>   And all good people say,
> All nice people, like Us, are We
>   And every one else is They:
> But if you cross over the sea,
>   Instead of over the way,
> You may end by (think of it!) looking on We
>   As only a sort of They!   (*DV* 764)

The two most persuasive challenges to Eliot's version of Kipling have come from Craig Raine and Jan Montefiore. In the introduction to his *Rudyard Kipling: Selected Poetry* (1992), Raine sums up Eliot's position: 'Kipling ... writes terrific tunes but misses out on melody; we like his songs, but where are his lieder?'[34] In place of Eliot's Kipling, Raine posits a poet of the 'underdog' and studs his own introductory essay with brilliant close readings: how, for instance, in the rhythmically shifty 'We put back to Sunderland 'cause our cargo shifted' (from 'The Ballad of the "Bolivar"'), 'the cargo's shift is embodied in the line itself'.[35] Raine puts forward such 'tiny miracle[s] of rhythmic subtlety', together with examples of Kipling's verbal alchemy, as evidence of 'the unremittingly alert language we call poetry'.[36] These indicators of Kipling as poet have gone unnoticed, claims Raine, 'because, like Eliot, we do not expect to discover them'.[37]

Raine's trump card is to claim Kipling as a modernist poet, to whom Eliot himself was significantly indebted (the cockney pub scene in *The Waste Land*, use of nursery rhyme in 'The Hollow Men'). Jan Montefiore, in her *Rudyard Kipling*, largely endorses Raine's view, but extends it. Montefiore affirms the 'extraordinarily wide imaginative sympathies' of Kipling's poetry but is less evasive about the often distasteful, sometimes repellent, power of the public poetry. She finds Kipling's modernity embodied not simply in his themes but, 'more subtly', in the 'interpretative uncertainty generated by the multiple voices and registers that speak his poems'.[38] Montefiore detects a self-reflexiveness in Kipling the 'brilliant stylistic magpie'; also a strong subversive streak in the underrated parodic sequence 'The Muse among the Motors' and in late secular hymns such as 'Hymn to Physical Pain'.[39] This demotically vital, pluralist, ventriloquist Kipling, Montefiore suggests, is less likely to raise 'anxieties about [his] aesthetic status' in an age of performance and rap poetry.[40]

*

Eliot insists that Kipling's verse did not 'revolutionize' poetry.[41] Raine casts him as at least a modernist fellow traveller. Montefiore points to the range of his poetic legacy. This legacy is indeed widespread. It is there, predictably, in Newbolt's thumping patriotics, 'Banjo' Paterson's Australian bush-ballads, Robert Service's gold-rush ballads, John Masefield's 'salt-water' ballads (and his demotic 'The Everlasting Mercy'). But Kipling also makes possible the soldier voices of Sassoon's '"They"' ('Poor Jim's shot through the lungs and like to die; / And Bert's gone syphilitic') and Wilfred Owen's 'The Chances': 'I 'mind as how the night before that show / Us five got talkin'; we was in the know'.[42]

Kipling's legacy hums through A. A. Milne's light verse, but also powerfully pulses through James Fenton's 'New Recklessness' poems of the 1980s – 'The Ballad of the Imam and the Shah' and the fierce 'Tiananmen':

> The cruel men
> Are old and deaf
> Ready to kill
> But short of breath
> And they will die
> Like other men
> And they'll lie in state
> In Tiananmen.[43]

'The Islanders' ghosts W. H. Auden's 1930s doomwatch poems: 'Shut up talking, charming in the best suits to be had in town, / Lecturing on navigation while the ship is going down'.[44] Brooke's favourite, 'Cities and Thrones and Powers' ('So Time that is o'er-kind / To all that be' (*DV* 487)), provides the key signature to Auden's famous pardon of Kipling in 'In Memory of W. B. Yeats' (1939): 'Time that with this strange excuse / Pardoned Kipling and his views'.[45] Kipling's technical virtuosity flashes out in Gavin Ewart's comic inventiveness, his parodic panache in Wendy Cope. Cope's witty send-up of twentieth-century poets from T. S. Eliot to Seamus Heaney in *Making Cocoa for Kingsley Amis* (1986) neatly complements the spoofs by Kipling and his sister a hundred years earlier. Singer-songwriter Billy Bragg cleverly redeploys Kipling's line 'And what should they know of England who only England know?' in 'The Few', a 1991 song against Union-Jack-wearing National Front supporters.[46] Bragg is suggesting both the logical consequence of the rampant nationalism of Kipling's poem 'The English Flag' and, less obviously, that Kipling's line makes a perennially important point: to understand one's own culture, one must experience other cultures.

*

Raine rounds off his introductory essay with a reading of 'If–' that manages to defamiliarise the overly familiar: 'The poem ... mimics the moral difficulty posed by Kipling – and yet the successful negotiation of the impossibly cumbered sentence to its end demonstrates, in miniature, the possibility of achieving something genuinely difficult'.[47] This deft defence may still, however, be an *under*-reading. A more ventriloquist approach might envisage 'If–' as a poetic echo chamber, reverberating not only with prescribed precepts but, more destabilisingly, with intimations of Gray's 'Ode to Adversity' and Donne's 'The Undertaking'.

Even Raine sees the final line ('And – which is more – you'll be a Man, my son!') as ultimately affirming (*DV* 577). But to hear behind the line the sobering conclusion to Gray's 'Ode to Adversity' ('Man' is also capitalised in some versions) is to enlarge and complicate any such affirmation:

Teach me to love and to forgive,
Exact my own defects to scan,
What others are to feel, and know myself a man.[48]

If the presence of Gray (himself echoing Pope, Terence and others) disrupts an overly reassuring reading of that famous conclusion, to recognise Donne's 'The Undertaking' as a primary model (Kipling had used the poem as an epigraph to his 1895–6 story 'William the Conqueror') is to admit the possibility of an altogether more perplexing overview:

> If, as I have, you also do
> Virtue attir'd in woman see,
> And dare love that, and say so too,
> And forget the He and She;
>
> And if this love, though placèd so,
> From profane men you hide,
> Which will no faith on this bestow,
> Or, if they do, deride:
>
> Then you have done a braver thing
> Than all the Worthies did;
> And a braver thence will spring,
> Which is, to keep that hid.[49]

The lover in Donne's poem directly parallels the child in Kipling's. Both face a tangle of impossible conditions. What is witty in Donne is rueful in Kipling (who observed the poem 'contained counsels of perfection most easy to give').[50] No one gets to be a 'Man' – that is, adult – if this is what it takes. This is the test everyone fails. But we do not detect these echoes of Gray and Donne because, as Raine said of Eliot, 'we do not expect to discover them'.[51]

Even if Hamilton is right that Kipling remains a candidate for oblivion, his poetry continues to command a popular readership and to encourage increasingly nuanced critical debate. C. H. Sisson could confidently claim in the early 1970s that Kipling 'seems to be after the irrefutable prose statement, whether the subject is important or not'.[52] Nearly forty years later, Montefiore's open-endedness seems more fitting: 'The "certain certainties" of Kipling's poetry are not as certain as all that, once you look at them closely'.[53]

Notes

1 Jan Montefiore, *Rudyard Kipling* (Tavistock: Northcote House, 2007), p. 104.
2 Max Beerbohm, *The Poets' Corner* (1904; London: The King Penguin Books, 1943), p. 24.
3 George Orwell, 'Rudyard Kipling', in George Packer (ed.), *George Orwell: Critical Essays* (London: Harvill Secker, 2009), pp. 188–9.

4 *Rudyard Kipling's Verse: Definitive Edition* (London: Hodder and Stoughton, 1940), p. 824. Subsequent references in the text as *DV*.

5 Andrew Rutherford, *Kipling's Mind and Art* (Edinburgh: Oliver & Boyd, 1964), p. 80.

6 Evelyn Waugh, *Unconditional Surrender* (London: Chapman and Hall, 1961), p. 290.

7 *Early Verse by Rudyard Kipling 1879–1889: Unpublished, Uncollected, and Rarely Collected Poems*, ed. Andrew Rutherford (Oxford University Press, 1986), p. 62. Subsequent references in the text as *EV*.

8 Roger Lancelyn Green (ed.), *Kipling: The Critical Heritage* (New York: Barnes and Noble, 1971), pp. 103, 124.

9 *The Letters of Rudyard Kipling, Volume 1, 1872–89*, ed. Thomas Pinney (Basingstoke: Macmillan, 1990), p. 282.

10 Green, *Kipling: The Critical Heritage*, pp. 192–5.

11 *Henry James Letters, Volume 4, 1895–1916*, ed. Leon Edel (Harvard: The Belknap Press, 1984), p. 40.

12 Green, *Kipling: The Critical Heritage*, pp. 193–4.

13 Craig Raine, Introduction to *Rudyard Kipling: Selected Poetry* (London: Penguin, 1992), p. xxv.

14 *The Letters of Rudyard Kipling, Volume 1*, p. 86.

15 Elliot L. Gilbert, *The Good Kipling: Studies in the Short Story* (Manchester University Press, 1972), p. 19.

16 Henry Labouchère, 'The Brown Man's Burden', *Truth* (London), reprinted in *Literary Digest*, 18 (25 February 1899).

17 Orwell, 'Rudyard Kipling', pp. 180–1; Rajeev S. Patke, *Postcolonial Poetry in English* (Oxford University Press, 2006), p. 4.

18 Raine, Introduction to *Rudyard Kipling: Selected Poetry*, p. 18.

19 Angus Wilson, *The Strange Ride of Rudyard Kipling: His Life and Works* (London: Secker & Warburg, 1977), p. 239.

20 Siegfried Sassoon, *The Weald of Youth* (London: Faber and Faber, 1942), p. 229.

21 Green, *Kipling: The Critical Heritage*, p. 322.

22 *Ibid.*, p. 323.

23 *Ibid.*, p. 325.

24 *The Letters of Rudyard Kipling, Volume 1*, p. 379.

25 T. S. Eliot, Introduction to *A Choice of Kipling's Verse* (London: Faber and Faber, 1941), p. 9.

26 *Ibid.*, p. 11.

27 *Ibid.*, p. 13.

28 *Ibid.*, pp. 34, 35.

29 *Ibid.*, pp. 30, 5.

30 *Ibid.*, pp. 36, 22.

31 Ian Hamilton, *Against Oblivion: Some Lives of the Twentieth-Century Poets* (London: Viking, 2002), p. 4.

32 Eliot, Introduction to *A Choice of Kipling's Verse*, pp. 5, 31; J. M. S. Tompkins, *The Art of Rudyard Kipling* (London: Methuen, 1959); C. A. Bodelsen, *Aspects of Kipling's Art* (Manchester University Press, 1964).

33 Rudyard Kipling, *Debits and Credits* (London: Macmillan, 1926), p. 145.

34 Raine, Introduction to *Rudyard Kipling: Selected Poetry*, p. xvii.

35 *Ibid.*, pp. xi, xviii.

36 *Ibid.*, pp. xvii, xiii.

37 *Ibid.*, p. xviii.

38 Montefiore, *Rudyard Kipling*, pp. 111, 115.

39 *Ibid.*, p 116.

40 *Ibid.*, p 109.

41 Eliot, Introduction to *A Choice of Kipling's Verse*, p. 34.

42 Siegfried Sassoon, *Collected Poems 1908–1956* (London: Faber and Faber, 1961), p. 24; Jon Stallworthy (ed.), *The Poems of Wilfred Owen* (London: Chatto and Windus, 1990), p. 148.

43 James Fenton, *Out of Danger* (London: Penguin, 1993), p. 41.

44 W. H. Auden, 'XXXI', in *The English Auden: Poems, Essays and Dramatic Writings, 1927–1939*, ed. Edward Mendelson (London: Faber and Faber, 1977), p. 49.

45 *Ibid.*, p. 242.

46 Billy Bragg, 'The Few', *Don't Try This At Home*, Elektra, 1991, track 8.

47 Raine, Introduction to *Rudyard Kipling: Selected Poetry*, p. xxvi.

48 *The Poems of Gray, Collins and Goldsmith*, ed. Roger Lonsdale (London: Longmans, 1969), p. 74.

49 *The Songs and Sonnets of John Donne*, 2nd edn, ed. Theodore Redpath (London: Methuen, 1983), pp. 289–90.

50 *The Letters of Rudyard Kipling, Volume 1*, p. 111.

51 Raine, Introduction to *Rudyard Kipling: Selected Poetry*, p. xiii.

52 C. H. Sisson, *English Poetry, 1900–1950: An Assessment* (London: Methuen, 1971), p. 35.

53 Montefiore, *Rudyard Kipling*, p. 122.

9

PATRICK BRANTLINGER

Kim

'Kim dived into the happy Asiatic disorder which, if you only allow time, will bring you everything that a simple man needs.'[1] Rudyard Kipling was far from being a 'simple man'. But in his most successful novel, he wrote about a boy whose enjoyment of 'happy Asiatic disorder' matched his own. The Irish orphan travels among all sorts of Indians with enviable freedom and street smarts while watched over by a diversity of caring father figures: the Teshoo Lama, Mahbub Ali, Lurgan Sahib, Hurree Chunder Mookerjee, Col. Creighton. These surrogate fathers are sure that Kim is the very person they need, either to play the Great Game or, in the case of the Lama, to help find the sacred River of the Arrow. And Kim does not disappoint. Kipling's ideal boy is 'Friend of all the World'. He is delighted by almost all aspects of India as well as by his own escapades: 'It was all pure delight ...' (*K* 207).

'*Kim* is many things', writes Fred Lerner: 'a spy story, a quest novel, a Bildungsroman, but above all, it is a love letter to India, a celebration of the sounds and smells and colours of the subcontinent.'[2] *Kim* is also an imperialist adventure tale with a boy-hero, akin to the novels of G. A. Henty. One of Kipling's major innovations is making Kim, though Irish and therefore a 'sahib', more like the Indians he lives among than like an Irish or British boy. Kim is so embedded in India that he appears to be the perfect spy, both for the Secret Service which comes to employ him and as an ethnographic spy for the non-Indian reader. 'All castes and kinds of men move here,' says the old sepoy (soldier) about life on the Grand Trunk Road; 'Look! Brahmins and chumars, bankers and tinkers, barbers and bunnias, pilgrims and potters – all the world going and coming' (*K* 81). Kim is the lens through which the reader observes what seems to be all of India coming and going.

The history of *Kim* and its critical reception

In his autobiography, Kipling writes that as early as 1892 'I had a vague notion of an Irish boy, born in India and mixed up with native life. I went as far as to make him the son of a private in an Irish Battalion, and christened him "Kim of the 'Rishti" – short, that is, for Irish.'[3] This 'vague notion' also included a Lama from Tibet.[4] Kipling started to write about his Irish boy several times, but, notes Charles Carrington, the novel 'was abandoned in favour of *"Captains Courageous"*'. In the fall of 1899, having finished with *Stalky*, he turned again to *Kim*.[5] Kipling remarks: 'In a gloomy, windy autumn *Kim* came back to me with insistence, and I took it to be smoked over with my Father. Under our united tobaccos it grew like the Djin released from the brass bottle. ... I do not know what proportion of an iceberg is below water-line, but *Kim* as it finally appeared was about one-tenth of what the first lavish specification called for' (*SM* 82).

Kipling mined parts of his unpublished novel *Mother Maturin* for *Kim*. The earlier story dealt with an Indian woman running an opium den, and it apparently depicted India much more negatively than does *Kim*. Rudyard told his aunt Edith that it 'is not one bit nice or proper but it carries a grim sort of a moral with it and tries to deal with the unutterable horrors of a lower-class Eurasian and native life as they exist outside the [official] reports'.[6] How much of *Kim* was drawn from *Mother Maturin* is uncertain, because Kipling apparently discarded its manuscript.[7]

Kim was completed in early August 1899, and first published as a serial in *McClure's Magazine* in America from December 1900, and in Britain in *Cassell's Magazine* from January 1901. It was then published in volume format the next autumn. Kipling's comment about 'smoking over' *Kim* with his father suggests that it was, to some degree, a collaborative project: 'There was a good deal of beauty in it, and not a little wisdom, the best in both sorts being owed to my Father' (*SM* 84). He also owed the illustrations for the 1902 edition of the novel to Lockwood: 'But the crown of the fun came when (in 1902) was issued an illustrated edition of my works, and the Father attended to *Kim*. He had the notion of making low-relief plaques and photographing them afterwards' (*SM* 63).

Most of the first reviewers of *Kim* recognised it as a masterpiece, and it continues to be held in high regard as Kipling's best novel. Jan Montefiore describes it as 'the most enchanting of Kipling's fictions and the only one ever to be compared with the great traditional names Dickens, Shakespeare, or Chaucer'.[8] And Nirad C. Chaudhuri declared that *Kim* is 'the finest novel in the English language with an Indian theme'.[9] Indian critics such as Chaudhuri, however, do not always agree that Kipling succeeded in expressing Indian perspectives. Thus, Salman Rushdie writes: 'I have never been able to read Kipling calmly. Anger and delight are incompatible emotions.' Yet Rushdie acknowledges that 'No other Western writer has ever known India as Kipling knew it, and it is this knowledge of place, and procedure, and detail that gives his stories their undeniable authority.'[10]

The racism and support of British imperialism, evident throughout *Kim*, are for Rushdie as for other postcolonial critics such as Edward Said its most limiting features. Said notes that Indian readers are likely to stress 'Kipling's stereotypical views ... on the Oriental character'.[11] He is referring to assertions such as: 'Kim could lie like an Oriental' (*K* 33). Nevertheless, under the heading 'The Pleasures of Imperialism', Said claims: 'Only Conrad ... can be considered along with Kipling ... to have rendered the experience of empire as the main subject of his work with such force ... they brought to a basically insular ... British audience the color, glamor, and romance of the British overseas enterprise' (*K* 132).

Kim appears to some commentators as a highly original work that bears little relationship to earlier writing about India. But Anglo-India had been producing its own distinctive literature since the eighteenth century, and aspects of *Kim* have a number of precedents. Thus, both John Lang's short story 'Who Was the Child?' (1859) and Sara Jeanette Duncan's *The Story of Sonny Sahib* (1894) feature European orphans raised by Indians. And F. M. Crawford's 1882 novel *Mr Isaacs* is based on a real-life Simla jeweller who also served as the model for Lurgan Sahib in *Kim*. Crawford's novel, like *Kim*, expresses anxiety about the security of India's north-western frontier. But 'whatever Kipling's debts to his predecessors,' writes Bart Moore-Gilbert, 'his remains the greatest achievement in nineteenth-century Anglo-Indian literature'.[12]

Carrington contends that the only other novel about India by a non-Indian comparable to *Kim* is E. M. Forster's *A Passage to India*, 'and in many respects *Kim* comes well out of the comparison. In this instance Forster, not Kipling, is the political writer, the observer of a passing phase.'[13] This suggests that *Kim* is not a political novel. Yet it is a spy story, based on the threat Russia posed to the British Raj. Kipling was hardly dismissive of that threat, but in the novel it is exorcised from the subcontinent by a boy and a self-styled 'fearful' Bengali without much difficulty. In a sense, Carrington is right: *Kim* is a political novel from which politics is banished.

A 'nakedly picaresque and plotless' story

When Rudyard announced that Cervantes was one of his models for *Kim*, his mother responded: 'You *know* you couldn't make a plot to save your soul' (*SM* 82). Whether she was encouraging him to emulate Cervantes is unclear, though Kipling asserted that *Kim* is 'nakedly picaresque and plotless' (*SM* 132). While *Kim* is hardly 'plotless', Kipling understood 'the picaresque connection with Cervantes', writes Angus Wilson, who adds that the Lama and Kim 'recall ... Quixote and Sancho Panza, a deeper, more original recall than Pickwick and Sam Weller'.[14] As a novel of the road, *Kim* is indeed a picaresque narrative like *Don Quixote* or, more exactly, like *Lazarillo de Tormes*, which depicts the adventures of a young rogue, a *pícaro*, as he travels from scene to scene in episodes that don't lead anywhere in particular, except to the next episode.

The picaresque form means that *Kim* is 'concerned with movement rather than with the goal', writes Phillip Mallett; it lacks a teleological structure, which would involve 'change and development' for the protagonist and perhaps for India.[15] It approximates an 'idyll', which is why it might seem apolitical to anyone apt to see the British Empire as transcending politics. Michael Gorra writes that racism, the Indian Rebellion of 1857–8 and 'the fledgling Indian National Congress' which Kipling 'often criticized' play little or no role in *Kim*.[16] He contends that, like all 'idylls', *Kim* excludes history, or the possibility that the Raj could be effectively challenged. John McLure also writes that Kipling leaves out history, stressing instead 'either side of the historical process ... the plenitude of the moment and the finality of the eternal'.[17] Kim is focused on 'the moment', the Lama on 'the eternal'. The kaleidoscope of races, creeds and cultures that Kim experiences seems in constant flux, and yet nothing fundamental changes. As Said observes, 'Dotting *Kim*'s fabric is a scattering of editorial asides on the immutable nature of the Oriental world ...'[18] Kipling wished to believe the British Empire was also immutable.

Kim is neither a typical boys' adventure novel nor a proto-modernist novel, like Conrad's *Lord Jim*. It has an omniscient, third-person narrator and utilises a version of antiquated English, coupled with amusing mispronunciations, malapropisms and a sprinkling of Indian words to represent the 'vernacular'.[19] 'I know the ways of the te-rain,' Kim says to the Lama about the railway; 'Never did *yogi* need *chela* as thou dost ... They would have flung thee out at Mian Mir but for me' (*K* 38). This manner of representing Indian speech suggests that India is itself far from modern, that the Lama is both innocent and holy (he sounds biblical), and that Indians in general are childlike. The last quality is emphasised when their speech is mixed with comical mistakes and confusions. Telling Kim about the advantages of education, Hurree Babu urges him to read Wordsworth, Shakespeare and 'Burke and Hare' (*K* 231). And the scribe who pens a letter for the Lama signs himself: 'Written by Sabrao Satai, Failed Entrance Allahabad University' (*K* 147).

The 'vernacular' in *Kim* is thus a blend of the archaic, comic and stereotypic. Kipling's method of characterisation, too, is often stereotypic and yet just as often complexly individualising. Mahbub Ali and Hurree Babu seem stereotypic, but they also challenge stereotypes, most notably by being effective spies in the service of the British Raj. Hurree in particular, a comic character of 'Falstaffian' dimensions,[20] is at once the much-maligned 'babu' or English-educated Bengali and a challenge to that racist construction. Preparing to accompany the foreign agents, he tells Kim:

> Of course I shall affeeliate myself to their camp in supernumerary capacity as perhaps interpreter, or person mentally impotent and hungree … Onlee – onlee – you see, Mister O'Hara, I am unfortunately Asiatic, which is serious detriment in some respects. And *allso* I am Bengali – a fearful man. (*K* 319)

Despite his self-stereotyping, and also despite his obesity, Hurree is an indefatigable hiker and a brave, crafty spy. Thus does Kipling simultaneously affirm and override the stereotype of the Bengali 'babu'.

Kim and the Lama also surpass stereotypes. The Lama is a Tibetan Buddhist, so in India he is exotic even to Kim, who is first attracted to him because of his novelty. Moreover, the Lama is the erudite head of a monastery, whom the curator of the Lahore Museum (Kipling's representation of his father) immediately respects. And the Lama's growing affection for Kim is the most subtly drawn of all the father-son relationships in the novel. Further, Kim is a Protean figure who can't be pinned down to a set of Irish, British, Indian or even adolescent traits.

As Kim and the Lama wend their way along the Grand Trunk Road, the story often reads like an exotic, beautifully written travelogue. When Kim first goes to St Xavier's, he orders his driver to take him around Lucknow, which the narrator describes in travelogue fashion: 'There is no city – except Bombay, the queen of all – more beautiful in her garish style than Lucknow … Kings have adorned her with fantastic buildings' (*K* 170). And as Kim and the Lama hike into the mountains toward Tibet, the prose sounds Wordsworthian: 'Along their track lay the villages of the hill-folk – mud and earth huts … clinging like swallows' nests against the steeps … jammed into a corner between cliffs that funnelled and focused every wandering blast' (*K* 330). Kipling effectively combines exotic characters and customs, scene-painting that is both realistic and romantic, and the exciting adventures of his eager boy-hero.

Kim may be picaresque, but it also depicts several quests, which constitute its plot. Besides the Lama's quest for the River and salvation, Kim's quest is at first for 'a Red Bull on a green field' (*K* 2), the symbol of his father's regiment, which would explain the three papers he carries as an amulet: his birth certificate and two documents indicating his father's Masonic membership. These might in turn lead to his being sent to 'the

Masonic Orphanage in the Hills' (*K* 3). When Kim is discovered by the regiment's chaplains, he is identified as Kimball O'Hara's son. But instead of the Masonic Orphanage, Kim is sent to St Xavier's School to become a 'sahib'. From there on, Kim's quest specifically concerns the 'Great Game' of espionage for the Secret Service.

Kim's 'parallel' worlds

Said writes that Kim inhabits 'parallel universes'.[21] He accepts the role of the Lama's *chela* or disciple; he also accepts the role of spy, serving Col. Creighton. The Lama and the Colonel represent the two 'universes', sacred and secular, Oriental and western, twinned and yet forever segregated. '*Oh, East is East, and West is West, and never the twain shall meet*', Kipling wrote in 'The Ballad of East and West'. Yet they meet all the time in his fiction and poetry, though without changing in any essential way, a hybridity that forestalls hybridity. With India firmly in British control (the Russian threat never seems very serious), India can simply be enjoyed. After all, Kim's 'actions', says Said, always 'result in victories not defeats'. 'Kipling assumes a basically uncontested empire,' writes Said; for him there was 'no conflict' in regard to India. Said claims to be disagreeing with Edmund Wilson's judgement that in *Kim* East and West represent 'two entirely different worlds existing side by side, with neither really understanding the other ... the parallel lines never meet; the alternating attractions felt by Kim never give rise to a genuine struggle', but this seems to be precisely what Said is saying. Wilson writes that the novel ends with a 'pair of victories' that don't affect each other.[22]

Both Kim and the Lama seem to be living in an 'idyll', or inhabiting a world in which they do not have to achieve any final, absolute 'victories'. If *Kim* is on one level a Bildungsroman, on another it is a culmination of the lengthy tradition of boys' adventure fiction, from Captain Marryat through H. Rider Haggard. In most adventure stories featuring boy-heroes, the protagonists are unmistakably British. John McBratney notes that even an imitation of Kim such as Harry Lindsay in Henty's *At the Point of the Bayonet: A Tale of the Mahratta War* (1902) is 'the plain, solid, English-grown type we find in so much adventure fiction of the time'. Yet, like Kim, Harry has been raised by Indians, speaks Mahratti as well as English, 'and disguises himself in native dress to spy for the British'.[23] Kim isn't English, of course: he is an Irish orphan growing up on the streets of Lahore, tended only by a poor Indian woman. Nevertheless, his white race gives him an advantage in most situations. In his other writings, Kipling sometimes portrays the Irish as a threat to imperial stability, as when he writes about Irish 'mutinies'.[24]

But in *Kim*, both the hero and his father's Irish regiment serve the British Raj without any major deviations.

Stressing Kim's 'remarkable personal abilities', John Kucich notes that his 'sadomasochistic omnipotence' is evident from the beginning, when Kim wins the contest over his Hindu and Muslim friends to sit astride Zam-Zammah, the cannon outside the Lahore Museum. Kucich points to other episodes in which Kim seems to exercise 'magical powers' or in which the Lama, Lurgan Sahib and other characters describe him as 'genie-like'.[25] The fantasy of youthful omnipotence characterises most adventure fiction that features boy-heroes. The imperialist belief in the absolute power and recti-tude of British rule is the political corollary of this fantasy. Joseph Bristow notes that 'Kim very nearly grows up. However, he does not quite reach an adult state of knowledge. He is instead contained by a trajectory of growth which thematises the youthful strength of what is supposed to be a still-maturing empire.' According to this interpretation, Kipling wishes to see the Empire itself as a youthful adventure. 'Kim represents the spectacular procession of empire,' Bristow continues, 'forever, longingly and innocently, developing.'[26]

Kim's shape-shifting, trickster character belies the fact that he is as fro-zen in time as James Barrie's Peter Pan: neither 'imperial boy' progresses towards a clear, satisfactory adulthood. True, Kim gets two educations, one from St Xavier's and the other from the Lama. But as the Lama's disciple, he can remain forever young, an image of Kipling's ideal self preserved in the amber of a changeless imperial order. Of course, the real Empire was constantly changing and often disappointing, as in the case of the Indian Rebellion or the South African War, but one purpose of the imperial boy, in Kipling and in other writers of imperialist adventure fiction, was to fore-stall or disavow change. Imperial boys stick their thumbs in the dykes of history. Donald Randall comments that Kim, 'still in the care of two par-tial and incompatible fathers, Mahbub [Ali] and Teshoo Lama, is left sus-pended on the brink of an impossible manhood. The predicament implied by Kim's truncated Bildung, his insuperable adolescence, mirrors the prob-lem of imperial consolidation', or of 'an empire that has not discovered ... its appropriate coming of age'.[27]

At the end of the novel, Kim is, at best, an incomplete sahib. Said insists that 'a Sahib is a Sahib, and no amount of friendship and camaraderie can change the rudiments of racial difference'. But Kim's utility to the Secret Service is based on his behaving like an Indian. Besides, he is Irish, and Kipling claimed that the Irish were 'the Orientals of the West'.[28] Moreover, when the Lama insists that Kim is a sahib, Kim gets upset: 'Thou hast said there is neither black nor white. Why plague me with this talk, Holy One?

... It vexes me. I am *not* a Sahib. I am thy *chela* ...' (*K* 386). Yet Kim is also a spy working for the British, who send him to school to try to turn him into a sahib. If anything makes Kim as happy as travelling on the Grand Trunk Road with the Lama, it is the praise he receives for rescuing E.23 from his pursuers: 'For the first time in his life, Kim thrilled to the clean pride ... of Departmental praise' (*K* 314). Nevertheless, turning Kim into a grown-up, fully fledged sahib seems either unimportant or retrograde. 'Therefore,' says the narrator, 'you would scarcely be interested in Kim's experiences as a St Xavier's boy ...' (*K* 175). The brief descriptions of the school make it sound like a prison: '"The Gates of Learning" shut with a clang' (*K* 174). For three years Kim manages to do well as a student, but only his adventures when he is on vacation or playing hooky are rendered in much detail.[29]

Kim remains adolescent, too, in regard to the women whom he encounters. Like most adventure fiction authored by men and aimed at youthful, male readers, *Kim* is at least mildly misogynistic. The Great Game, writes Said, 'is best played by men alone'. Kim's is 'a masculine' and 'a celibate world', in which travelling, war, espionage and expert religious knowledge are male-dominated. 'At best,' Said continues, 'women help things along: they buy you a ticket, they cook, they tend the ill, and ... they molest men.'[30] The Game may be 'played by men alone', yet Daniel Bivona observes that in *Kim* the idea expressed by the word 'game' never loses the connotation of 'trivial child's play'.[31] In imperialist adventure fiction, boys will be boys.

When Lispeth or the Woman of Shamlegh proposes to Kim, he thinks: 'How can a man follow the Way or the Great Game when he is eternally pestered by women?' (*K* 366).[32] Yet the few women characters are sympathetic and kindly. Kim himself, writes Angus Wilson, is 'physically beautiful and, in a way that is successfully kept by Kipling from being fully sexual, flirtatious with all and sundry'. Wilson points to the frequency with which Kim is found attractive by women, including various prostitutes. Kim's relations with the men in his life also evoke love and, at times, jealousy. 'Yet all this sensuality is without an explicit sexual tinge', except, Wilson notes, 'for the scene where a prostitute tries to steal from Mahbub Ali'.[33] The last sentence of the novel suggests that the homosocial bond between the Lama and Kim is especially strong. The Lama 'crossed his hands on his lap and smiled, as a man may who has won Salvation for himself and his beloved' (*K* 413). The Lama and Kim have grown to love each other as father and son.

Buddhism and Kipling's beliefs

Noting that 'few if any interpretations of *Kim* have given substantial attention' to its Buddhist elements, J. Jeffrey Franklin also points out that 'the

Friend of all the World' 'is able to embrace and move between a variety of religious positions. [Kipling] was careful to give Kim a father figure of every religious stripe: a Buddhist Lama, a Muslim in Mahbub Ali, and a hybridised Hindu in Hurree Babu', who claims he is also a Spencerian materialist.[34] There are as well 'an occultist' (Lurgan Sahib), a Roman Catholic (Father Victor), and an Anglican (Revd Arthur Bennett). The least sympathetic of these characters is Bennett. Father Victor is more understanding, but his desire to turn Kim into a Catholic and Bennett's closed-mindedness are expressions of Kipling's general dislike of missionary endeavours in India. Kim 'lived in a life wild as that of the Arabian Nights, but missionaries and secretaries of charitable societies could not see the beauty of it' (K 3–4).

If Kipling was not sympathetic to missionaries and to orthodox brands of Christianity, neither was he sympathetic to Hinduism. David Gilmour asserts that Kipling 'despised Hindu mythology', because it 'seemed to encourage fatalism, apathy and a fundamental escapism. Besides, Kipling held it responsible for most of India's social problems.'[35] He had greater respect for Islam. In Kim, through the Lama and the curator of the Lahore Museum, Buddhism is the only traditional religion that is given serious attention, though it isn't clear that Kim views it as more than just another intriguing game. Nor is it clear that Kipling ever considered himself a Buddhist or held any very definite religious beliefs.

Nevertheless, Charles Allen argues that, at the end of the novel, with Kim seemingly 'a committed disciple of a Tibetan Buddhist Lama', the story has shifted from 'a political allegory about the defence of British India and, by implication, of Western values', to 'the vehicle for a very different Law, that of the Buddhist *Dharma*'.[36] Perhaps so, though what this says about Kipling's interest in Buddhism is uncertain. The Lama may be 'one of the most sympathetic figures in the long tradition of the holy fool', as Mallett calls him,[37] though that may support rather than negate the possibility that he can lead his *chela* to salvation. 'I was made wise by thee, Holy One,' Kim tells the Lama, 'forgetting St Xavier's; forgetting his white blood; forgetting even the Great Game as he stooped, Mohammedan-fashion, to touch his master's feet in the dust of the Jain temple. "My teaching I owe to thee …"' (K 271). But just what that 'teaching' has been, apart from accepting and respecting all of the people and the experiences he meets along the Road of Life, seems finally unimportant.

Whatever he believes by the end of the story, Kim takes seriously his role as the Lama's *chela*. He recognises the Lama's kindness, honesty and innocence of the ways of the world, but that doesn't mean that he becomes a fully fledged Buddhist. Kim is on his way, however, to becoming a full-time employee of the Secret Service. 'Kim is a spy,' George Moore remarked, 'but spying is called the Great Game, and nothing matters so long as you are not taken in.'[38] And Kim is rarely 'taken in'. Kipling, too, hoped he was rarely 'taken in', including by false religions. That is perhaps one reason why Buddhism appealed to him; it was an ethical practice rather than a theological orthodoxy or bundle of quarreling orthodoxies. For that reason, too, as Franklin demonstrates, Buddhism appealed to many Victorians, in part because it seemed reconcilable with scientific materialism and the theory of evolution.

But Kipling may also have viewed Buddhism as just an attractive alternative in the 'game' of competing religions. The two Great Games – both spying and going on pilgrimage with the Lama – keep Kim in the whirl and excitement that is India, and that is finally what the novel is about. T. S. Eliot wrote that, because of Kipling's 'craftsmanship' and 'versatility', it is easy to view him as 'no more than a performer'. The 'unity in variety' that binds the works of 'a great writer' together, Eliot continued, is 'more difficult to discern' in Kipling than in any other writer 'of equal eminence'.[39] Eliot is aware, however, that there is a 'unity' in Kipling's very diverse writings. This is his belief in the ultimate justice and virtue of the British Empire and of the English in their dealings with the rest of the world. For Kipling, it was the duty of the white servants of empire and civilisation to try to bring the 'Law' to what he called, in 'Recessional', 'the lesser breeds without the Law'. Because of the racial inferiority of those 'lesser breeds', empire was an unending, perhaps ultimately tragic endeavour. Hard work, honesty and selfless devotion to duty were the qualities that redeemed imperialism and its servants in India and elsewhere, even if the ultimate goals of the full civilisation and independence of India were – as Kipling seems always to have believed – unreachable. For Kipling, imperialism did not mean primarily political domination or a system of economic exploitation, but a moral ideal, even a surrogate religion, similar in this respect to how many Europeans understood Buddhism.

A happy unending

Even before he engages in the Great Game of imperial policing and espionage, Kim 'loved ... the game for its own sake' (*K* 4). His chameleon-like character allows him to slip in and out of disguises, speak various languages, befuddle authorities, beg food for himself and the Lama without ever going hungry, and successfully foil the foreign intruders. Against Kim's seemingly magical abilities, and with Hurree Babu's also remarkable abilities, the foreigners don't stand a chance. Mentioned in passing is the conspiracy of 'the five confederated Kings, the sympathetic Northern Power [Russia], a Hindu banker in Peshawur, a firm of gun-makers in Belgium, and an important, semi-independent Mohammedan ruler to the south' (*K* 31). But as Angus Wilson puts it, 'evil … is strikingly absent' from *Kim*, 'as may be measured by the unimportance of the "villains", the Russian and French spies. They are bad men',[40] but Kim and Hurree Babu have little trouble sending them packing, leaving Kim in possession of all of their surveying instruments and their valuable documents.

The India depicted in *Kim* is like Prospero's magic island, an ideal colony in which the Rebellion of 1857–8 was merely a passing 'madness'. Yet at least from the time he was a student at the United Services College, Kipling studied Russian and took the threat of Russian designs on Afghanistan and India quite seriously. The Great Game was a real game, and Thomas Richards calls *Kim* 'the first sustained narrative of state nomadology', in which diverse, mobile agents are employed in a complex strategy to protect and prolong the Raj.[41] There are several episodes, including the attempted assassination of Mahbub Ali and the narrow escape of E.23, that suggest its perils. However, Kim is able to help Mahbub Ali foil the assassins and E.23 to disguise himself as a Saddhu, who thus evades his pursuers. Hurree Babu may be 'a fearful man', as he calls himself, yet Kim never seems afraid of anything or anyone (though he is perhaps somewhat intimidated by Lurgan Sahib and his jealous and apparently murderous Hindu apprentice). *Kim* is indeed a spy novel or a 'romance of surveillance', as Gautam Chakravarty calls it.[42] Yet its protagonist is happiness personified; he is 'entirely happy to be out chewing *pan* and seeing new people in the great good-tempered world' (*K* 48). How many spy novels can also be described as happy?

From this point of view, at the end of the story Kim is not necessarily on the verge of having to choose between the Lama's Buddhism and the British Secret Service; he is left in a still-adolescent state which is also one of the pleasures of the text – he can have his cake and eat it, too. And yet from the outset, when he works for Mahbub Ali and becomes the Lama's *chela*, Kim is aware that there *is* a conflict in regard to his identity ('Who is Kim?') and that what is at stake is his future. The conflict perhaps becomes clearest when he is sent to St Xavier's. As Zohreh T. Sullivan puts it, Kim's 'journey towards "education" will also be a journey towards loss'.[43] Prominent in the St Xavier's episodes is the bullying the drummer boy inflicts on Kim. Sullivan observes:

> The life of a Sahib in school, or out of it, is inevitably a life of cold competition whose final reward will be Kim's function as a cog in the imperial machine. His life on the road with the lama, on the contrary, is a carnival that inverts and democratizes the imperial hierarchy of class, creed, color and race.[44]

Sahibs may be unhappy. But, with sahibs in full control of India, whatever Kim's future may be, it is unlikely to be unhappy. The spies including Kim employed by the Secret Service are engaged in 'a war without friction, a peacetime war', as Richards calls it, 'in which the calculations of pure strategy entail and provoke almost no violence'.[45] Sahibs are nevertheless necessary for ruling India and for keeping a watchful eye out against intruders. And their rule seems to be appreciated by most of the Indians Kim meets, including the loyal old sepoy that he and the Lama encounter. The sepoy speaks of the Rebellion of 1857–8 as 'the madness', and when the Lama asks 'What madness was that, then?' he responds:

> The Gods, who sent it for a plague, alone know. A madness ate into all the Army, and they turned against their officers. That was the first evil, but not past remedy if they had then held their hands. But they chose to kill the Sahibs' wives and children. Then came the Sahibs from over the sea and called them to most strict account. (*K* 74)

Wounded nine times, the old sepoy was awarded several medals, including 'the Order of Berittish India', as well as a parcel of land for his heroic service to the Raj (*K* 75).

'The Anglo-Indians who taught Rudyard Kipling his political philosophy believed that the Indian people required protection because of their ignorance,' writes Peter Havholm; 'it was the duty of Britain's servants in India to care for them, care enough to devote lives to learning their infinite variety so that they might best be protected from themselves.'[46] So confident was Kipling in expressing the Anglo-Indians' 'political philosophy' that his version of the Raj takes on utopian, dream-world overtones. The Raj is threatened from without, but within it is stable and unchallenged by any threat of unrest from Indians themselves. The Irish are also there to serve the Empire. Yet Kipling wrote *Kim* forty years after the Rebellion of 1857–8, twenty years after the Ilbert Bill crisis of the 1880s, and as Indian nationalism, via the Indian National Congress and many other organisations, was on the rise. And of course Indian nationalism was matched by Irish nationalism.[47]

In conclusion, *Kim* expresses 'a lost dream of possibility for an eternal childhood in an imagined India', as Sullivan puts it, 'a fantasy of integration between the oppositional roles of colonizer and colonized and of the master who rules and the child who desires'.[48] The novel also 'integrates' – or rather, presents as 'parallel universes' – the secular and the sacred, the British Raj and Buddhism, as non-conflictual antitheses (or opposites that aren't really opposites). There are thus two 'games' that Kipling's boy-hero can play and win, without fully growing up and without having to make a final choice between them. Perched between these non-antitheses, Kim is 'awake' to the entire subcontinent. Among all of Kipling's writings, *Kim* best expresses the ethnographically curious, tolerant and even admiring side of Kipling – that is, Kipling at his best. Though he called his masterpiece 'nakedly picaresque and plotless', it is precisely its 'picaresque' openness to cultural difference and its lack of teleological structure – the 'Great Game' played on the 'Road of Life' with no self-evident closure – that allows Kim, despite his role as a spy, and Kipling through him, despite his authoritarian politics, to be the 'Friend of all the World'. And Kim's companion on the Road, the Teshoo Lama, offers a non-authoritarian model of how to approach the world: not in a possessive, imperialist way, but just the reverse – an unworldly way of appreciating and getting along with everyone in it.

Lerner notes that after writing *Kim*, and especially after the First World War, Kipling 'lost much of his appreciation for the Diversity of Creatures that populated God's creation'. He became increasingly 'an intolerant chauvinist',[49] anti-Semitic, anti-Irish and xenophobic, as well as the supporter at all costs of the British Empire. But did Kipling's views change all that much between the 1890s and 1930? Part of what gives *Kim* its delight in India and Indians is its author's confidence in the rightness and permanence of British rule. Kim acts, after all, for the British Secret Service as well as for the Teshoo Lama and, just as importantly, for himself. That an Irish orphan behaving like an Indian scamp can help to foil an international conspiracy expresses faith not just in Kim but also in what Kipling hoped would be the happy endlessness of the British Raj.

Notes

1 Rudyard Kipling, *Kim* (1901; London: Macmillan, 1919), p. 91. Subsequent references in the text as *K*.

2 Fred Lerner, 'The Tragedy of Rudyard Kipling', *Kipling Journal*, 82 (September 2008), p. 12.

3 Rudyard Kipling, *Something of Myself and Other Autobiographical Writings*, ed. Thomas Pinney (Cambridge University Press, 1990), p. 81. Subsequent references in the text as *SM*.

4 Andrew Lycett, *Rudyard Kipling* (London: Weidenfeld & Nicolson, 1999), p. 253.

5 Charles Carrington, *Rudyard Kipling: His Life and Work* (London: Macmillan, 1986), p. 424.

6 Cited in Lycett, *Rudyard Kipling*, p. 102.

7 'To Be Filed for Reference', in *Plain Tales from the Hills*, tells the story of McIntosh Jellaludin, who on his deathbed gives a book called 'Mother Maturin' to the narrator. McIntosh calls it his 'treasure', his 'only baby' and 'a great work', which he has 'paid for' through 'seven years' damnation' (p. 241). The Oxford-educated McIntosh has converted to Islam, married an Indian woman and succumbed to alcoholism.

8 Jan Montefiore, *Rudyard Kipling* (Tavistock: Northcote House, 2007), p. 81.

9 Nirad C. Chaudhuri in Roger Lancelyn Green (ed.), *Kipling: The Critical Heritage* (London: Routledge and Kegan Paul, 1971), p. 29.

10 Salman Rushdie, *Imaginary Homelands: Essays and Criticism, 1981–91* (London: Penguin, 1991), pp. 74–5.

11 Edward Said, *Culture and Imperialism* (New York: Knopf, 1993), p. 135.

12 These examples come from Bart Moore-Gilbert, *Kipling and 'Orientalism'* (New York: St Martin's Press, 1986), pp. 24–6. Charles Allen notes that among Kipling's friends was Mahbab Ali, an Afghan horse dealer whom he met in 1886 in Lahore's Sultan Sarai (Charles Allen, *Kipling Sahib: India and the Making of Rudyard Kipling* (London: Little, Brown, 2007), pp. 208–10); and Thomas Richards points to both Colonel Thomas Holdich, Superintendant of Frontier Surveys in India from 1892 to 1898, and Captain Thomas Montgomerie, head of the survey of Tibet, as models for Colonel Creighton, while Sarat Chandra Das, author of *Journey to Lhasa and Central Tibet* (1902), may have been a model for Hurree Babu (Thomas Richards, *The Imperial Archive: Knowledge and the Fantasy of Empire* (London: Verso, 1993), pp. 18–19, 155 n. 11).

13 Carrington, *Rudyard Kipling*, p. 425.

14 Angus Wilson, *The Strange Ride of Rudyard Kipling: His Life and Works* (London: Secker & Warburg, 1977), p. 129.

15 Phillip Mallett, *Rudyard Kipling: A Literary Life* (New York: Palgrave Macmillan, 2003), p. 118.

16 Michael Gorra, 'Rudyard Kipling to Salman Rushdie: Imperialism to Postcolonialism', in John Richetti (ed.), *The Columbia History of the British Novel* (New York: Columbia University Press, 1994), p. 640.

17 John McClure, *Kipling and Conrad: The Colonial Fiction* (Cambridge, MA: Harvard University Press, 1981), p. 80.

18 Said, *Culture and Imperialism*, p. 149.

19 Montefiore, *Rudyard Kipling*, p. 100.

20 *Ibid.*, p. 94.

21 Said, *Culture and Imperialism*, p. 132.

22 Said, *Culture and Imperialism*, pp. 157, 134, 146; Edmund Wilson, 'The Kipling That Nobody Read', in *The Wound and the Bow: Seven Studies in Literature* (New York: Oxford University Press, 1947), pp. 86–147.

23 John McBratney, *Imperial Subjects, Imperial Space: Rudyard Kipling's Fiction of the Native-Born* (Columbus: The Ohio State University Press, 2002), p. 44.

24 Kaori Nagai writes: 'Kipling, by representing his imperial hero as Irish, at once contains Irish rebellion and reclaims the Irish as loyal subjects' (Kaori Nagai, *Empire of Analogies: Kipling, India and Ireland* (Cork University Press, 2006), p. 10). At several points, Nagai refers to Kipling's portrayals of potential or actual Irish 'mutinies', including 'The Mutiny of the Mavericks' – Kim's father's regiment.

25 John Kucich, *Imperial Masochism: British Fiction, Fantasy, and Social Class* (Princeton University Press, 2007), p. 161.

26 Joseph Bristow, *Empire Boys: Adventures in a Man's World* (London: HarperCollins Academic, 1991), p. 198.

27 Donald Randall, *Kipling's Imperial Boy: Adolescence and Cultural Hybridity* (New York: Palgrave, 2000), p. 158.

28 Said, *Culture and Imperialism*, p. 135; Kipling quoted in David Gilmour, *The Long Recessional: The Imperial Life of Rudyard Kipling* (New York: Farrar, Straus and Giroux, 2002), p. 242.

29 The use Robert Baden-Powell made of *Kim* for the Boy Scouts is also noteworthy in regard to the issues of adolescence, adventure and masculinity. See Hugh Brogan, *Mowgli's Sons: Kipling and Baden-Powell's Scouts* (London: Jonathan Cape, 1987).

30 Said, *Culture and Imperialism*, p. 237.

31 Daniel Bivona, *British Imperial Literature 1870–1940: Writing and the Administration of Empire* (Cambridge University Press, 1998), p. 70.

32 In 'Lispeth', a beautiful, light-skinned Afghan girl is wooed and then jilted by a 'sahib'. In *Kim*, Lispeth – or the Woman of Shamlegh – though she has several indigenous husbands, sees in Kim a second chance at winning the love of an attractive sahib: 'I am the Woman of Shamlegh, and I hold from the Rajah. I am no common bearer of babes. Shamlegh is thine: hoof and horn and hide, milk and butter. Take or leave' (*K* 366).

33 Angus Wilson, *The Strange Ride of Rudyard Kipling*, p. 131.

34 J. Jeffrey Franklin, *The Lotus and the Lion: Buddhism and the British Empire* (Ithaca, NY: Cornell University Press, 2008), p. 130.

35 Gilmour, *The Long Recessional*, p. 57.

36 Allen, *Kipling Sahib*, p. 362.

37 Mallett, *Rudyard Kipling: A Literary Life*, p. 118.

38 George Moore in Green, *Kipling: The Critical Heritage*, p. 288.

39 T. S. Eliot, 'Rudyard Kipling', *On Poetry and Poets* (New York: Farrar, Strauss and Giroux, 1943), pp. 274–5.

40 Angus Wilson, *The Strange Ride of Rudyard Kipling*, p. 132.

41 Richards, *The Imperial Archive*, pp. 19–22.

42 Gautam Chakravarty, *The Indian Mutiny and the British Imagination* (Cambridge University Press, 2005), p. 159.

43 Zohreh T. Sullivan, *Narratives of Empire: The Fictions of Rudyard Kipling* (Cambridge University Press, 1993), p. 166.

44 Sullivan, *Narratives of Empire*, p. 172.

45 Richards, *The Imperial Archive*, p. 31.

46 Peter Havholm, *Politics and Awe in Rudyard Kipling's Fiction* (Aldershot: Ashgate, 2008), p. 9.

47 See Nagai, *Empire of Analogies*.

48 Sullivan, *Narratives of Empire*, p. 148.

49 Lerner, 'The Tragedy of Rudyard Kipling', p. 14.

10

HOWARD J. BOOTH

The later short fiction

A line of Kipling critics have identified the late short fiction as his best writing. Although this remains a minority view, the later collections are central to debate on his relationship to modernism. Kipling's extended career meant that he had a worldwide reputation at the end of the nineteenth century, but was still publishing new work in the 1930s at the end of the modernist period. Here the focus will be on evaluating the later fiction precisely as 'late' and 'untimely' work.

Little or no reference is made to Kipling's later writing in a number of classic accounts of the short story. H. E. Bates in his 1941 study only refers to Kipling's Indian writing and dismisses him for his support for imperialism. Indeed Bates finds Kipling no more than 'an interesting pathological study', with no signs of 'fine quality' in the writing.[1] Frank O'Connor offers more in the way of engagement with Kipling's writing in his *The Lonely Voice* (1962). He notices that Kipling was more interested in groups and on the effect his tales had on his readers than on internal character development. Seen as in flight from the loneliness in his own life and therefore afraid of depicting isolation in his stories, Kipling is seen by O'Connor as unable to become 'the lonely voice', the truly modern short fiction writer who expresses the isolation of the modern individual.[2]

More recent accounts want to relate Kipling to the modernist short story but find him hard to place. According to Adrian Hunter in his 2007 volume on the short story, Kipling straddles the Victorian and modern periods but belongs to neither. Hunter sees the modern short story in Britain as emerging in the last decades of the nineteenth century, making an advance over the short stories of Charles Dickens, Elizabeth Gaskell and Thomas Hardy. These Victorian writers of short fiction used techniques more fitted to the novel and considered the shorter form a constraint. Some of the plots available did appeal, with tales of the supernatural used to protest against the increasingly ordered, known world ushered in by modernity and mechanisation. At the end of the nineteenth century, though, the short story form was given a considerable boost by commercial conditions. Many periodicals were competing in a rapidly growing market where self-contained stories rather than serialised novels became the norm.[3]

New approaches to the short story centred on how they were narrated, with a move away from the omniscient third-person narrator. The short story was becoming increasingly 'plotless' and undidactic. A focus on dis-continuous and intense moments in a life was used to register how old world views were fracturing and giving way. The short story was becoming a cen-tral modernist form able to capture modern conditions.[4] Though Hunter acknowledges that Kipling's stories make technical advances in the modern short story around narration, and also share many of its themes, he is unable to find a clear place for Kipling in his account and ends up declaring him to be inconsistent:

> [F]or the student of the short story, there remains the nagging difficulty of assessing Kipling's contribution to the development of the form. He seems at once an inveterate traditionalist and a bold experimenter, a writer as fond of familiar story structures as he was elsewhere determined to break them down … Such range and inconsistency gives rise to critical hesitation, for depending on which stories one refers to, it is as easy to champion Kipling as a peripheral modernist as it is to dismiss him, *pace* Bates and O'Connor, as an outmoded conventionalist, faltering well into the new century under the artistic and ideo-logical burdens of the old.[5]

Hunter does not explore why he finds some stories to be fully 'modern' and others not; he does acknowledge, though, that Kipling cannot simply be seen as a transitional figure. A fuller sense of Kipling and the short story requires an investigation of his development and how he used the form.

The influential American liberal critic Edmund Wilson, in a long piece from 1941 entitled 'The Kipling that Nobody Read', argued that Kipling's best work is to be found in his late stories.[6] The quality of the final collections had gone unrecognised because early readers and critics had come to them with fixed and settled views of what to expect from Kipling. They saw only what they expected to see, and not what was there. Though Kipling's repu-tation had reached its height around 1910,[7] Wilson suggests that he had, largely unnoticed, continued to grow as a writer. Noting that at this time there was 'so much wreckage around, political, social and moral', Wilson observed that 'the Kipling who limped out of the wreckage, shrunken and wry though he looks, has in a sense had his development as an artist. Some of these stories are the most intense in feeling as they are among the most concentrated in form that Kipling ever wrote; to a writer, they are perhaps the most interesting.' Wilson's recourse to imagery leaves what is being said about Kipling's 'development' in thought and writing unclear. Indeed, though he identifies the Kipling that nobody read, Wilson does not really read that work either. Mainly concerned with an account of Kipling's life and career, the nearest he comes to setting out what characterises the late writing is to see it as 'disinterested' and to identify 'five classes of stories': 'tales of hatred, farces based on practical jokes, studies of neurotic cases, tales of fellowship in religion, and tales of personal development'.[8] The problem here is that these concerns are found throughout Kipling's output. J. M. S. Tompkins organised her highly regarded 1959 study using themes found across Kipling's oeuvre, though she too felt that his greatest work came in his last collections, when his art had 'deepened'.[9]

What might be meant by 'late' career is explored in Edward Said's book *On Late Style* (2006) – it was itself a late work, published posthumously. Said observed that one form of late career sees reconciliation with the processes of ageing and of death; Shakespeare's final comedies are the most often cited example. However, Said's main focus is a rather pricklier form of late career. He sees this as 'a kind of self-imposed exile from what is generally acceptable, coming after it, and surviving beyond it'. It involves not only what the texts say, but also matters of style: 'There is therefore an inherent tension in late style that abjures mere bourgeois ageing and that insists on the increasing sense of apartness and exile and anachronism, which late style expresses and, more important uses, to formally sustain itself.'[10] The readings Said offers – the examples are mostly from music – often see the artist finding forms that reflect their apartness, rejecting the normal rules of genre and forgoing wholeness. Said on lateness forces us beyond the view that artists in late career are simply nostalgic for an old order and to be set aside in a rush for the new and emergent, as well as demanding an attention to form. Kipling does not fully fit Said's model, however; while themes of reconciliation and the rejection of the age are often in tension, the late stories are both carefully organised and highly polished. Again, this brings us back to the specificities of Kipling's use of the short story form.

At the risk of simplification, Kipling's career as a short story writer can be divided into four periods. The first ends with his departure from India and his arrival in London in 1889, and the gradual move away from his Indian subject matter and Anglo-Indian audience. For some, such as Charles Allen and Harish Trivedi (in his chapter in this volume), the end of this first period marks the start of a decline.[11] Others, while abjuring qualitative judgements, have analysed how Kipling's writing changed in this second period. David Sergeant has seen it as the 'most significant' shift in Kipling's career, with the result that he produced two kinds of story: some seek to instruct a wide audience about the Empire, while others showed marked formal development.[12]

With the start of the third period around the turn of the new century, Kipling entered 'late career'. Circumstances precipitated this at an early age, though there was an extended transitional period. After the row with his wife's family that ended his time in Vermont came the death, during a further visit to the United States in 1899, of his beloved daughter Josephine, in New York. By September 1902, when the Kiplings moved into Bateman's, Kipling had an established reputation, was financially independent – and was still only thirty-six. Though he continued to work hard, his short stories began to appear less regularly. The author who could write a 'turn over' at speed with a high fever in his Indian days was increasingly producing work that had matured over many years. The stories of this third period reached a new level of complexity, and certain themes recur. In the later Kipling there are many older characters, the focus is often on social groups other than the family, and the plots do not usually address the development of the young or end in marriage.

Tales from the start of the century often featured themes of technological change and the possible proximity of other worlds. Examples include '"Wireless"', '"They"' and 'Mrs Bathurst' in *Traffics and Discoveries*. In her major study of the relationship between literature and film in the modern period, Laura Marcus sees 'Mrs Bathurst' as exploring changed ways of looking, repetition, an excess of the visual and the frame.[13] With *Actions and Reactions* in 1909, the organisation of the short story collection reached a new level (a point that could also be made with recourse to the collections of short stories for children that flank it, *Puck of Pook's Hill* and *Rewards and Fairies*). Stories can be related both to the other fiction and to the poems interspersed through the collection. The reader also has to consider how the stories related to the (often doublet) volume titles. Links are established with neighbouring volumes, and other parts of Kipling's career.[14]

In a 1909 letter to Henry Seidel Canby, Kipling made it very clear whom he most admired as a short story writer. Canby had praised Kipling, in his *The Short Story in English*, as 'on the whole, the most vigorous, versatile, and highly endowed among contemporary writers of fiction'.[15] But Kipling felt that Canby had not fully recognised Henry James's talent, where he would have 'liked a long chapter on [James]': 'In spite of all you say about Henry James you don't seem to me to admit what I believe to be the case – that he is head and shoulders the biggest of them all and will in the end be found to be perhaps the most enduring influence.' (Kipling also praises Edgar Allan Poe while placing him in a different category: Poe is '*the* poet of America'; the fact that he 'chose prose instead of verse for his tales was merely an accident'.)[16] Though James first praised and then criticised Kipling,[17] the two remained on good terms, if at a distance, and Kipling clearly learned much from the older author. A number of their tales can be compared productively: for example, both Kipling's '"They"' and James's *The Turn of the Screw* explore place, childhood and alternative realities. Kipling shared James's stress on French literature, and would have approved of his observations, in his 1888 essay on Guy de Maupassant, on how brevity could be turned to aesthetic advantage.[18] While James's own tales, though highly innovative, are often close to being novellas, Kipling practised what Baudelaire called 'the infinitely beneficial influence of constraint'.[19]

Though rarely mentioned in accounts of 'early modernism', Kipling deployed carefully controlled narratives and the symbol in an attempt to represent the experience of living in modernity. Kipling shared a stress on the significance of the 'impression' with writers such as Ford Madox Hueffer (later Ford Madox Ford) and Joseph Conrad.[20] G. K. Chesterton observed: 'Our modern attraction to the short story is not an accident of form; it is a sign of real fleetingness and fragility; it means that existence is only an impression, and, perhaps, only an illusion ... We have no instinct of anything ultimate and enduring beyond the episode.'[21] While Kipling registers this same 'fleetingness and fragility', though, his response to modern conditions was to advocate holding ever more firmly onto the forms, social groups and traditions that help hold self and society together. To return to Frank O'Connor's terms, Kipling simply refused to accept that he should become 'the lonely voice'.

Kipling's strong sense of the distinction between art and life means that we do not see in the stories of this third period the levels of vituperation that are found in his letters, where he fulminates against, among others, Liberals, reformers of empire and Germany. In the stories, as Daniel Karlin has noted in a fascinating exploration of *Actions and Reactions*, we can point both to the sense of resolution and acceptance found by the Jewish M'Leod family in 'The House Surgeon' *and* to the harshly negative treatment of another settler, Mr Sangres, in 'An Habitation Enforced'. If themes of homecoming and restored health are stressed in that latter story – though all does not seem down to the free will of the American couple, as the word 'enforced' in the title suggests – the collection also includes the harsh allegory of what happens when order and duty are not respected in the anti-socialist story 'The Mother Hive', and the sour caricature of Lethabie Groombride, MP, with his advanced views on colonial governance, in 'Little Foxes'.[22]

The fourth and final period of Kipling's career as a short story writer, and the second of his extended lateness, began with the First World War, the death of his only son and the onset of the chronic ill health of his final decades. Written just before John Kipling's death in 1915, 'Mary Postgate' explores, in the words of the poem that follows the story at the end of *A*

Diversity of Creatures, what happens when 'the English began to hate'.[23] However, the dominant notes of the final collections, *Debits and Credits* and *Limits and Renewals*, are reconnection and healing; Kipling was, as Edmund Wilson put it, now 'losing his hatred'.[24] Examples include the stories set in the Masonic training lodge in which first soldiers and then ex-soldiers work over their experiences and reconnect with everyday life, and 'On the Gate: A Tale of '16' in *Debits and Credits* and 'Uncovenanted Mercies' in *Limits and Renewals*, both set in heaven during wartime. The first of these sees a successful effort to bring a man shot for desertion across the void and into heaven. However, the absence of the German dead from these two stories – none seem heaven-bound – reminds us that sympathy in Kipling's final phase is not unconfined.

This can be demonstrated by examining 'The Church That Was at Antioch' in *Limits and Renewals*, which was the favourite Kipling short story of the great Argentinean writer Jean Luis Borges.[25] It tells the story of Valens, a young Roman officer. Discovering that he has joined the cult of Mithras, his mother has used her influence to have him transferred to 'civil duty' in Antioch.[26] Under his uncle Serga, the local Prefect of Police, his task is to keep order on the streets of the city. The Christians are in dispute over whether to preserve Jewish dietary laws, and the Jews – those, it is said, from Jerusalem rather than Antioch itself (*LR* 98, 108) – are trying to take advantage of this internal division to cause difficulties for the Christians. A first-time reader might well assume that the Christian leaders Petrus and Paulus (St Peter and St Paul) will come to be the real focus for the story, where they will be viewed from Valens's perspective. However, when Valens is mortally wounded and forgives his attacker, Petrus and Paulus soon realise that it is he who has shown Christ-like virtues. The loyalty and devotion he produces in '[h]is girl' (*LR* 106), whom he rescued from slave-dealers in Constantinople, shows both the power of human love and that compassion reaches across social barriers (there are echoes here of Jesus and Mary Magdalene). Where in 'The Manner of Men' Kipling seems to identify himself with St Paul, here, as Sergeant has argued, Paulus is seen in terms of a self-regarding dogmatism.[27] Perhaps Kipling is even venturing a self-criticism.

However, forgiveness is not the only theme of the story. Harry Ricketts has rightly argued that the story is 'at heart deeply anti-Semitic'.[28] Valens says of the Jews' response to the Christians' debate on diet that '[t]rade feeling's at the bottom of most of it'. Those protecting Valens are drawn off by an 'impudent little Jew boy' before he is stabbed by the brother of a Cilicean brigand he had killed on his journey to Antioch (*LR* 101, 111). The story is pervaded by the suggestion that social disorder is fermented by Jews, and is organised to exclude their perspective on events; they are always a threatening presence, just out of view. When Serga says that 'Every crowd is crazy', he is outlining what the forces of law and order always have to deal with, but the statement comes in a discussion of how the current problems have been stoked by rumour and suggestion from the Jews (*LR* 108). It seems that for Kipling trying to help bind the group together does not preclude a fear of threats from within and without.

At the level of the individual, too, fixed structures and patterns of behaviour are needed if breakdown is to be avoided. Work and the social interaction that goes with it are the greatest support, where C. S. Lewis further observed that 'I think he loves work for the sake of professional brotherhood'.[29] The interest in the group in part explains Kipling's affection for stories that feature practical jokes, though their prevalence must have fatigued even his most ardent admirers. Though Kipling does seem to have believed that young men (and it does appear to be a male phenomenon) require periods spent lying on the floor laughing, these stories also suggest the need for play and release. Suspensions and inversions of hierarchy are temporary, however; the status quo is re-established after a point is made, a lesson learned or a problem resolved.[30] The carefully controlled narrative, the use of capital letters and the fixed symbols that accrete meaning all serve to reveal the existence of an underlying order that can sustain the reader.[31]

The role of art and literature in providing support can be seen in 'The Janeites' in *Debits and Credits*. It is set during cleaning work at the training lodge, with Brother Anthony and Humberstall acting as narrators. Part of a Heavy Artillery battery just before the dramatic German advances of late 1917, Humberstall is made aware that certain advantages will accrue from joining the society of Janeites. He sets about gaining knowledge of Jane, though he never becomes aware of the wider fame and reputation of Jane Austen. Initially he really cannot see the attraction of the novels, and Kipling mines the comic potential of the situation – all in a context of possible sudden death. His own reverence and sympathies are reflected though – for example, we are told that the greatest of all Jane's novels is *Persuasion* (1818), and Humberstall reports the suggestion of one Janeite that 'She *did* leave lawful issue in the shape o' one son; an' 'is name was 'Enery James' (he does not know who the 'sire' of this ''Enery James-man' was, though).[32] Humberstall reflects that 'It *was* a 'appy little Group. I wouldn't 'a changed with any other' (*DC* 165). The meaning of the '*was*' here is more fully understood when we learn that soon afterwards the gun battery took a series of direct hits, leaving Humberstall 'the on'y Janeite left' (*DC* 171). His knowledge of Jane still comes in useful, though: branding one nurse 'Miss Bates' leads another, who feels this is a highly apposite name for her colleague, to squeeze him onto a hospital train. Humberstall tells his audience of two at the Lodge that he is still reading the novels: 'You take it from me, Brethren, there's no one to touch Jane when you're in a tight place. Gawd bless 'er, whoever she was' (*DC* 173). Brother Anthony adds further information gained from Humberstall's sister. Shell-shocked earlier in the war after a munitions explosion at Étaples, Humberstall made an unofficial return to his unit. The suggestion, indeed, is that the whole Janeite society and programme of reading was made up by his fellow soldiers in order to help Humberstall continue to function. The inference can be drawn that the role of literature is to hold readers together in mind and body.

A stress on tradition was, of course, important to the writers of the modern movement. Writing about *Debits and Credits*, Ricketts sees Kipling as modernism's 'literary father'.[33] He cites Edmund Wilson's claim in his *New Republic* review that the 'Cyclops' chapter of James Joyce's *Ulysses* (1922) could only be written by someone who knew their Kipling.[34] There is a gathering of materials from different cultural texts that can be compared with that other classic of 'high modernism' published in the same year, T. S. Eliot's *The Waste Land*. For Ricketts, among the 'quintessentially modernist features' of *Debits and Credits* is its

> intense literary self-consciousness ... reflected in the constant allusions to earlier writers, but also in the subversive games that were played. Official literature (Jane Austen, Swinburne, Shakespeare) was regularly placed in conventionally unliterary contexts (the officers' mess, the Navy, the trenches, school) and mixed up with unofficial literature (*Uncle Remus*, limericks, hymns), so that there were no firm boundaries between high and low culture, no fixed categories ... Again as with Eliot's poem, there was continual parody and pastiche of past writers. Enjoyable as a virtuoso performance in itself, this also served a double function – of giving the illusion of collapsing the distance between present and past, so that the two appeared contemporaneous, while at the same time reinforcing the sense that everything was running down and fragmenting – that after the war all a writer could do was recycle the past.[35]

While this is highly insightful, it rather suggests that Kipling welcomed the 'subversive' and things 'running down and fragmenting'. Though recognising these forces, he wanted to bulwark self and society. Kipling's conservatism and understanding of tradition, it can be added, were different from Eliot's in later career, the main difference being that Kipling did not find the same consolation in orthodox religion.

Kipling's relationship to modernism, indeed, can be compared to Austen's relationship to Romanticism. The novels of Jane Austen, in Marilyn Butler's influential reading, have been seen as novels for the gentry, educating them to take up their role in times that threaten their class.[36] Kipling, while not so class-bound, is also engaged in supporting the connective tissue of society. Literature is not a special realm which raises authors above the common ruck. In 'Dayspring Mishandled' in *Limits and Renewals*, literary scholarship and a writing career lead not to self-improvement through the proximity to greatness, but to all kinds of obsessions, vanities, prevarications and moral failings large and small. Often in late Kipling, there are warnings of the damage unchecked individualism will do to the self and the wider community if the old forms and structures are dismantled entirely. Kipling saw a stress on self-development as a contemporary trend, where it would have unintended consequences. As he observed to Sir Almroth Wright during the First World War, the 'movement had many names – "toleration", "the larger outlook", "self-realization" (you know all the labels) and it led, naturally and inevitably to mental and moral slackness'.[37] The control in the writing and the way texts are always seen partaking in a set of relationships with other texts mirror Kipling's views on the need for mental discipline and for social structures.

John Lee has argued that Kipling's artistic honesty means that though he gives his allegiance to fixed positions, the texts nevertheless register his 'frailty', the difficulties he had in keeping steady.[38] Using psychoanalysis to provide a language, Jan Montefiore argues that 'Modernity, it would seem, is Kipling's unconscious, the other side of his apparently unswerving conservative imperialism'.[39] Kipling's goal, to continue to use psychoanalytic terminology, is like that of American 'ego psychology', namely to support those structures that keep the unconscious in check and that help the individual to cope. Without contesting these powerful readings, they do perhaps suggest that only localised and short-term rear-guard actions are in play. The stories set in the past are used by Kipling to reflect upon major periods of cultural transition; he clearly felt that he was witnessing just such a time himself. In late career, from a position slightly to one side, he is able to examine and critique the new episteme.

A key text here is 'The Eye of Allah' in *Debits and Credits*. The story is preceded by 'Untimely', a didactic piece of verse which argues that a scientific advance requires the right climate of reception. 'The Eye of Allah' explores a moment when a discovery – the microscope – was made before its time and it is realised that the medieval Church is not yet ready to deal with the discovery of the existence of microorganisms. John Otho is working on an illuminated St Luke's gospel in a monastery in southern England. He is about to travel to the south of Spain in search of new ways of treating his subject matter from a culture where Christianity, Islam and Judaism co-exist; he also wants to see the non-Christian woman he loves. As John receives requests for materials and talks with the abbot – who was held in Egypt for two years after a crusade and also has a relationship, this time with a local woman of good family, Ann of Norton – a number of the story's main themes are introduced, including craftsmanship, medicine, love and the role of the Church.

Returning twenty months later, John has secured many of the materials and drugs he had been looking for; however, his lover has died in childbirth along with their baby, and back at the monastery Ann of Norton is very ill. Staying at the monastery are two important figures (Kipling is drawing on real people, though they were not active at the same time): Roger Bacon, the Oxford philosopher, and the surgeon, Roger of Salerno (he has been called upon to examine Ann of Norton). Issues of art, science and the possibility of healing come together when John reveals that he has been using, to help him develop his images of the devils expelled by Jesus from the Gadarene swine, a microscope (the 'eye of Allah') to examine the forms found in stagnant water. The doctors are excited by what they see but, fearing the immanent possibility of coming to heretical conclusions that the Church will punish, the abbot intervenes and destroys the instrument.

Kipling, in response to a query, said, 'Yes, the Eye of Allah *was* an allegory. Several of my tales are.'[40] It is, though, a particularly complex, involved and suggestive example of its kind. C. A. Bodelsen saw it as

> on one level, a story about what happens to a group of people in a mediaeval monastery; on another level it is a story about a premature discovery; on a third it is about the impact of the Renaissance on the mediaeval world picture; on a fourth about the attitude of the artist, the physician, and the philosopher to science; and on the fifth about four aspects of civilisation, personified as the artist, the scientist, the philosopher and the church dignitary and statesman, and illustrated by confronting them with an emblem of the new science: the microscope.[41]

Even talking in terms of five levels omits important themes in the story – including cultural difference, illness (specifically cancer), healing and the need for love – as well as the story's historical context.

Though the microscope plot is historical fantasy as the earliest known examples date from after 1600, Kipling's sense of the context is highly developed. Internal evidence suggests a date of 1266 or 1267 for the story, and in an absorbing article John Coates has linked the tale to Jean de Joinville's *Life of St Louis*. In that text, King Louis IX of France, defeated on a chaotic crusade at the battle of Mansura in 1250, was held in Cairo. It is this Kipling used for the experiences of Abbot Stephen, and to suggest how knowledge from the Moslem world could disrupt the belief systems operating in an

English monastery. Coates also explores the wider implications for intellectual history, relating the story to the impact of the ideas of the Moslem thinker Averroes. They called into question the Aristotelian world view that the Church still held, where at the time of the story is set Thomas Aquinas was composing his books in support of orthodoxy, the *Summa Contra Gentiles* and the *Summa Theologica*. As Coates thus observes, 'Kipling demonstrates not merely the psychological perception and deliberate ambivalence all readers detect and most readers admire in his later fiction, but a depth of historical and cultural understanding less often noticed but equally striking.'[42]

Abbot Stephen's destruction of the microscope, in line with the poem 'Untimely', occurs because the right time for it has not yet come. Acknowledging the teaming life seen under the lens – 'There *is* no end' (*DC* 389), he says – would damage the authority of the medieval Church. That said, the story recognises that the intellectual conditions for the Renaissance were emerging. The two Rogers would like to have continued to use the instrument, though Roger of Salerno is held back by fear of the stake. John Otho, on the other hand, has the detachment of the artist: 'I have my patterns ... In my craft, a thing done is done with. We go on to new shapes after that' (*DC* 392). Perhaps the most interesting figure of all, though, is the character with the lowest status, Thomas the Infirmarian. He lacks John Otho's breeding, and has never taken orders, it is suggested, because he cannot square his insights with orthodox belief. He follows Varro in believing that 'certain small animals which the eye cannot follow enter the body by the nose and mouth, and set up grave diseases' (*DC* 379). Though feelings of relief come with the confirmation of his suppositions, he is seen as losing his equipoise and starting to define his own religious faith and practice: '"Life create and rejoicing – the work of the Creator ..." He flung himself on his knees and began hysterically the *Benedicite omnia Opera*' (*DC* 389–90). The role of the Church in securing meaning and a particular world is shown in the account of the view from the upper cloister, 'three English counties laid out in evening sunshine around them; church upon church, monastery upon monastery, cell after cell, and the bulk of a vast cathedral moored on the edge of the banked shoals of sunset' (*DC* 272–3). From the disciples who gave up fishing to become 'fishers of men' the Church has come to order minds and space,[43] producing along the way an achieved civilisation that should not be given up lightly.

The poem that follows 'The Eye of Allah' is, unsurprisingly after such a story, much more open than 'Untimely'. 'The Last Ode' is one of Kipling's imitations of Horace and explores life after death and cultural change.[44] Its final lines, 'And shall this dawn return us, Virgil mine, / To dawn? Beneath what sky?' (*DC* 395), evoke both our usual confidence that 'dawn' follows 'dawn', and doubt about the form the future will take. For all its complexity – compassion co-existing with prejudice, creativity and intelligence operating within bounds – late Kipling asks a clear question of the newly emerged modern hegemony: what will happen to both individual and society if they are left without anchor?

Notes

1 H. E. Bates, *The Modern Short Story: A Critical Survey* (London: Thomas Nelson, 1941), p. 112.
2 Frank O'Connor, *The Lonely Voice: A Study of the Short Story* (1962; London: Macmillan, 1963), pp. 99–112.
3 Adrian Hunter, *The Cambridge Introduction to the Short Story in English* (Cambridge University Press, 2007), pp. 5–31. See also Dominic Head, *The Modernist Short Story* (Cambridge University Press, 1992). On the dramatic expansion in writing, publishing and reading at this time see P. J. Keating, *The Haunted Study: A Social History of the English Novel, 1875–1914* (London: Secker & Warburg, 1989).
4 Hunter, *The Cambridge Introduction to the Short Story in English*, pp. 7–8.
5 *Ibid.*, p. 21.
6 Edmund Wilson, 'The Kipling that Nobody Read', in Andrew Rutherford (ed.), *Kipling's Mind and Art* (Edinburgh: Oliver & Boyd, 1964), pp. 17–69. First published in the *Atlantic Monthly* in 1941, it was collected in Wilson's *The Wound and the Bow* of that same year.
7 *Ibid.*, p. 17.
8 *Ibid.*, p. 63.
9 J. M. S. Tompkins, *The Art of Rudyard Kipling* (London: Methuen, 1959), p. 258.
10 Edward W. Said, *On Late Style: Music and Literature Against the Grain* (London: Bloomsbury, 2007), pp. 16, 17.
11 Charles Allen, *Kipling Sahib: India and the Making of Rudyard Kipling* (London: Abacus, 2008), p. 364.
12 David Sergeant, 'Changes in Kipling's Fiction Upon his Return to Britain', *English Literature in Transition, 1880–1920*, 52:2 (2009), pp. 144–59, p. 157.
13 Laura Marcus, *The Tenth Muse: Writing About Cinema in the Modernist Period* (New York: Oxford University Press, 2007), pp. 80–6.
14 For example, both 'Garm – a Hostage' in *Actions and Reactions* and 'The Debt' in *Limits and Renewals* are set in India, and there were further Stalky stories. The first story in *A Diversity of Creatures*, 'As Easy as A.B.C.', begins with a quotation from 'With the Night Mail' from *Actions and Reactions* (Rudyard Kipling, *A Diversity of Creatures* (1917; London: Macmillan, 1918), p. 1).
15 Henry Seidel Canby, *The Short Story in English* (New York: H. Holt, 1909), p. 300.
16 *The Letters of Rudyard Kipling, Volume 3, 1900–10*, ed. Thomas Pinney (Basingstoke: Macmillan, 1996), p. 394.

17 For references to Kipling in James's letters and his introduction to Kipling's *Mine Own People* (1891) see Roger Lancelyn Green, *Kipling: The Critical Heritage* (London: Routledge and Kegan Paul, 1971), pp. 67–70, 159–67.

18 Henry James, *Selected Literary Criticism*, ed. Morris Shapira (London: Heinemann, 1963), pp. 98–9.

19 Siân Miles, Introduction to Guy de Maupassant, *A Parisian Affair and Other Stories* (London: Penguin, 2004), p. xxv; Charles Baudelaire, *Œuvres Complètes II* (Paris: Gallimard, 1976), p. 119.

20 See Peter Brooker, 'Early Modernism', in Morag Shiach (ed.) *The Cambridge Companion to the Modernist Novel* (Cambridge University Press, 2007), pp. 32–40.

21 G. K. Chesterton, *Charles Dickens* (London: Methuen, 1906), p. 85.

22 Daniel Karlin, '*Actions and Reactions*: Kipling's Edwardian Summer', *Kipling Journal*, 84 (April 2010), pp. 8–23.

23 Rudyard Kipling, 'The Beginnings', in *A Diversity of Creatures*, p. 442.

24 Wilson, 'The Kipling that Nobody Read', p. 66.

25 Paul Theroux, *The Old Patagonian Express: By Train Through the Americas* (1975; London: Penguin 2008), p. 391.

26 Rudyard Kipling, *Limits and Renewals* (London: Macmillan, 1932), p. 89. Subsequent references in the text as *LR*.

27 David Sergeant, '"The Church That Was at Antioch": A Reading', *Kipling Journal*, 83 (March 2009), pp. 39–40.

28 Harry Ricketts, *Rudyard Kipling: A Life* (1999; New York: Carroll and Graf, 2000), p. 381.

29 C. S. Lewis, 'Kipling's World', in *They Asked for a Paper* (London: Geoffrey Bles, 1962), p. 87.

30 In his speech opening the Men's Student Union at St Andrews University on 11 October 1923, Kipling noted that the new building would provide a 'place for those suddenly begotten eruptions of jest, extravagance, and absurdity that reduce all concerned in them to the helpless, aching, speechless mirth which is as necessary to the health of a young man's mind as grit to the gizzard of a fowl'. *Rudyard Kipling's Uncollected Speeches: A Second Book of Words* (Greensboro, NC: ELT Press, 2008), p. 115. See Phillip Mallett's 'Kipling and the Hoax' in his edited collection *Kipling Considered* (Basingstoke: Macmillan, 1989), pp. 98–114.

31 See Adrian Poole, 'Kipling's Upper Case', in Mallett (ed.), *Kipling Considered*, pp. 135–59, and Sergeant, '"The Church That Was at Antioch": A Reading', pp. 37–8.

32 Rudyard Kipling, *Debits and Credits* (London: Macmillan, 1926), pp. 154–5. Subsequent references in the text as *DC*.

33 Ricketts, *Rudyard Kipling: A Life*, p. 364. Sandra Kemp also claims Kipling as a modernist in her *Kipling's Hidden Narratives* (Basingstoke: Basil Blackwell, 1988), pp. 1, 67–81.

34 Edmund Wilson, 'Kipling's Debits and Credits', *New Republic* (6 October 1926).

35 Ricketts, *Rudyard Kipling: A Life*, p. 363.

36 Marilyn Butler, *Jane Austen and the War of Ideas*, 2nd edn (Oxford University Press, 1987).

37 *The Letters of Rudyard Kipling, Volume 4, 1911–19*, ed. Thomas Pinney (Basingstoke: Macmillan, 1999), p. 420.

38 John Lee, 'Kipling's Frailty and "With the Night Mail"', *Kipling Journal*, 84 (April 2010), pp. 25–43.

39 Janet Montefiore, 'Latin, Arithmetic and Mastery: A Reading of Two Kipling Fictions', in Howard J. Booth and Nigel Rigby (eds.), *Modernism and Empire* (Manchester University Press, 2000), p. 130.

40 *The Letters of Rudyard Kipling, Volume 6, 1931–36*, ed. Thomas Pinney (Basingstoke: Palgrave Macmillan, 2004), p. 54.

41 C. A. Bodelsen, *Aspects of Kipling's Art* (Manchester University Press, 1964), pp. 91–2.

42 John Coates, 'Memories of Mansura: the "Tints and Textures" of Kipling's Late Art in "The Eye of Allah"', *The Modern Language Review*, 85:3 (July 1990), pp. 555–69, p. 569.

43 Mark 1.17.

44 On Kipling and Horace see Stephen Medcalf, 'Horace's Kipling', in Charles Martindale and David Hopkins (eds.), *Horace Made New: Horatian Influences on British Writing from the Renaissance to the Twentieth Century* (Cambridge University Press, 1993), pp. 217–35.

11

BART MOORE-GILBERT

Kipling and postcolonial literature

Insofar as postcolonialism is so often used as a synonym for anti-colonialism,[1] one might infer that the relationship between the terms in my title is one of binary opposition rather than negotiation or conjunction. In such a reading (which will be contested in due course), Kipling might be understood simply as a figure whom later non-western writers engage with only to dismiss. There is certainly evidence to support such a reading. Given his long association with India, hostility towards Kipling is, understandably perhaps, especially apparent in the subcontinent and its diasporas, with *Kim* and *The Jungle Books* – the main focus of the discussion below – often identified by critics as embodying the most demeaning properties of colonial discourse.[2]

Antipathy to Kipling is perhaps most widely evident amongst later South Asian writers with explicitly nationalist sympathies. An early example of such antipathy is Sarath Kumar Ghosh's epic novel *The Prince of Destiny* (1909). While never explicitly named, Kipling and his supposed imperial politics are recurrently the object of biting commentary, notably in the denunciations made by the protagonist Barath and his friend Naren, who complains: 'For twenty years [the banjo-poet] and his hundred imitators ... who write of India by his inspiration, have abused us and insulted us most deeply.'[3] If this suggests little scope for seeing Kipling as anything other than a whipping boy for later Indian writers in English, the same apparently holds true for literature in indigenous languages. According to a recent biography of the most celebrated such writer, Rabindranath Tagore's work in the early 1900s was in part a reaction against 'the effusions of imperial poets like Rudyard Kipling'.[4] After winning the 1913 Nobel Prize, Tagore was furious at being described as 'India's Kipling'. He dismissed *Kim*, which he read in 1902, as exemplifying 'western exaggeration' about India.[5] *Gora* (1910) – translated from Bengali into English in the same year as *A Passage to India* (1924) – is a specific riposte to *Kim*, which anticipates the argument of Forster's novel that Britain had lost the moral authority to rule India.

The same pattern of disavowal is observable in the interwar period. Nationalist writers like Mulk Raj Anand could be extremely disobliging about Kipling. Implicated in disturbances preceding the Amritsar massacre in 1919, for which, Anand's memoir *Conversations in Bloomsbury* records, he received 'seven stripes of the cane [which] made me hate British rule',[6] he was subsequently jailed for agitation on behalf of Gandhi. On release, Anand came to England in 1925 to continue his education, becoming friends with the Bloomsbury set, many of whom were, of course, deeply suspicious of Kipling. Little wonder that Anand should echo their hostility; thus he recalls that the relationship which he and fellow exiles enjoyed with Bloomsbury 'compensated us for Rudyard Kipling's contempt for the "lesser breeds"'.[7] With those sympathetic to Kipling, notably Bonamy Dobrée and T. S. Eliot, Anand sometimes had heated exchanges, and he took the latter's 'siding with Kipling as an insult'.[8] Echoing Tagore, Anand asserted that 'Kipling's writings seemed fantastic but small-minded' and he dismissed *Kim* as 'a fairy tale glorifying ... a fantasy boy'.[9]

Such attitudes persist into more recent times. Thus Timeri Murari's novels, *The Imperial Agent* (1987) and *The Last Victory* (1988), follow Kim's career well beyond the confines of Kipling's text, both temporally and geographically. While producing Anglo-Indian characters of some complexity and providing an intermittent critique of elements of conventional nationalist mythography (for example, its characteristic masculinism), the anti-colonial politics of Murari's texts are unequivocal. British rule is repeatedly represented as unjust, humiliating to every class of Indian and too quick to rely on violence, even when not obviously threatened. Murari has commented: 'I've always thought, even when reading him as a child, that Kipling was colonial and a racist.'[10] Consequently, his Creighton plays a far more important role than Kipling's as a ruthless and reactionary political manipulator, not least of Kim, and it is he who gives General Dyer the green light for the Amritsar massacre. Little wonder that Murari's Kim, in later life married to an Indian and a father, becomes progressively disillusioned with British rule and throws in his lot with Gandhi, before being killed in the Jallianwala Bagh.

In Shashi Tharoor's *The Great Indian Novel* (1989) – a much-praised, Rushdie-esque national comic-epic tracing twentieth-century Indian history – Kipling appears in a double guise, each facet being equally negative. In one incarnation, he represents the western scholarship decried in Said's *Orientalism*.[11] Professor Kipling's grounding in a supposedly humanist tradition of research does not inhibit his articulation of the most degrading stereotypes about Indians. His other avatar is Colonel Rudyard who, like General Dyer, orchestrates a bloody attack on civilian protestors. Presenting 'Kipling' in this double guise, Tharoor appears to corroborate *Orientalism*'s

arguments about the intimate and reciprocal relationship between representation, knowledge and power in the service of colonialism. Another dig at
Kipling is evident in Tharoor's choice of name for his principal protagonist, the Gandhi-esque leader who succeeds in winning Indian independence.
Naming him Ganga, Tharoor alludes pointedly to the figure of Gunga Din
from *Barrack-Room Ballads*, Kipling's paradigmatically loyal servant of the
raj, who is now appropriated in the service of quite different ideologies

More recently still, Amit Chaudhuri's review of Harry Ricketts's biog-
raphy of Kipling further cautions against any assumption that Kipling has
been fully rehabilitated in contemporary Indian letters. Author of a number
of works which have propelled him to the forefront of the post-*Midnight's
Children* generation of diasporic Indian novelists, Chaudhuri insists that
Kipling 'was a spokesman for a particularly unpleasant racial theory'.[12]
Like many previous commentators, and more specifically Bengali observers,
Chaudhuri deplores Kipling's caricatures of western-educated Indians, seeing them as indicative of his forebear's wilful failure to recognise India's
incipient modernity. Indeed, in his supposedly strident opposition to its
development, Chaudhuri presents Kipling as an 'often deranged racial
supremacist'.[13]

Such voices cannot be ignored, for they include some of the most illustrious figures in modern Indian literature. Nonetheless, a large measure of
indebtedness to Kipling is evident even among those most hostile towards
him. Like Ghosh's *The Prince of Destiny*, Tagore's *Gora* appropriates many
of *Kim*'s themes and tropes to challenge Kipling's political vision as well
as what are deemed to be his general cultural misconceptions about India.
Meanwhile, Anand acknowledges: 'I am going to rewrite Kipling's *Kim* ...
from the opposite point of view.'[14] More recently, Murari confesses: 'I did
certainly use *Kim* for my own purposes – both as a riposte and as a template
to work off in a very revisionary way. By taking on Kim as the central figure of my text, I wanted to finally turn him against his creator.'[15] Without
Kipling to kick against, or 'write back' to,[16] one might argue, modern Indian
literature might have developed quite differently and his work has consequently shaped even nationalist writing to a considerable degree.

However, attitudes towards Kipling of a more ostensibly positive nature
are widely pervasive among later Indian writers. Independence seems to
have been instrumental in generating the revaluation. As Nirad Chaudhuri
argued in 1957, 'the disappearance of British rule has emancipated some, if
not all, of us from the ... inhibition against Kipling'.[17] Indeed, he went on: 'It
is the easiest thing to wash out the free acid of Kiplingian politics from his
finished goods.'[18] Perhaps the earliest corroboration of Chaudhuri's claim is
G. V. Desani's *All About H. Hatterr* (1948), which gives the clearest signs of

its debts when the eponymous narrator visits a lending library: 'I happen to pick up R. Kipling's autobiographical *Kim* ... Dam' true to *Life*, if anything is!'[19] *Kim* is unquestionably the principal template for Desani's comic-epic description of the rites of passage of his youthful, racially mixed, culturally hybrid protagonist who also battles to establish his relation to the nation and his own truth system amid the clamorous claims of competing political and religious creeds. If Desani largely ignores the text's imperial politics to focus on other aspects of *Kim*, the further rehabilitation of Kipling conversely owes something to a growing recognition that Kipling's politics were in fact more nuanced and contradictory than was generally admitted earlier in the century. Thus Salman Rushdie emphasises the psychological and ideological conflicts in Kipling's writing, so that of 'On the City Wall' (*Soldiers Three*), for example, he can suggest persuasively that 'the Indian Kipling manages to subvert what the English Kipling takes to be the meaning of the tale'.[20]

Of all Kipling's writings, *Kim* has perhaps proved most enabling for later authors. Several factors underlie its continuing appeal. The first is that, as Parama Roy argues, one of Kipling's preoccupations 'is to produce the idea of the nation and of the citizen'.[21] Whereas Kipling seeks 'to make the Anglo-Indian perform as first citizen'[22] – a trajectory which no Indian author is, understandably, prepared to follow – he also constitutes a crucial precedent in his concern with the idea of India as a single entity, defined by clear boundaries (discursive and material), sustained by the common obligations it demands of its subjects, whoever they are and wherever they reside. Further, Kipling provides a model for subsequent authors in terms of the form of his text, which provides the potential terms of a nationalist allegory. The use of the Bildungsroman and quest narrative to allegorise the emergence towards independence and autonomy of its protagonist is a common trope in Indian literature after Kipling. Thus while writers like Tagore, Rushdie or Murari contest his political vision, time and again they use the structure of the maturing Kim's journey across the subcontinent as a framework on which to hang sometimes very different elaborations of the nation, citizenship and appropriate economies of power.

Perhaps the single most productive template which Kipling provides for later writers is *Kim*'s negotiations with the multicultural nature of India and the implications of its ethnic, religious and cultural diversity for national identity and belonging. Many more recent Indian writers echo Kipling's recognition of the challenge of integrating sometimes highly disparate social constituencies within a single coherent national community and polity (signified by the octopus-like trope of the 'Great Game'). Crucially, while deeply preoccupied by spiritual issues, *Kim* insists on the equality of the many faiths which make up India, anticipating the future consolidation of independent India as a theoretically secular state. In more recent decades, Kipling proves particularly useful for those wishing to contest the increasing influence of narrow and homogenising conceptions of Indian identity. Thus he speaks to literary representatives of several constituencies anxious about their place or apparent lack of it within the independent, Hindu-dominated, nation. This is in fact evident even among those hostile to Kipling, such as Murari, who is preoccupied by the marginalisation of South India's role in the independence struggle in dominant (North Indian) versions of nationalist historiography. It is partly in the service of extending the reader's awareness of the role of areas like Tamil Nadu within the history of modern India. In doing this, there is an implicit acknowledgement that while Kipling rarely sets his fiction much further south than central India, nonetheless he offers in principle a genuinely pan-Indian vision of the nation, recognising all the regions and cultures of India Kim travels through as equally constituent weaves of the same fabric.

In a further twist to this theme, Nirad Chaudhuri has anathematised the failure of dominant (Hindu) nationalist historiography to recognise the crucial importance of the contributions made by non-Hindu constituencies to modern India.[23] Consonant with these arguments, from a critic he much admires, Salman Rushdie has used Kipling to broach issues surrounding the legacy of British rule, for better and worse. Taking up *Kim*'s trope of 'pedigree', *Midnight's Children* (1981) insists in a sometimes ironic but essentially affirmative way on the constitutive part played by the Methwold family in the emergence of modern Bombay (now Mumbai). In the ambiguities surrounding Saleem Sinai's paternity, Rushdie suggests that the contribution to modern India of its British past cannot be wished away. A less optimistic vision of this legacy is provided by *Shame* (1983) which to some extent attributes the travails of modern Pakistan to the influence of colonial history. Omar Shakil, the anti-hero, is of mixed race and his trajectory involves elements of parody of *The Jungle Books*. Early on, he is described as resembling a 'wolf-child'; although the narrator disavows the appropriateness of seeing Omar as 'the mowgli, the junglee boy',[24] this is perhaps primarily because of the protagonist's flagrant violation of 'the law', both divine and human. If this is partly a function of being caught between two worlds in the way Mowgli sometimes is, the negative consequences of the behaviour he represents are embodied in Sufiya Zenobia whose destructiveness later becomes identified, in another echo of Kipling's text, with the panther of Bagheeragali. Either way, Rushdie insists that the contribution of the British cannot be ignored in the manner of certain kinds of Hindu supremacist discourse in particular.

The British, of course, left behind not just discursive legacies and infrastructure but significant numbers of mixed-race subjects. I. Allan Sealy's
The Trotter-Nama (1988) draws on Kipling in seeking to admit to national
belonging a constituency often regarded with suspicion in nationalist mythography. Kipling makes an appearance in the text as the author of a peevish
newspaper article on 'half-castes', which provokes Alex Alexander-Trotter
to threaten the commissioning editor with a horse-whip; and the narrator
Eugene clearly regards 'His Chance in Life' (*Plain Tales from the Hills*) as
a slight on those of mixed race like himself. Nonetheless, Kipling provides
Sealy with some crucial templates. Perhaps the most notable of the early
Trotters is Mik, whose name evokes not only Kipling's protagonist (and his
part-Irish provenance?), but the idea of 'mix'. This often highly poignant
'Raj novel gone wrong'[25] clearly turns to *Kim* to forward its exploration of
the conflict of loyalties generated by the 'in-between' position of Eurasians
as 'the hyphen in Anglo-India'.[26] Thus after being dismissed by his Maratha
masters, Mik reluctantly goes over to the British and has to renegotiate
his sense of both himself and India. In following his subsequent trajectory,
The Trotter-Nama invokes the sometimes tortured questing after identity of
Kipling's protagonist. Like *Kim*, *The Trotter-Nama*'s ending is unresolved,
with Mik's contemporary descendant Eugene dislocated, both physically
and psychically, allegorising the deeply uncertain future course of his community within India a generation after independence.

The title of Sealy's text further represents a symbolic attempt to weave
together the history of the Eurasians and India with Islamic culture, the
nama being an epic narrative form imported by the Mughals from Persia.
Much the most substantial minority in India historically, Muslims like
Mahbub Ali play a crucial role in Kim's development and occupy a pivotal
place in Kipling's vision of the *raj*. Their right to belong as equal citizens
in post-partition, independent India has, however, come under increasing
pressure with the rise of the Hindu Right. A Kiplingesque insistence on
their 'Indianness' is asserted with particular force not just by Sealy, but by
Rushdie's *Midnight's Children*, where the Kim-like central protagonist is a
Kashmiri of Muslim descent.[27] Rushdie thereby engages with both the predicament of the larger Indian Muslim constituency and the liminal nature
of Kashmiri identity more specifically, as something increasingly threatened by India's and Pakistan's claims to the territory. While Rushdie's text
supports the Nehruvian ideal of a secular Indian state, Saleem's Muslim
identity asserts itself throughout the text in ways which are represented as
entirely legitimate. One notable example is the narration of the 1965 India–
Pakistan war (over Kashmir) which Saleem interprets specifically as a *jihad*
against him, punishment for his failure to maintain ritual purity. In making

a Muslim his main protagonist, Rushdie insists on the centrality of Islam to contemporary Indian identity and the contribution of its adherents within the multicultural weave of the nation. Rushdie's secularism has famously led him into conflict with Islamists. Nonetheless, his respect for the cultural, if not theological, legacies of Islamic culture in India is clear in novels from *Midnight's Children* through *The Moor's Last Sigh* (1995) to *Shalimar the Clown* (2005).

Another important example of the use of Kipling in contemporary Indian writing to advocate multicultural models of the nation is Arundhati Roy's *The God of Small Things* (1997). Set predominantly in the Syrian Christian community of Kerala, the text in part anatomises the beleaguered position of confessional and ethnic minorities in an era when Hindu revivalism is entering a new phase of intensity, even in traditionally Communist-ruled areas. There are several clear echoes of Kipling. For example, the failed relationship between Baby Kochamma and Father Mulligan invokes 'Lispeth' (*Plain Tales from the Hills*) with a similarly biting critique of the ethnocentrism of modern western missionaries. The title of the text alludes to Kipling's 'God of Things as They Are' ('When Earth's Last Picture is Painted') and Ammu spends considerable time reading *The Jungle Books* to her children. However, Roy's critique of the predicament of the Christian minority in India extends to a much broader issue: the place of caste in contemporary Indian society. It is the inflexible 'law' of custom which prohibits the cross-caste relationship between Ammu and Velutha. But Roy emphasises that this is a human law, the actual inhumanity of which is in strong contrast to the 'natural' law of Mowgli's jungle. The latter is also, by contrast, incumbent on *all* the denizens of the jungle *equally*, rather than being used to promote unjust and discriminatory hierarchies.

Many such conflicts surrounding cultural and national (self-)identification are echoed in the experiences of diasporic Indians, who also find in Kipling a productive precedent for their exploration. Thus for Rushdie, one might infer, Kipling constitutes the first serious exploration in literature of a recognisably modern diasporic sensibility. For example, *The Moor's Last Sigh* reproduces verbatim almost a whole page of 'On the City Wall', on which Rushdie focused his 1990 essay on Kipling.[28] While certainly used in part to illuminate the obduracy of colonial government towards the challenge of nationalism in the 1930s, Rushdie balances this with a sympathetic discussion between one colonial official and his nationalist interlocutor about 'Kipling's almost schizophrenic early stories of the Indiannesses and Englishnesses that struggled within him'.[29] To this extent, it is hard to agree with Michael Gorra that 'Kipling's belief in both an essential India and an essential England made him – like most servants of the Raj – contemptuous of ... cultural hybrids'.[30] Even Amit Chaudhuri (contradicting his primary emphasis on Kipling's essentialising and dichotomising vision) concedes that *Kim* 'tells us casually that colonial India was a comedy of inversions and unstable identities'.[31] In light of such comments, Kim's endless self-questioning about his identity and adoption of multiple personae can be understood as a symptom of Kipling's sympathetic appreciation of some 'in-between' cultural positions, at least, with Kim fully assimilated to neither his culture of origin nor his culture of destination. *Kim*'s performative model of identity, above all, helps to inspire a range of diasporic Indian writers, from G. V. Desani to Hari Kunzru. Many such figures find in Kipling's work a template for their own conceptions of the fluidity, decentredness and multiply determined nature of identity, especially when subjects are 'translated' in diaspora.

One striking example of the use of Kipling in this regard is *The Buddha of Suburbia*, Hanif Kureishi's Bildungsroman set in contemporary south London. Several critics have remarked on the affinities between it and *Midnight's Children*,[32] not least among which is their re-articulation of elements of *Kim*. Karim, the protagonist of Kureishi's novel, whose very name echoes that of Kipling's hero, acts as a reluctant *chela* to his father, the eponymous 'Buddha'. Like the Lama, Haroon is a figure of spiritual authority – at least to his circle of white friends – and is often helpless in the face of the baffling modern world. Like Kim, Karim is a spy on a number of levels, from his sexual voyeurism to his infiltration of Pyke's house on behalf of Terry's radical set. While, as with Sealy's *The Trotter-Nama*, there are certainly elements of parody of *Kim*, *The Buddha* also takes many of its forerunner's interests entirely seriously in the context of diaspora. The mixed-race Karim faces similar dilemmas to many of the Trotters and Kim in respect of his divided cultural identities and loyalties. In seeking to resolve their contradictory claims, Karim restlessly reinvents himself, a process symbolised in his endless renewing of his wardrobe (recalling Kim's multiple disguises), figuring difficulties of (self-)identification no less pressing than in *Kim*.

In the *Buddha*, however, perhaps the principal intertext is *The Jungle Books*, the social and moral geographies of which are cunningly mapped onto contemporary London. This is represented as a dangerous jungle in which the youthful narrator Karim must survive if he is to successfully mature. The 'fringe' production of *The Jungle Books* which launches Karim as an actor is used not, as one might expect, to attack Kipling but primarily to expose the often coercive 'benevolence' of white radicals. In attempting to demarcate a space for the ethnic 'Other' to represent him/herself they are represented as often only re-consigning that 'Other' in the straight-jacket of an 'authentic' identity defined by the dominant. To this extent, the criticisms which Haroon and Jamila make of Karim's role in the production are clearly represented as misdirected.

Kureishi's use of Kipling to negotiate a way between the competing demands of culture of origin and host nation is taken up in Michael Ondaatje's *The English Patient* (1992), which cites whole chunks of *Kim*. As with *The Trotter-Nama* and *The Buddha*, one obvious parallel concerns the question of 'pedigree' (the English Patient's identity is as elusive as Kim's). Kip, the protagonist whose name evokes Kipling's, as well as Kim's, initially venerates the English patient as a Lama-figure, seeing him as a 'wise old teacher', in what Hana describes as 'a reversal of *Kim*'.[33] Elsewhere, in another reversal, Hana sees herself as playing the role of Kim to Kip's Creighton. Other links include the theme of spying, the motif of 'mapping' and several verbal echoes: for example, Almasy has been 'burned black',[34] the exact description of Kim at the outset of Kipling's text. Kim's dilemmas over his 'hybridity' are rearticulated in the predicament of the Indian bomb-disposal expert Kip, who has initially thoroughly assimilated himself to 'Englishness' through contact with Lord Suffolk. As with Kureishi and others, Ondaatje undoubtedly provides elements of a critique of Kipling's vision. For example, it is perhaps no coincidence that Kip is a Sikh, and as such provides a counter-discursive perspective on the loyalist veteran whom Kim meets early on his travels.

However, Kip's trajectory does not amount to an uncomplicated espousal of anti-colonial nationalism or a fetishisation of his culture of origin as something pure or immemorial. Ondaatje's critique of nationalism is emphatic, with various kinds of *transnational* communities, from the desert explorers to the inhabitants of the villa, being privileged over those who root themselves in singularising models of national identity. For all his sometimes biting critique of 'western' values, it is significant that Kip leaves behind the photo of his nationalist brother, in an apparent act of disavowal, when he quits the villa. Neither 'western' values nor 'Third World' cultural nationalism, one infers, are affirmed. Indeed, Kip's final destination is unclear; he has gone back somewhere in the subcontinent, certainly, but whether to the Punjab or even to which nation state, is never specified. Fittingly, for a novel which also invokes Melville's *Pierre: or, the Ambiguities*, the cultural/political meanings of *The English Patient* and especially of its ending are as ambivalent in their own way as *Kim*'s.

A further aspect of the turn to Kipling in diasporic Indian writing is the desire to provide a critique of tendencies to homogeneity and essentialism in host cultures, notably Britain. Thus Kureishi's *The Buddha* adapts the virtues of its protagonist's Kim-like hybridity to the reconceptualisation

of Britain itself, famously attempting to expand conventional defini-
tions of 'Englishness' by adumbrating 'a new [more inclusive] breed' of
Englishman.[35] Perhaps the most effective example in this regard, however, is
The Impressionist (2002), by Hari Kunzru – like Kureishi, British-born and
of mixed race. The novel follows the (mis)fortunes of Pran Nath, the orphan
son of an English colonial officer and Indian woman, through a succession
of changes of identity, in India, England and Africa, during the early decades
of the twentieth century. The radical indeterminacy of the protagonist's origins haunt him throughout his life as he transforms himself, through his 'talent for mimicry',[36] from adoptive son of a Brahmin who uses the Allahabad
Pioneer to promote his traditionalist views, to child sex-slave, to Bombay
street tough and thence progressively into an epitome of 'Englishness'. So
convincing is this last 'impersonation' that, to his mortification, his bohe-
mian lover at Oxford jilts him in favour of a more 'exotic' Black American.

Often hilarious and replete with at times superb pastiches of a variety of
metropolitan writings about empire, from Haggard to Evelyn Waugh, J.G.
Farrell and William Boyd, Kunzru comments that 'my book has ended up
being in dialogue with a really major strand of British literary writing.'[37]
The dialogic nature of Kunzru's relations with this tradition is nowhere
more clear than in his engagement with *Kim*, which provides the text's epigraph and many of its themes. For example, 'Bridgeman', as he later (significantly) becomes, teams up with an anthropological expedition which is
partly engaged by the Colonial Office in mapping an area of Africa disputed
with another European power. The ending of the text is as open as Kim's
or *The English Patient*'s, with 'Bridgeman' fleeing into the Sahara, his final
destination and cultural identity equally unclear as he seeks to escape the
overdeterminations of traditional conceptions of 'Britishness' and, by extension, of national belonging more generally.

Sometimes subtending the use of Kipling among writers in the subcontinent and diaspora alike is the theme of the conflict between (indigenous) tradition and (western) modernity. If *Kim* and *The Jungle Books* have
thus far proved the most important intertexts in terms of Kipling's relationship with modern Indian writing, Kamala Markandaya's *The Coffer
Dams* (1969) provides something refreshingly different in this regard. The
novel engages substantially with one of Kipling's most important short
stories, 'The Bridge-Builders' (*The Day's Work*), as well as 'In Flood Time'
(*Soldiers Three*) and 'The Undertakers' (*The Jungle Books*), in its exploration of the conflict between tradition and modernity in independent India.
Markandaya's novel certainly offers a biting critique of the ethnocentric
attitudes of some of the expatriate workers on the dam, which are shown to
have their roots in colonial history; and it also provides an implicit critique

of Kipling's characteristic masculinism (which perhaps helps to explain why he has been taken up by more male Indian writers than female ones). But such elements do not efface the extent to which Kipling's tale provides an enabling precedent. Markandaya repeats Kipling's triangular relationship between Findlayson, Hitchcock and Peroo in that between Clinton, Mackendrick and Bashiam. Bashiam is a tragic reworking of Peroo – another crane specialist who deifies machinery. Just as Findlayson suffers grievously at the hands of an indifferent colonial administration, so the bureaucracy of independent India increasingly frustrates Markandaya's bridge-builders. Interestingly, her representation of Helen Clinton and Bashiam as the prime 'bridge-builders' between West and East is possibly less radical in its implications than Kipling's privileging of Peroo as the figure who most fully represents the process of cross-cultural synthesis. In this respect he is clearly superior to Findlayson, whose materialist philosophy and position within the imperial hierarchy mean that the engineer is unable to appreciate fully his subordinate's contribution to the project or the challenge which this represents to conventional colonialist hierarchies and dichotomies (compare Clinton's similar limitations vis-à-vis Bashiam).

Finally, Kipling has provided important leads in terms of the styles of later Indian writing. Among those hostile to Kipling, Amit Chaudhuri is prepared to concede that 'Kipling is a very great writer'[38] without at any point suggesting that, in this guise, he might have anything to offer authors like himself (partly, perhaps, because Chaudhuri positions himself in relation to a tradition quite different to that represented by admirers of Kipling such as Rushdie).[39] However, it is clear that Kipling's work provides stylistic templates for many others. Nirad Chaudhuri has commented astutely on *Kim*'s 'combination of romance and actuality'.[40] Certainly its generic flexibility anticipates precisely the rapid transpositions from realism to fantasy typical of so much recent South Asian literature, especially of the diaspora. While Kipling cannot be described strictly as 'a magic realist', there is nonetheless a strong sense of the 'marvellousness of the real' and its associated epistemological instability in *Kim*, as events in Lurgan's shop, for example, suggest. Kipling's orality provides another template. *Kim*'s narrative voice (compare that of *The Jungle Books* and *Just So Stories*) often draws on the conventions of orature, and Kim – like many of his avatars – spends considerable time telling, or listening to, stories. From Desani to Rushdie and Roy, South Asian fiction is often marked by a similar attachment to oral tradition. The picaresque elements of *Kim* have proved equally appealing to recent South Asian writers, with digressive quest plots characterising texts as diverse as *Hatterr*, *Midnight's Children* and *Trotter-Nama*. Kipling's linguistic experimentation is equally prophetic. The variety of *Kim*'s narrative register, which combines diction and syntactic patterns from standard and non-standard Englishes as well as indigenous Indian tongues, anticipates what Rushdie calls the 'chutnification' of register and languages characteristic of many of his contemporaries. Indeed, Feroza Jussawalla suggests that Kipling employs a 'code-mixed, code-switched Hindi-English that linguists today identify as Indian English'.[41] Thus Anand's incorporation of Punjabi diction and syntax, and Roy's of Malayalam, are alike anticipated in Kipling's work. A further precedent lies in Kipling's amalgamation of western and non-western narrative traditions (as well as of 'high' and 'popular' narrative forms). In *Kim*, the latter include *The Thousand and One Nights*, the Buddhist *Jataka* cycle and *The Mahabharata*. The same is true of *Hatterr*, *Midnight's Children*, *The Trotter-Nama* and *The Buddha*.[42] Even a figure hostile to Kipling such as Murari follows his forerunner's example in weaving his own Kim-narrative together with elements of traditional narrative, notably the *Ramayana*.

Clearly, one must guard against the temptation to represent Indian writing as paradigmatic of the many varieties of postcolonial literature, and thereby to generalise too readily about Kipling's relationship to postcolonialism as a whole. However, it is worth noting other positive responses to him from a variety of figures outside South Asia, including even some whose politics have at times been redoubtably anti-colonial. The 'Black Marxist' C. L. R. James adapted one of Kipling's most famously disobliging questions to his domestic British audience as an epigraph to his genre-breaking 'cricketing autobiography', *Beyond A Boundary*: '*What do they know of cricket who only cricket know?*'[43] At an age when he already 'carried within [him] the seeds of revolt', James won two volumes of Kipling's stories as a school prize: 'One vacation I picked them up and for two years they [were] my perpetual companions.'[44] Edward Said, the founding figure in Postcolonial Studies, recalls of his childhood in Egypt: 'My mother didn't like what she took to be the militarization of my spirit; having read about Mowgli, Kaa, Akela, and even Rikki-tikki-tavi with me, she couldn't accept the hierarchies and authorities imposed on her boy by the English [school-masters in Cairo].'[45] Aung San Suu Kyi, the focus of opposition to the junta in Myanmar, and daughter of one of the figures who led the country to independence from Britain, has echoed Hilda Said's association of Kipling with the principle of freedom. She has always loved *Kim*, in particular, to the point of naming one son after Kipling's hero. Further, she insists that 'the poem ['If–'] that in England is often dismissed as the epitome of imperialist bombast is a great poem for dissidents'.[46]

All this indicates that there has always been sufficient complexity within Kipling's work, and sufficient distance between the views of Kipling the man and what his writing expresses, for it to be no real surprise that he has been taken up in later postcolonial writing in the productive ways identified above. The irony for many western readers, perhaps especially left-liberals, ironically, is that it is only with the advent of a more nuanced understanding of postcolonialism as a process of negotiation as well as contestation that this is becoming fully apparent. Such a constituency has much to learn from the attitude exemplified in *The English Patient*. In advising Hana to 'read Kipling slowly', advice which leads her to a greater appreciation of 'its delicate and holy sentences',[47] Almasy hints at depths in the 'laureate of empire' which many other postcolonial writers have also rightly insisted on.

Notes

1 For discussions of the varied and changing meanings of 'postcolonialism', see my *Postcolonial Theory: Contexts, Practices, Politics* (London: Verso, 1997).

2 See, for example, Gayatri C. Spivak, 'Imperialism and Sexual Difference' (1986), in Robert Con Davis and Ronald Schleifer (eds.), *Contemporary Literary Criticism: Literary and Cultural Studies* (2nd edn; Harlow: Longman, 1989), pp. 522–5; Fawzia Afzal-Khan, *Cultural Imperialism and the Indo-British Novel: Genre and Ideology in R. K. Narayan, Anita Desai, Kamala Markandaya, and Salman Rushdie* (Philadelphia: Penn State University Press, 1993), p. 129; and K. D. Verma, *The Indian Imagination: Critical Essays on Indian Writing in English* (Basingstoke: Palgrave, 2000), p. 24.

3 S. K. Ghosh, *The Prince of Destiny: The New Krishna* (London: Rebman, 1909), p. 560.

4 Krishna Dutta and Andrew Robinson, *Rabindranath Tagore: The Myriad-Minded Man* (London: Bloomsbury, 1995), p. 129.

5 *Ibid.*, p. 142.

6 Mulk Raj Anand, *Conversations in Bloomsbury* (New Delhi: Arnold-Heinemann, 1981), p. 39.

7 *Ibid.*, p. 21.

8 *Ibid.*, p. 28.

9 *Ibid.*, p. 6.

10 E-mail from Murari to the author, February 2002.

11 Edward W. Said, *Orientalism* (London: Routledge and Kegan Paul, 1978).

12 Amit Chaudhuri, 'A Feather! A Very Feather Upon the Face!', *London Review of Books*, 22:1 (6 January 2000), p. 21.

13 *Ibid.*, p. 24.

14 Anand, *Conversations in Bloomsbury*, p. 52.

15 E-mail from Murari to the author, February 2002.

16 See Bill Ashcroft, Gareth Griffiths and Helen Tiffin, *The Empire Writes Back: Theory and Practice in Post-Colonial Literatures* (London: Routledge, 1989).

17 Nirad C. Chaudhuri, 'The Finest Story About India – in English', *Encounter*, 8:4 (April 1957), p. 47.

18 *Ibid.*, p. 48.

19 G. V. Desani, *All About H. Hatterr* (1948; New Delhi: Arnold-Heinemann, 1985), p. 199.

20 Salman Rushdie, *Imaginary Homelands: Essays and Criticism, 1981–1991* (1991; London: Penguin, 1992), p. 78.

21 Parama Roy, *Indian Traffic: Identities in Question in Colonial and Postcolonial India* (London: University of California Press, 1998), p. 79.

22 *Ibid.*, p. 86.

23 Nirad C. Chaudhuri, *The Autobiography of an Unknown Indian* (1951; London: Picador, 1999), pp. 465ff.

24 Salman Rushdie, *Shame* (New York: Knopf, 1983), p. 28.

25 I. Allan Sealy, *The Trotter-Nama* (1988; New Delhi: India Ink, 1999), p. 560.

26 *Ibid.*, p. 547.

27 On the manifold links between *Kim* and *Midnight's Children* see, for example, Richard Cronin, 'The Indian English Novel: *Kim* and *Midnight's Children*', *Modern Fiction Studies*, 33:2 (1987), pp. 201–13; Michael Gorra, 'Rudyard Kipling to Salman Rushdie: Imperialism to Postcolonialism', in John Richetti *et al.* (eds.), *The Columbia History of the British Novel* (New York: Columbia University Press, 1994), pp. 631–57.

28 Salman Rushdie, *The Moor's Last Sigh* (1995; London: Vintage, 1996), pp. 39–40.

29 *Ibid.*, p. 39.

30 Gorra, 'Rudyard Kipling to Salman Rushdie', pp. 633–4.

31 Amit Chaudhuri, 'A Feather!', p. 23.

32 For further discussion, see my *Hanif Kureishi* (Manchester University Press, 2001), pp. 28, 124–9.

33 Michael Ondaatje, *The English Patient* (1992; London: Picador, 1993), p. 111.

34 *Ibid.*, p. 85.

35 Hanif Kureishi, *The Buddha of Suburbia* (London: Faber and Faber, 1990), p. 3.

36 Hari Kunzru, *The Impressionist* (London: Hamish Hamilton, 2002), p. 28.

37 Hari Kunzru on www.penguin.co.uk/static/packages/articles/booksfor2002.html

38 Amit Chaudhuri, 'A Feather!', p. 21

39 See Amit Chaudhuri, Introduction to *The Picador Book of Modern Indian Literature* (London: Picador, 2001), pp. xv–xxxiv.

40 Nirad C. Chaudhuri, 'The Finest Story About India', p. 50.

41 Feroza Jussawalla, '(Re)reading *Kim*: Defining Kipling's Masterpiece as Postcolonial', *Journal of Commonwealth and Postcolonial Studies*, 5:2 (Fall 1998), pp. 115–16.

42 For more detailed discussion of Kipling's style in all these regards see my *Writing India: British Representations of India, 1757–1990* (Manchester University Press, 1996), pp. 125ff.

43 C. L. R. James, *Beyond A Boundary* (1963; London: Serpent's Tail, 1994), p. ix.

44 *Ibid.*, p. 23.

45 Edward Said, *Out of Place: A Memoir* (1999; London: Granta, 2000), p. 48.

46 Timothy Garton Ash, 'Beauty and the Beast', *The Guardian* (27 March 2001), G2, 2.

47 Ondaatje, *The English Patient*, p. 94.

12

MONICA TURCI

Kipling and the visual: illustrations and adaptations

Many nineteenth-century writers have entered our visual age, one dominated by cinema and television; a number have managed to survive; only a few have positively thrived. Rudyard Kipling is in the latter group. The popularity of cinematic adaptations of his work has drawn fresh attention to his texts, reworking them within new cultural, historical and political contexts. Work in film studies has informed the closely related field that addresses the relationship between word and image; it can aid the exploration of illustrated editions of Kipling.[1]

While film adaptations of Kipling began to be made in the 1910s, Kipling's works often appeared illustrated when they were first published. For the first Macmillan edition of Kipling's works published between 1894 and 1902, professional illustrators were commissioned including I. W. Taber, who worked on *'Captains Courageous'* (1896), and H. A. Millar, who illustrated *Puck of Pook's Hill* (1906) and *Rewards and Fairies* (1910). The illustration of this edition was not left to professional illustrators alone, however. Kipling's father, John Lockwood Kipling, co-illustrated *The Jungle Book* (1894) and was the sole illustrator of *The Second Jungle Book* (1895) and *Kim* (1901), while Kipling himself provided images for the *Just So Stories*(1902).[2]

All illustrations in the Macmillan edition were short-lived, with the sole exception of those for the *Just So Stories*.[3] In the 1950s Macmillan replaced Lockwood's illustrations for *The Jungle Books* and *Kim* with images by Stuart Tresilian. Though popular in their time, these too proved ephemeral; recent editions have often been wholly devoid of images. The demise of illustrations in Kipling's books coincided with – and perhaps was gradually brought about by – film adaptations. Moving images appealed more than static illustrations, colour more than black-and-white. Clearly, publishers no longer saw images as adding to the commercial value or demand for their books.

For some, illustrations are superfluous decorations that adulterate the text. Likewise, early commentators on film adaptations saw them as artistically inferior 'translations' that bore little resemblance to the originals. This chapter is aligned with work that questions such views. The visual was an important aspect of Kipling's writing and has long played a part in how he has been read and understood. Here attention will focus on the illustrations by Lockwood and Rudyard Kipling for *The Jungle Books*, *Kim* and *Just So Stories*, and on film adaptations of *Gunga Din* (1939), two versions of *The Jungle Book* (1942 and 1967) and *The Man Who Would Be King* (1975).

Illustrations

Rudyard and Lockwood Kipling responded to the revival of the illustrated book at the end of the nineteenth century, a period Janzen Lorraine Kooistra has described as 'a "golden age" of illustration second only to the illustrious [eighteen] sixties'. Her work challenges the assumption that illustrations are of limited importance.[4] Lockwood's images are visual commentaries that have oriented readers' interpretations as well as accomplished works of art in their own right. Image and text are inextricably connected in Kipling's illustrations for his *Just So Stories*. Though the *Just So Stories* was the only book Kipling himself illustrated, texts from throughout his career show him exploring the relationship between word and image.

Lockwood Kipling's approach to book illustration can be compared with that of William Morris, Walter Crane and the Arts and Crafts Movement. Lockwood's biographer, Arthur A. Ankers, has seen him as an 'art work-man', operating at the interface of the decorative arts, architecture and sculpture.[5] Lockwood's intention, like Morris's when he was designing for his Kelmscott Press, was to transform the book into an object that was both useful and beautiful. While he was working on the illustrations for *Kim*, Kipling recalled Lockwood quoting from Robert Browning's 'Fra Lippo Lippi': 'If you get simple beauty and naught else, / You get about the best thing God invents.'[6] Lockwood was also influenced by oriental traditions of decorative design. In India, he not only taught architectural sculpture and design at the Bombay School of Art, but he also learned about Indian art and culture while acting as curator of the Art Museum in Lahore. Charles Allen has noted that his curatorial experience had a significant impact on his art. Developing an exceptional knowledge of Buddhist iconography, art and culture, Lockwood sought a synthesis of oriental and occidental traditions.[7]

These elements are in play in his illustrations for his son's texts. Several of his illustrations in *The Jungle Book* have a frame showing architectural motifs. The title page of 'Kaa's Hunting', for example, has a woodcut imitating a plaque with representations in relief; it depicts Kaa, Bagheera, Baloo and Mowgli (Figure 1).[8] The elaborately intricate design, with every inch of the woodblock filled, is reminiscent of the illustrations the Pre-Raphaelites

Figure 1 Title illustration by John Lockwood Kipling for 'Kaa's Hunting'. (Rudyard Kipling, *The Jungle Book* (London: Macmillan, 1902), p. 45.)

undertook for the Kelmscott Press, and also the work of Walter Crane. In *The Second Jungle Book* Lockwood's work exemplifies the expanded scope of illustration in the 1890s. As Kooistra has noted, this included not just illustrations, but also the 'binding, cover design, endpapers, title pages and page layout'.[9] Initial decorative letters with ornamental motifs appear at the start of each story, for example at the start of the 'Letting in the Jungle' chapter of *The Second Jungle Book* (Figure 2). Decorative title letters were used in Old English manuscripts and remained, for Crane, 'the primal element' for the decorative illustrator.[10] Lockwood was well aware of comparable traditions in other cultures. In his *Beast and Man in India* (1891) he wrote that 'it has long been a practice of Oriental penmen, who are often artists, to weave the fine forms of Persian letters into the outline of animals or birds'.[11]

Lockwood's illustrations, for all his commitment to an aesthetic idea of beauty as something sufficient in itself, are also in dialogue with the text and serve an important structural role in binding the narrative together. In *The Second Jungle Book* three of the decorative first letters depict Mowgli as he grows from child to man.[12] They help make the volume cohere around the figure of Mowgli, despite stories about him being interspersed with others. The focus on Mowgli's maturation that Lockwood establishes can be found in later film adaptations by Disney (1967) and Stephen Sommers (1994).

The illustrations for *Kim* consist of ten full-page photographic reproductions of terracotta plaques in low bas-relief inserted into the book as sepia plates. These show a selection of the most important characters set in a

Figure 2 Illustrated first letter 'Y' by John Lockwood Kipling at the beginning of 'Letting in the Jungle'. (Rudyard Kipling, *The Second Jungle Book* (London: Macmillan, 1903), p. 61.)

decorative landscape. As with the ornamental first letters in *The Second Jungle Book*, the style seeks to combine the western and the oriental; that is, the realistic representation of figures within a decorative context typical of Arts and Crafts illustrators on the one hand, and a flat and linear design reminiscent of oriental illustration on the other.[13]

Some have seen the relationship between text and image in these early illustrations for *Kim* as dissonant. For Rachel Fleming, the illustrations

Figure 3 'The Jat and his Sick Child' by John Lockwood Kipling. (Rudyard Kipling, *Kim* (London: Macmillan, 1901), p. 268.)

offer reactionary and racist views that contrast with those in the text. She notes that Lockwood's illustrations are strikingly similar to those found in colonial ethnographic studies, such as *The People of India* (1868) by John Forbes Watson and John Kayes. Illustrations such as 'The Jat and His Sick Child'[14] present 'the viewer with the appearance of Indian life as something to be observed and deciphered' rather than being inspired by characters in the novel (Figure 3).[15]

Others have seen illustrations and text in *Kim* as in a more harmonious relationship, indeed as transcending stereotypes to establish a picture of Indian life that is at once realistic and poetic. Janice Leoshko argues that text and image provide proof of Lockwood's detailed and deep understanding of Buddhist religion, art and influence on Indian life. Leoshko's argument focuses on the illustrations that portray the Lama, in particular the first and last. In that captioned 'The Lama' (*K* 21) he is shown with a pair of glasses perched on his head. The detail can be explained in relation to a Buddhist practice mentioned frequently in the novel: these are indeed the glasses that have been given him by the museum curator as part of the practice of 'gift-giving'. Leoshko notes that in Buddhism and also in the novel 'gift-giving' is 'a central concern … acquiring merit (punya) – but is also an acknowledgment of those who are spiritually special'.[16] The depiction of the cross-legged Lama in an illustration near the end captioned 'The End of the Search' (*K* 404) – Kim, just recovered from illness, reclines in the foreground – is seen by Leoshko as drawing directly on a sculpture of Buddha in the Lahore Museum mentioned at the beginning of the novel.[17]

Kipling follows his father in that his illustrations for the *Just So Stories* also engage with a broad range of western and oriental art. They are informed not only by Arts and Crafts but also by the illustrative work of art nouveau, which was in turn heavily influenced by Japanese woodblock prints. As Lisa Lewis has noted, Kipling's illustrations recall the work of a number of specific artists including Edward Burne-Jones (one of Kipling's uncles), Aubrey Beardsley and Katsushika Hokusai.[18] Lockwood clearly stimulated his son's interest in art and illustration. Elsie Bambridge, Kipling's daughter, remembered that Rudyard 'inherited a great deal of his own father's artistic ability and was often busy with pencil and paint-brush illuminating, for instance, his various copies of Horace's *Odes* with designs and pictures'.[19] Indeed, Jim Cheff includes Kipling, along with William Blake, William Makepeace Thackeray and Max Beerbohm, among those 'author-artists' whose 'combination of literary and illustrative skill gave readers a special insight into their thoughts and imaginings'.[20]

The illustrations for the *Just So Stories* – thirty-five drawings and thirty-three sketches – demonstrate the interrelatedness of the visual and the written in Kipling. Assumptions that the two are separate and have a hierarchical relationship are challenged in a number of ways: the narrative sees both as having the same origins, the use of decorative capital letters is playfully manipulated and the one is asked to do the work of the other.

The two central stories of the collection, 'How the First Letter was Written' and 'How the Alphabet was Made', show Taffy, a little girl of the Neolithic Tegumai tribe, developing the alphabet.[21] The stories depict, as Yin Liu suggests, the 'moment at the beginning of literacy when … image became text' according to the 'classic' or 'traditional' theory in which picture-writing, pictograms and ideograms are the precursors of writing and modern alphabetic systems. This theory was popularised in Kipling's time by Isaac Taylor in his influential study *The Alphabet* (1883).[22] Taffy invents a picture-writing that sees letters drawn as pictures in the first story, and then, in the story on the alphabet, associates those letters with a particular speech sound.

Letters as pictures provide one of the structuring leitmotifs of the collection. In the stories 'How the Whale Got his Throat' (*JSS* 1–13) and 'How the Leopard Got his Spots' (*JSS* 43–61), the almost identical initial capital 'I' is an example of how a letter of the alphabet can also become a picture. In both cases it is drawn as a knife (Figure 4). The physicality of the object, conveyed through an intense attention to detail, co-exists with its abstract symbolic function as a letter. By incorporating a sign that functions simultaneously as object and letter, Kipling shows that picture-writing is not limited to the distant past of medieval manuscripts or Persian letter writing; an author-artist can create examples in the present.

Another way in which the dichotomy between image and text is challenged comes in 'The Beginning of the Armadilloes' (*JSS* 105) with the representation of a map that mixes text, icons and indexical signs such as arrows. Maps of course usually include both image and text, but this one challenges expectations about the way each conveys meaning. Hillis Miller noted that illustrations make present and immediate what the text only evokes.[23] The map of the Amazon, however, with its confusing signposting and fragments of text, refuses representational immediacy and clarity. Understanding only comes with the set of captions on the facing page that provide a way to view the map, 'You begin at the bottom left-hand corner and follow the little arrows …' (*JSS* 104). Reversing the function of illustration and text provides readers with an illustration that fails to make present the text, and a text that 'illustrates' the illustration.

The theme of the relationship between word and image in Kipling, seen in the pictorial and textual playfulness of *Just So Stories*, can also be found in writing from throughout his career. For example, the protagonist of *The Light That Failed* is a war artist; indeed, in *Something of Myself* Kipling saw that novel as a verbal-visual creation inspired by both Abbé Prévost's novel *Manon Lescaut* and Pascal Dagnan-Bouveret's painting of the death of Manon.[24] Near the end of his career, Kipling's story 'The Eye of Allah' in *Debits and Credits* (1926) depicts an illustrator of manuscripts in a medieval monastery whose work registers wider shifts in art, science and thought. However, for the best example of all we can return to *Kim* and the account of the Lama's drawing of the 'Wheel of Life'. A specimen of a brush-pen

How the Leopard got his Spots

N the days when everybody started fair, Best Beloved, the Leopard lived in a place called the High Veldt. 'Member it wasn't the Low Veldt, or the Bush Veldt, or the Sour Veldt, but the 'sclusively bare, hot, shiny High Veldt, where there was sand and sandy-coloured rock and 'sclusively tufts of sandy-yellowish grass. The Giraffe and the Zebra and the Eland and the Koodoo and the Hartebeest lived there ; and they were 'sclusively sandy-yellow-brownish all over ; but the Leopard, he was the 'sclusivest sandiest-yellowest-brownest of them all—a greyish-yellowish catty-shaped kind of beast, and he matched the 'sclusively yellowish-greyish-brownish colour of the High Veldt to one hair. This was

Figure 4 Detail of the first page of 'How the Leopard got his Spots' with illustrated first letter 'I' by Rudyard Kipling. (Rudyard Kipling, *Just So Stories* (1902; London: Macmillan, 1930), p. 39.)

Buddhist image for the initiation of his *chela*, the Lama defines it as a 'written picture' and the curator of the Lahore Museum as an example of those 'pictures which are, as it were, half written and half drawn' (*K* 17). With the 'Wheel of Life' the picture-writing that Kipling himself practised in the *Just So Stories* is being described and used in the fiction.

Adaptations

Films based on Kipling's work take us beyond the context in which the texts were produced. (Though Kipling sold the rights to a number of his works, and was involved in plans for adaptations, none of those made in his lifetime survive complete.)[25] In the first critical commentary on Kipling adaptations from 1974, Philip French dismissed them en masse as gross simplifications that had created a misleading and superficial portrait of the author. Kipling became 'the man who wrote about children, animals, patriotism, the Empire, the mystic East and the White Man's Burden'.[26] The adaptations cannot be so easily dismissed, however; they have opened up Kipling's works to new audiences, interpretations and meanings.

Here a number of the most influential and popular adaptations of Kipling from an extended period are considered.[27] All are products of the commercial American film industry. They are treated as cultural objects in their own right, and not solely as reincarnations, translations, interpretations or deconstructions of the source text. In Dudley Andrew's words, they are seen in terms of 'the complex interchange among eras, style, nations and subjects'.[28] The way in which directors, producers, screenwriters and film companies re-presented and re-worked Kipling's stories was informed by the context in which they were made, audience expectations and filmic convention.

Between 1937 and 1939, Kipling adaptations played a central role in 'British Empire cinema' in Hollywood. This emergent genre was rooted in shared Anglo-American cultural values and the consequences of the Depression. As Chapman and Cull have noted, domestic distribution in the United States alone was not enough to fund expensive productions. As Britain accounted for about a half of all Hollywood's overseas revenues, there was a strong incentive to develop films that would appeal to audiences on both sides of the Atlantic.[29] That these years therefore marked the high-water mark of Kipling adaptations is not surprising; his texts were popular throughout the anglophone world. Films included *Wee Willie Winkie* (1937), *Elephant Boy* (1937) – based on the short story 'Toomai of the Elephants' from *The Jungle Book*[30] – and, most successful of all, *Gunga Din* (1939).[31]

Directed by George Stevens, *Gunga Din* had proved hard to make. Various drafts of the script, including one by William Faulkner in 1936, were rejected and, in the end, Joel Sayre and Fred Guiol hastily assembled the final script just weeks before shooting started. As with other Kipling adaptations of this period, *Gunga Din* was not faithful to its source. As Rudy Behlmer has noted, 'There was hardly enough narrative in the poem for a full-fledged commercial feature film, so perhaps the often-used phrase "inspired by" is more accurate.'[32] The script drew on Kipling's poem, *Soldiers Three* (1888), Empire movies of the 1930s, popular American dramas and Westerns.

Kipling's 'Gunga Din' is the best-known poem in *Barrack-Room Ballads* (1892). It is a bleak portrait of an Indian water carrier, or *bhisti*, who follows British soldiers in battle. The tone of the poem is ambivalent and alternates between contempt and admiration for Gunga Din, ending with the famous line retained in the film version: 'You're a better man than I am, Gunga Din!'[33] The film refers to the poem at the beginning and at the end, but replaces its complexity with a straightforward racial hierarchy in which Gunga Din and other Indians are inferior to the British soldiers both culturally and morally. This narrative underpins the two interlinked stories that make up the plot: the narrative of Gunga Din and the struggle of the British army against the Thugees, a group of religious fanatics who are devotees of the goddess Kali.

In the film, Gunga Din (Sam Jaffe) wants to become a bugler in a British regiment. Introducing this wish for self-improvement aligns Gunga Din with a characteristically American masterplot, one exemplified by the novels of Horatio Alger. Gunga Din does not identify with other Indians and indeed takes pride when the officers declare him to be different from his fellow countrymen. When shown imitating soldiers in battle by waving a broken sword, or copying the steps of a military drill, Gunga Din appears a comical, eager simpleton, the colonised child who mimics the British colonisers but can never be their equal. As Davinia Thornley has noted, he exemplifies the trope in which 'racism works within and between exploited groups' that Albert Memmi named the 'pyramid of tyrannies'.[34] Gunga Din is allowed heroism only in death, blowing his cherished bugle to alert the British to an ambush. Another significant departure from the poem, this death scene was introduced, as Behlmer notes, for dramatic purposes and echoes earlier Empire films such as *The Lives of a Bengal Lancer* (1935) and *The Charge of the Light Brigade* (1936).[35]

The British soldiers' struggle against the religious fanaticism of the Thugees was the result of Joel Sayre's late attempt to stitch the plot together, and followed some hasty reading on Indian religion.[36] The dark skin of the Thugees and their dishevelled robes are contrasted with the white uniforms of the British soldiers, who march in an orderly fashion and sing with a hearty openness of expression. From the first the Thugees are presented as deceitful and cowardly, attacking the British at night while everyone is asleep and spreading terror in the villages. Though colonial occupiers, the British are never portrayed as aggressors or invaders. Rather, they fight to defend themselves and their comrades in the name of patriotic ideals and the cause of civilisation.

The protagonists of the film, Cutter (Cary Grant), Ballantine (Douglas Fairbanks Jr.) and McChesney (Victor McLaglen), are reminiscent of Kipling's characters Learoyd, Mulvaney and Ortheris. Their adventures establish a set of connections between colonialism, the exotic and male friendship, where the strength of that friendship is used to suggest what makes the British strong as a race. The bond between them is threatened when Ballantine plans to marry Emmy (Joan Fontaine); this occurs just at the time when the British are most threatened by the Thugees. The suggestion is that both other races and women endanger the colonial project, though this is not developed at length.[37] When Emmy disappears and the Thugees are defeated, the white male world is restored and reasserted.

The film clearly went down well in Britain and America, as its box office returns were second only to those of *Jesse James* that year. There is no evidence of adverse critical reaction as its nostalgia for the heyday of British imperialism helped distract audiences from the Depression, the prospect of another world war and the tears that were appearing in the fabric of colonialism. Elsewhere in the world, though, *Gunga Din* was seen differently from the start: it was banned in Japan, Malaya and, indeed, British India.[38]

The end of the first period of Empire movies came when Britain went to war in September 1939. Even recent films that celebrated the Empire lost favour with the public and the press. In 1942 the US Office of War Information prevented *Gunga Din*'s re-release; in the same year, MGM temporarily shelved production of a film version of *Kim*.[39] In Britain, the initially popular *Four Feathers* (1939) by the Korda brothers was criticised by *The Times* on its reissue in 1943 for 'its juvenile attitude to war'. It was said to maintain 'the "sadistic Englishman" idea so prevalent on the Continent'.[40] There was a perception that such cultural products might damage efforts to win friends and build alliances – were other countries being asked to fight Nazi aggression or to help sustain the British Empire? – and help stoke nationalist movements in India and elsewhere.

For their adaptation of *The Jungle Book* (1942), the Kordas moved to Hollywood and refashioned the Empire film genre that had made their reputation. They developed a romanticised and idealised vision of India supposedly from an Indian perspective. The film opens with an old Indian storyteller, Buldeo (Joseph Calleia), narrating the story of Mowgli. Kipling's own texts have an omniscient narrator who cannot be located in either the village or the jungle. The impression is therefore created that the film belongs to a tradition of Indian oral culture instead of being inspired by a text by a British author from the Victorian period. Where in *Gunga Din* Kipling made an appearance in the process of composing his poem, in *The Jungle Book* he is only mentioned in the credits. Indeed the British are marginal; the only British character is a woman addressed by the storyteller as 'Memsahib', a passer-by who appears only in a couple of opening and closing shots. Her role, though, is an important one, offering an initial point of identification for a western audience that helps to vouch for the respectability and interest of the story.

While in the Kipling, Buldeo makes only a brief appearance in 'Tiger! Tiger!' and 'Letting in the Jungle',[41] in the Korda adaptation he features throughout. He provides the viewer with the film's preferred mode of interpretation, and takes the place occupied by Mowgli in Kipling's stories. Where Kipling examines Mowgli's rite of passage from childhood to maturity, the film provides an Indian version as Buldeo moves from greedy hunter to wise storyteller, where the act of retelling his past helps him understand it. At a more general level, a narrative is being constructed in which India is said to be growing from oriental primitive barbarism towards civilised western values.

Little more than twenty years separate the Korda brothers' adaptation from that of Walt Disney.[42] The most popular of all Kipling's adaptations, Deborah Cartmell has noted that 'the film overtakes the source text as the "original" in most people's minds.'[43] The Korda and the Disney films have little in common: where the Korda film focuses attention on Buldeo and the Indian village, the Disney film concentrates on the jungle. As a cartoon it can focus on the animals and, like Kipling's own stories, endow them with language. But where the animals in Kipling's book use a uniform vernacular English augmented with a rhetorical elegance that defines the jungle as certainly other, different and perhaps superior, the animals in the Disney film adopt different forms of ordinary speech.

The plot of the Disney adaptation is on the whole close to Kipling's stories, and there are even visual references to the early illustrations. The representation of the wolves' meeting at Council Rock echoes the relevant illustration in the Macmillan first edition, even down to the detail of the full moon.[44] For all the similarities between adaptation and original, the animation avoids focusing on Mowgli's problematic identification with both humans and animals. To the fore instead are Bagheera's attempts to take a reluctant Mowgli back to the village – and therefore to mankind and civilisation – where he will be protected from Shere Khan.

For Chapman and Cull this adaptation says more about America and the demise of the British Empire than about Kipling's vision of India.[45] Mowgli's humorous encounters with the animals show a particular response to political and racial issues in the post-war United States. Colonel Hathi, the Elephant, is a parody of the British Empire of Kipling's time. Hathi imitates a British officer, even speaking with an upper class English accent as he reminisces about how, back in 1888, he received a commission in the Maharajah's Fifth Pachyderm Brigade. In the post-independence India of the Disney adaptation, Hathi and the elephants represent an empire long past its best. Shown marching through the jungle with a motley small regiment of ageing pachyderms that includes Hathi's long-suffering wife and young son, they sing loudly in an echo of English soldiers in the Empire films of the 1930s such as *Gunga Din*. The parodic effect is further heightened by the musical refrain, which defines the elephants' military goal as 'a question rather droll' of aimless and destructive marches through the jungle. Colonel Hathi's idealisation of hard work and duty invoked by Kipling's famous writings such as 'The White Man's Burden' (1899) is ridiculed and made fun of by Mowgli, who defiantly declares that the jungle no longer belongs to Hathi. The British might have been in charge of India in 1888, but in Disney's Americanised jungle the British Empire is an old and pompous elephant that provides a few minutes comic relief. His final march towards the setting sun symbolises the end of the Empire on which the sun was said never to set.

The real hero of this jungle is not someone who works hard but laidback Balloo the bear. He has a bigger role than in Kipling's stories, not only teaching Mowgli how to live and survive in the jungle but also saving him from the *bandar-log* monkeys and Shere Khan. Balloo represents the ascendant post-war American culture. Scott Schaffer has noted that he sounds and acts like 'The Duke', John Wayne, the star of many Westerns.[46] Unlike Hathi, Balloo does not claim any military authority over the jungle; he is portrayed as lazy, jovial and irresponsible – or, to use the words of Bagheera, as 'a shiftless, stupid, jungle bum'. However, the presentation of a carefree existence may mask the ideological work that is being done here. The song 'The Bare Necessities' that Balloo uses to teach Mowgli about survival in the jungle can be said to suggest the form taken by American economic power in this period, which many would characterise as another form of imperialism. The 'bare necessities' song offers the prospect of an easy and contented life in a jungle that spontaneously and inexhaustibly provides fruits and insects. Balloo and the inhabitants of this rich land stand in allegorically for the still youthful and diverse American nation, and the birds and insects for the commodities and comforts of the post-war United States. The vision offered to the world – not least in Disney films such as this – masks the economic power, labour and environmental degradation involved in sustaining such an organisation of the economy, instead trying to pass it off as easy, natural and right.

Mowgli's adventures with the *bandar-log* monkeys bring into play issues of race in America. In Kipling's stories the monkeys are portrayed as the outsiders of the jungle. Unlike other animals, 'they have no speech of their own, but use the stolen words which they overhear'.[47] In the adaptation, their leader King Louie is among the Black-coded characters who, as Susan Miller and Greg Rode argue, 'speak a jazz lingo that reflects the most stereotypic African American dialect'.[48] Linking King Louie with African Americans and Louis Armstrong suggests that a whole set of racial stereotypes are in play. In pseudo-scientific evolutionary 'race theory', people of African descent were seen as less 'evolved' than those of white European heritage – indeed, as closer to monkeys. In the lyrics of King Louie's song 'I Wanna Be Like You', he sings of his desire to emulate Mowgli and to possess the Promethean gift of fire.

The final message of the Disney adaptation is that everyone should stay where they belong with their own kind: the monkeys ghettoised, as Miller and Rode note, 'in the abandoned remains of some now extinct, supposedly "primitive" culture',[49] the animals in the jungle and Mowgli in the human village where he will settle into heterosexuality, marriage and family life.

The Man Who Would Be King (1975), a labour of love for John Huston, is both the most acclaimed film to adapt Kipling and the most faithful to the original. Huston had been trying to take the story to the screen since the 1950s. The final script was written by Huston and Gladys Hill; producer John Foreman was responsible for the light-hearted 'buddy movie' material (in 1969 he had produced *Butch Cassidy and the Sundance Kid*). It would be simplistic to see it as a film made by an Irishman, with no love of the British, drawn to a tale about a failed imperial venture. Sarah Kozloff notes the different and indeed contrasting forces that animated Huston: liberalism, love of 1930s Empire movies, devotion to Kipling's works and an admiration for the British in India.[50] The film is highly ambivalent, alternating between ironic distance and celebrating courage and the love of adventure.

In short story and film, Peachy Carnehan and Daniel Dravot, two ex-army sergeants, decide that India constrains them and set off to make their fortune. (In the film, these roles are taken by Michael Caine and Sean Connery.) They travel to Kafiristan – the mountainous region north-east of Afghanistan, known today as Nuristan – and try to set themselves up as kings and plunder the country. The story ends with the death of Dravot and the crucifixion of Carnehan, who miraculously survives and returns to India to tell his story to a young journalist he had met before setting off. Though the protagonists are smugglers, swindlers and blackmailers, they are depicted as proud of their country, enterprising and even courageous. They have no time for what they regard as the petty laws imposed by the grey, unimaginative and corrupt colonial administrators. At the start of the film the Indians offer a stark contrast; they are seen as lawless, superstitious and uncivilised. As Richard Voeltz notes, the film opens 'with images of cities teeming with unruly people, with beggars; blind men; snake charmers; a man who puts scorpions in his mouth; "crazy" holy men; a man who first drinks, then washes himself, in boiling water; starving children; and buffoonish Indians'.[51] In Kafiristan, the contrast between the protagonists and the population becomes even starker. With the exception of Billy Fish (Saeed Jaffrey), a Gunga Din-like figure, the native population is represented as practising savage and cruel customs, such as slaughtering enemies or playing polo with a severed human head.

Dravot and Carnehan conquer village after village, become kings of the whole of Kafiristan and find the treasure of Alexander the Great. However, they fall out: Carnehan wants to keep to the initial plan, taking Alexander's treasure and returning to England. The local people would soon, as he puts it, 'go back to slaughtering babes, and playing stick-ball with one another's heads and pissing on their neighbours'. Dravot, like Kurtz in *Heart of Darkness* (1901), decides to stay to bring 'enlightenment to the darker regions of the earth'. The end of Dravot's dream comes about when he marries a local beauty, played by Shakira Caine. Afraid that she will die when Dravot touches her, she bites him on the cheek. The blood leads the Kafiris to realise that he is an ordinary mortal, and not a god or a devil. They kill Billy Fish – who, like Gunga Din remains loyal to the British to the end – and force Dravot out onto a rope bridge before cutting the rope. Dravot's fall is, as Jim Beckerman has noted, not just a personal fall from power, rather it symbolises the collapse of the myth of the civilising mission and of the Empire.[52] Shortly before dying, Dravot recognises his mistakes and is reconciled with Carnehan. The ending of the film celebrates ideals of male friendship, loyalty and self-abnegation and, like *Gunga Din*, portrays women and the racial Other as a threat.

The Man Who Would Be King has produced conflicting interpretations. For Lesley Brill, the film explores timeless themes such as immortality, heroism and community.[53] Chapman and Cull note that Huston implied that 'the film had contemporary significance', probably referring to the Watergate crisis.[54] For Voeltz, *The Man Who Would Be King* can be related to more recent events and the war in Afghanistan. He sees it as part of a subgenre, along with *Gunga Din*, that he calls the North West Frontier film. These films share a similar setting in the border region between the far north of British India, today's Pakistan and Afghanistan, and Russia. This is a territory that is represented not only as a physical place but also as 'a collective fictive mental arena for the representation of the "other"'. In terms of form, he sees *The Man Who Would Be King*, like other films from the same period such as *Zulu Dawn* (1979), as 'a conflicted film *in* the older Empire genre but not *of* it'.[55] He notes that these films see a shift beyond a politicised dichotomy between the colonial and the anti-colonial: 'although they purport to deplore imperialism's aggressions and injustices, they tend to serve up battles, massacres, exoticisms, and even executions in grand style, as thoroughly compelling entertainment that leads to a wonderful adventure and a marvelous spree'.[56]

Kipling's texts, then, have not only been adapted after the concerns of later periods and contexts. They have also shown themselves able to take on the new cultural forms produced in economies and societies very different from those of Kipling's time.

Notes

1 For a study of illustration and adaptation see Kamilla Elliott, *Rethinking the Novel/Film Debate* (Cambridge University Press, 2003). On the role of film studies in thought on the relationship between word and image see J. Hillis Miller, *Illustrations* (Cambridge, MA: Harvard University Press, 1992), p. 61.
2 Lockwood Kipling also did illustrations for 18 of the 21 volumes of the Outward Bound edition. See *The Letters of Rudyard Kipling, Volume 2, 1890–99*, ed. Thomas Pinney (London: Macmillan, 1990), pp. 263–4. Electronic versions of early illustrated editions of Kipling's works are available at www.archive.org
3 For a detailed account of the rare editions of *Just So Stories* that are not illustrated by Kipling, see Brian Alderson, 'Just-So Pictures: Illustrated Versions of *Just So Stories for Little Children*', *Children's Literature*, 20 (1992), pp. 147–74.
4 Janzen Lorraine Kooistra, *The Artist as Critic: Bitextuality in Fin-de-Siècle Illustrated Books* (Brookfield Vermont: Ashgate, 1995), p. 1.
5 Arthur A. Ankers, *The Pater: John Lockwood Kipling, His Life and Times, 1837–1911* (Otford: Pond View Books, 1988), p. 29.
6 Rudyard Kipling, *Something of Myself and Other Autobiographical Writings*, ed. Thomas Pinney (Cambridge University Press, 1990), p. 83.
7 Charles Allen, *Kipling Sahib: India and the Making of Rudyard Kipling* (London: Abacus, 2007), pp. 357–8.
8 Rudyard Kipling, *The Jungle Book* (London: Macmillan, 1899), ill. p. 45. The illustrations for this edition were by John Lockwood Kipling, W. H. Drake, and P. Frenzeny.
9 *Ibid.*, p. 3.
10 Walter Crane, *Of the Decorative Illustration of Books Old and New* (1896; London: Bracken Books, 1984), p. 207.
11 John Lockwood Kipling, *Beast and Man in India: A Popular Sketch of Indian Animals in Their Relations with the People* (London: Macmillan, 1891), p. 362.
12 Rudyard Kipling, *The Second Jungle Book* (London: Macmillan, 1899), ill. pp. 61, 221, 263. The title page has 'with decorations by J. L. Kipling, C. I.E'.
13 See Crane, *Of the Decorative Illustration of Books Old and New*, passim, and Kooistra, *The Artist as Critic*, p. 28.
14 Kipling, *Kim* (London: Macmillan, 1901), ill. pp. 81 and 268. Subsequent references in the text as *K*.
15 Rachel Fleming, 'John Lockwood Kipling and *Kim*', *Athanor*, 21 (2003), p. 42.
16 Janice Leoshko, 'What is in *Kim*? Rudyard Kipling and Tibetan Buddhist Traditions', *South Asia Research*, 21:1 (2001), p. 62.
17 *Ibid.*, p. 61.

18 Lisa Lewis, Introduction to her edition of Rudyard Kipling, *Just So Stories* (1902; Oxford University Press, 1998), p. xxiii.

19 Elsie Bambridge, 'Memoir', in Charles Carrington, *Rudyard Kipling: His Life and Work* (London: Penguin, 1986), pp. 587–97. Quote from p. 593.

20 Jim Cheff, '"With Illustrations by the Author": Some Author-Artists of the Nineteenth Century', *American Book Collector*, 8:2 (February 1987), p. 13.

21 Rudyard Kipling, '*Just So Stories For Little Children* with illustrations by the author' (1902; London: Macmillan, 1930), pp. 123–43, 145–69. Subsequent references in the text as *JSS*.

22 See Yin Liu, 'Text as Image in Kipling's *Just So Stories*', *Papers on Language and Literature*, 44: 3 (2008), p. 247.

23 As Miller succinctly put it, 'The word evokes. The illustration presents.' Miller, *Illustrations*, p. 67.

24 Kipling had seen the painting with his father at the Salon in 1878. Kipling, *Something of Myself*, p. 132.

25 For Kipling's involvement in planned adaptations of his work see *The Letters of Rudyard Kipling, Volume 2*, pp. 356–7, 409–12, 384–6, and *The Letters of Rudyard Kipling, Volume 6, 1931–36*, ed. Thomas Pinney (London: Macmillan, 2004), pp. 305–10, 312–14, 326–9.

26 Philip French, 'Kipling and the Movies', in John Gross (ed.), *Rudyard Kipling: The Man, his Work and his World* (London: Weidenfeld & Nicolson, 1972), pp. 162–9. Quote from p. 163.

27 For reasons of space it is impossible here to deal with all adaptations of Kipling's works. For a full list see Philip Leibfried, *Rudyard Kipling and Sir Henry Rider Haggard on Screen, Stage, Radio and Television* (London: McFarland, 1999), pp. 13–94.

28 Dudley Andrew, 'The Well-Worn Muse: Adaptation in Film History and Theory', in Syndy Conger and Janice Welsch (eds.), *Narrative Strategies: Original Essays in Film and Prose Fiction* (Macomb, IL.: Western Illinois University Libraries, 1980), pp. 9–17. Quote from p. 16.

29 James Chapman and Nicholas J. Cull, *Projecting Empire: Imperialism and Popular Cinema* (London and New York: I. B. Tauris, 2009), p. 7.

30 Kipling, *The Jungle Book*, pp. 201–45.

31 Dir. George Stevens (USA, 1939).

32 Rudy Behlmer, *America's Favourite Movies: Behind the Scenes* (New York: Frederick Ungar, 1982), p. 88.

33 Rudyard Kipling, *Barrack-Room Ballads and Other Verses* (1892; London: Macmillan, 1900), p. 26.

34 Davinia Thornley, 'Conceptions of Empire: Three Colonial War Films', *Quarterly Review of Film and Video*, 21 (2004), p. 108.

35 Behlmer, *America's Favourite Movies*, p. 98.

36 *Ibid.*, p. 94.

37 The marriage was one of the interpolations in this adaptation. Behlmer notes that it was borrowed from *The Front Page* (1928), a highly successful play by Hecht and MacArthur. *Ibid.*, pp. 90–1.

38 Chapman and Cull, *Projecting Empire*, p. 43.

39 *Kim* finally appeared in 1951 (dir. Victor Saville). For an account of the making of the film see William Blackburn, 'All About a Boy: Kipling's Novel, MGM's

Film', in Douglas Street (ed.), *Children's Novels and the Movies* (New York: Frederick Ungar, 1983), pp. 101–10.

40 Chapman and Cull, *Projecting Empire*, p. 27.

41 'Tiger! Tiger!' is included in Kipling, *The Jungle Book*, pp. 87–124; 'Letting in the Jungle' is in *The Second Jungle Book*, pp. 61–105.

42 Dir. Wolfgang Reitherman (USA, 1967).

43 Deborah Cartmell, 'Adapting Children's Literature', in Deborah Cartmell and Imelda Whelehan (eds.), *The Cambridge Companion to Literature on Screen* (Cambridge University Press, 2007), pp. 167–80. Quote from p. 172.

44 Kipling, *The Jungle Book*, p. 51.

45 Chapman and Cull, *Projecting Empire*, p. 44.

46 Scott Schaffer, 'Disney and the Imagineering of Histories', *Postmodern Culture*, 6:3 (1996), p. 7.

47 Kipling, *The Jungle Book*, p. 51.

48 Susan Miller and Greg Rode, 'The Movie You See, The Movie You Don't: How Disney Do's That Old Time Derision', in Elizabeth Bell, Lynda Haas and Laura Sells (eds.), *From Mouse to Mermaid: The Politics of Film, Gender and Culture* (Bloomington: Indiana University Press, 1995), pp. 86–103. Quote from p. 92.

49 *Ibid.*, p. 92.

50 Sarah Kozloff, 'Taking Us Along on *The Man Who Would Be King*', in Stephen Cooper (ed.), *Perspectives on John Huston* (New York: G. K. Hall, 1994), p. 184–96.

51 Richard A. Voeltz, 'John Huston, Sean Connery, Michael Caine, and the Epiphany of *The Man Who Would be King*', *The McNeese Review*, 40 (2002), p. 46.

52 Jim Beckerman, 'On Adapting "The Most Audacious Thing in Fiction"', in Michael Klein and Gillian Parker (eds.), *The English Novel and the Movies* (New York: Frederick Ungar, 1981), pp. 180–6. Quote from p. 186.

53 Lesley Brill, *John Huston's Filmmaking* (Cambridge University Press, 1997), pp. 32–48.

54 Chapman and Cull, *Projecting Empire*, p. 162.

55 Richard A. Voeltz, 'Rambo, Kipling, and Shirley Temple: From Hollywood to Afghanistan with Love', *The Mid-Atlantic Almanack*, 13 (2004), p. 55.

56 Voeltz, 'John Huston, Sean Connery, Michael Caine', p. 49.

13

HARISH TRIVEDI

Reading Kipling in India

Reading Kipling in India may seem as natural an activity as reading Kipling in England, or perhaps only a little less so, for he was an English writer with a crucial Indian dimension. Born in Bombay, he grew up speaking an Indian language, Hindustani, more fluently than he did English and was molly-coddled and indulged by a small army of Indian servants that included a dear ayah and a bearer.[1] Kipling was sent (back?) to England at the age of six, as nearly all children of the Raj were, to prevent them from being con-taminated in their formative years. He then spent the next six years of his life in the boarding-house in Southsea that he later described as the 'House of Desolation' where he had been introduced to 'Hell ... in all its terrors'.[2]

In contrast, Kipling's initial years in India came to be seen by him as a lost paradise, which he later revisited in fantasy and by proxy through the child-hero of his greatest work, *Kim* (1901). Thirteen when the novel begins and seventeen when it ends, Kim leads a carefree, footloose, hybridised and adventurous life, which takes him over vast tracts of India in the company of a richly varied array of surrogate father figures and avuncular well-wishers, including the Lama, Mahbub Ali and, to a lesser extent, Colonel Creighton and Hurree Babu. During this period in his own life Kipling was away from his family at a minor public school in Devon. He later called it a 'caste-school' where seventy-five per cent of the boys were, like himself, born outside England. In conformity with public school norms, the place was '[n]aturally ... brutal enough' and Kipling was a short, swarthy and weak boy with poor eyesight.[3] Gradually, though, he learned to enjoy his time there with his cohort of close friends; his experiences at school later provided the basis for his Stalky stories. But his schoolboy pranks and adventures seem but a molehill when compared with the high mountains and the extensive plains that Kim traverses.

Denied a university education because his father could not afford it, Kipling returned to India for a longer second innings as a young man. He worked as a reporter, and later also as a contributor of verses and short stories and sketches, on two English-language newspapers that served as mouthpieces of the British establishment, the *Civil and Military Gazette* in Lahore (from 1882 to 1887) and its bigger and far more influential stable-mate, the *Pioneer* in Allahabad (from 1887 to 1889). He had already published eight volumes of short stories and verse by the time he left India in March 1889 at the age of twenty-three, and was acclaimed on arrival in England as the next great literary star if not, at least in some quarters, already a proven genius.

There are not many instances in the history of world literature of a major writer with such an intricately intertwined relationship between two countries. He belonged to one country by lineage and race but was born and bred in the other, was schooled in the one but began his working and literary career in the other, initially won fame in the one for work written entirely in and about the other, and continued to write best about the other even after he had left it for good. Indeed, it may be difficult to determine which Kipling's own country was and which the other, at least in the first half of his life.[4] His later sojourns in the United States of America and in South Africa, before he settled for good in Sussex in 1902, never amounted to feeling at home in either place. Kipling 'belonged' to England and wrote in English, but he became a writer in India and wrote best about India. After he left India first as his physical home and then as his great métier, he may have gone on gaining in eminence as an oracle of the Empire but he clearly declined as a writer. India made him; he would have been half the writer he was without India.

But does India know this, and does India care? How is Kipling read in India and by what kind of Indians? How is he received and what is the nature of the response to him? Is the way he is read in India inflected by the complex and conflicted colonial history that England and India shared from 1757 to 1947? Is Kipling tainted in the Indian mind by his association with the high noon of empire that coincided with his rise to fame, and by his own major role as an ideologue of the Empire? Has the rise of postcolonial critical discourse brought about a depreciation of Kipling? Finally, is there a distinctly 'Indian' response to Kipling that differs from that in England and the rest of the world?

Young readers and the common reader

Kipling – or for that matter any writer in English, whether western or Indian – cannot possibly address a large part of the Indian population. Those who read literary works constitute a small segment of the population in all countries and languages, but in India one-third of the population is still illiterate. According to the latest census of India in 2001, the number of

Indians who declared English to be their mother tongue was 226,449 while, in comparison, the number of native speakers of the most populous language in India, Hindi, was 422 million and even the tenth biggest language, Oriya, had 33 million native speakers. Though figures vary widely on what proportion of the population 'knows' English, it would be safe to say that no more than one per cent of the total population can, or is likely to, read a book in English for pleasure. However, even one per cent of the Indian population is more than ten million people.[5]

Though some children in India have grown up reading the *Jungle Books*, they are mostly the 'baba-log' – that is, from an elite minority of affluent and anglicised families. An early and eminent example of such a reader was Jawaharlal Nehru (1889–1964), the first Prime Minister of independent India. The only son of one of the most successful lawyers in India of the time, he was brought up by English governesses, and never went to an Indian school but between the ages of eleven and fourteen had, instead, a resident British tutor. At this time he read a 'great many English books' including '*The Jungle Books* and *Kim*' as well as works by a dozen other authors including Walter Scott, Charles Dickens, Arthur Conan Doyle, Jerome K. Jerome and George du Maurier.[6] Nehru was later educated in England at Harrow, Cambridge and the Inner Temple; unlike Gandhi, whose favourite disciple he was, he went on to write all his books in English.

A considerably larger group of Kipling's readers in India would be students at school and college, especially the small fraction that go to English-medium schools and the larger number who are taught English as a second language – with the help of books such as a version of *Kim* 'retold' and reorganised into seventeen chapters using a limited vocabulary.[7] At the college and university level, on the English Honours course or an MA in English – which is nearly always a two-year taught degree in India, with little required in the way of specialisation or research – E. M. Forster's *A Passage to India* is usually the novel by a British writer about India that is set; prescriptions of it must outnumber those for *Kim* by at least ten to one.[8]

Beyond this captive readership of students lies the domain of the common reader. The veteran Indian-English novelist Khushwant Singh edited in 1994 what was claimed to be the first anthology of Kipling's short stories 'wholly brought out' – that is, edited and published – in India.[9] Another Indian editor of Kipling is Sudhakar Marathe, who has taken every opportunity to use texts by Kipling to teach both language and literature in the Department of English at the University of Hyderabad, and supervised an MPhil. dissertation which puts forward inter alia the thesis that 'without exception every human society has at some time colonized another'. Dismayed by the neglect of Kipling generally – 'as far as I know virtually no one reads Kipling in India'[10] – Marathe has attempted to remedy the situation by editing two collections of Kipling's short stories, *Stories of India* (2003) and a selection for children, *The Elephant's Child and Other Stories* (2005), both published by Penguin India. In his introduction to the former volume, he speaks of Kipling's many English characters 'who endear themselves to us because they seem to know and care for India even better than most Indians'. He argues that if Kipling 'on occasion ... happens to be wrong' that is because 'he loved India', that his readers 'will need to make allowances for Kipling's context', and that reading him now may 'test us' because 'reading carelessly, we may misunderstand Kipling' even though his stories 'by and large ... very fairly represent the historical situation'.[11] Such statements betray a partisan's zeal as well as a certain anxiety and special pleading.

Heedless of such complex postcolonial considerations, another Indian publisher, Rupa and Co., has over the last decade reprinted without the addition of prefatory or editorial matter of any kind over fifteen volumes by Kipling, including not only *The Jungle Book*, *Just So Stories* and *Kim*, but also works with no special Indian appeal such as *'Captains Courageous'* and *Puck of Pook's Hill*. It has also published *Humorous Tales from Rudyard Kipling* in five volumes (also issued together as the *Humorous Tales Omnibus*) and the misleadingly titled *Rajasthan Stories* in three volumes. (The latter are 'culled from' a series of reports of travels in 'Rajputana', now Rajasthan, that Kipling wrote for the *Pioneer* in late 1887 and early 1888 under the obscure and eccentric title 'Letters of Marque'.)[12] It appears that this major exercise in reprinting Kipling at prices ranging for most single volumes from 50 to 95 rupees – which is exceptionally low even in Indian terms – stems from a commercial confidence that Kipling has sufficient name-recognition as an entertaining and readable writer, especially for children and young adults.

Comparing Kipling

Regardless of what his critics may think of Kipling, numerous creative writers including those of Indian origin have shown a more positive regard for him. In his chapter in this volume, Bart Moore-Gilbert surveys an impressively vast array of responses to Kipling by postcolonial writers from South Asia and the diverse inventive uses to which they have put Kipling's texts. Such intertextual salaams in the direction of Kipling by Indian writers, however, constitute an exclusively anglophone durbar. As Moore-Gilbert points out, the one Indian-language writer in that assembly, Rabindranath Tagore, hated to be called 'the Indian Kipling', which he was presumably for no other reason than that he became the second writer from the British Empire to win the Nobel Prize in 1913 after Kipling in 1907.

More significantly, Tagore wrote a novel, *Gora* (published in Bengali in 1910, and in an English translation in 1924 with the title left untranslated: it means 'whitey'), in which the eponymous hero is an Irish orphan from the 'Mutiny' of 1857 who is adopted and brought up by an orthodox Brahmin couple. Gora grows up passionately engaged in the contemporary debates to reform Hindu society and is obliged to realign his identity in a major way when his origins are revealed at the end of the novel. Some readers of *Gora* have interpreted it as a direct counter-thrust to *Kim*, where the hero is similarly an Irish orphan, but as often happens with literary rejoinders – for example, Samuel Richardson's *Pamela* and Henry Fielding's *Joseph Andrews* – the later work soon veers away from its initial motivation and assumes a life of its own. Though one could wish for more such reactions to Kipling from writers and readers in the Indian languages, they are almost entirely lacking. One possible reason for this may be that Kipling has hardly been translated into the Indian languages, but then, for that matter, nor have many other writers in English though their texts may be of special interest to Indians; even Rushdie's *Midnight's Children* (1980) remained untranslated into Hindi until 1997. In this and other respects there are still two Indias, the anglophone and the non-anglophone, with neither one speaking to the other.

Anyhow, comparative sidelights to Kipling can be provided by reference to a couple of Indian writers in English (besides those discussed by Moore-Gilbert). Dhan Gopal Mukerji (1890–1936) was an Indian writer of fiction in English who appears to have been adopted by America in the 1920s as an authentic indigenous counterpart to Kipling.[13] Mukerji was sent out of India to escape the fate of his brother, who was apparently associated with a group of 'terrorists' or militant revolutionaries working to overthrow British rule; arrested, he spent five years in jail without trial. Dhan Gopal Mukerji went initially to Tokyo as a student, and shortly afterwards to the United States – Berkeley and Stanford – before marrying an American and moving to New York. He contributed fiction about India to *St Nicholas Magazine*, the journal for children that had serialised Kipling's own *Jungle Books*. Earlier still, in 1892, it was to this magazine's editor that Kipling had first broached the idea of a story about 'a small boy' and 'a Thibetan Lama' that eventually became *Kim*.[14]

Mukerji went on to write several books for the American publisher E. P. Dutton, including some deploying Kiplingesque themes such as *Kari the Elephant* (1921), *Hari the Jungle Lad* (1924) and *Ghond the Hunter* (1928). He also wrote the autobiographical *Caste and Outcaste* (1923) and *My Brother's Face* (1924). *Gay-neck, the Story of a Pigeon* (1927), his most successful novel, narrates the adventures of an Indian carrier pigeon and its keeper deployed with the Indian forces in Flanders and France during the First World War; both pigeon and keeper then journey to a lamassery in Tibet to recoup from their wounds. The novel was awarded the Newbery Medal 'for the most distinguished American Children's book' the year after its publication; Mukerji is apparently the only non-western writer to have so far won the award. (The odd-sounding 'Gay-neck' is in fact a deep allusion to a pigeon named 'Chitragriva', literally 'one with a variegated neck', in the Sanskrit collection of animal fables by Vishnu Sharma, the *Panchatantra*, from the third century BCE.) In his last years Mukerji, a true – that is, enforced and not voluntary – and unhappy exile, produced English versions of several scriptural and metaphysical texts from Sanskrit and underwent psychotherapy. He hanged himself at the age of forty-six.

A detailed comparative study of the treatment of similar themes by both Mukerji and Kipling, and by Mukerji necessarily in the context of Kipling as a spectacularly successful predecessor, is thus likely to throw interesting light on Kipling's jungle tales and the ways in which an Indian writer imbibed his influence or resisted his example. Meanwhile, we have teasing little remarks of Mukerji's such as the tiger being 'cunning as a Christian', and Kipling being 'a brilliant painter of Indian life', with a serious qualification:

> I use the word painter advisedly, for everything that the eye alone takes in, that Mr Kipling not only sees but takes in. No one however, except a Hindu, to whom the religion of his country is more real than all material aspects put together, can understand Indian life from within.[15]

Another writer of relevance here is R. K. Narayan (1906–2001), as famous as Mukerji is obscure; indeed, in India he remains the most popular and esteemed of all Indian novelists in English. Narayan stands at the opposite pole from Kipling, writing in a gentle comic tone about unremarkable and unadventurous mild men who quietly go with the flow of life in a small town in South India. His locale, too, is a far cry from Kipling's favourite region, the wild North West, with its legendary machismo.[16] It is not a direct comparison between Kipling and Narayan that is of interest here – for there are hardly any grounds for such a comparison – but rather the role Kipling played in the early Indian and British responses to Narayan's work.

In an introduction to an edition of Narayan's second novel *The Bachelor of Arts* (1937), Graham Greene confessed that the impression of India he had formed from writers such as Kipling and Forster had needed serious modification when he read Narayan. Kipling's India was 'the romantic playground of the Raj', where he 'romanticises the Indian as much as he romanticises the administrators of the Empire'. E. M. Forster in his depiction of India was in turn 'funny and tender' and 'severely ironic', yet 'India escaped him all the same'. In contrast, it was in the writings of the Indian Narayan – whom he did not 'hesitate to name' with Tolstoy, Henry James, Turgenev, Chekhov and Conrad – that Greene said he had found 'a second home', so much so that the fictional town where nearly all of Narayan's works are set, Malgudi, 'seems to me now more familiar than Battersea or the Euston Road', actual spaces where Greene had set some of his own fiction. A major point of contrast between Kipling and Narayan was that 'though the Raj still existed during the first dozen years of [Narayan's] literary career', the few English characters in his fiction were 'peripheral' and indeed 'hopelessly unimportant'. In the end, Greene speculated: 'How Kipling would have detested Narayan's books ...'[17]

An Indian who reviewed the same novel, *The Bachelor of Arts*, on its first publication, B. Appasamy, also offered a comparison between Narayan and Kipling. While Kipling 'knew his public' and exploited 'the varied possibilities of his own language', Appasamy argued that an Indian writer such as Narayan faced the double challenge of 'writing in a foreign language ... for an unknown public', and yet he had managed 'in a remarkable and mysterious way, to convey the flavour of the Tamil mind of his hero', with an inwardness denied to a foreign writer like Kipling.[18] But the most devastating criticism of using Kipling as a touchstone for the literary representation of India came in a review by the novelist Compton Mackenzie of Narayan's next novel, *The English Teacher* (1945), in the Glasgow *Evening News*. Mackenzie declared that having read Narayan, he could not forgive Kipling's portrayal of India, and that the only novels about India he wished to read now were those written by Indians. Modifying one of Kipling's most famous dicta to telling effect, Mackenzie asked: 'What should they know of India who only Kipling know?'[19]

The common thread that ran through these three early responses to Narayan was that Kipling's depiction of India carried conviction only until Indians themselves began to write about India in English, as if Kipling had been no more than the one-eyed man who is king in the country of the blind. It may be added that both Mukerji and Narayan were perfect bilinguals with English added on to Bengali and Tamil respectively, while Kipling's Hindustani was never more than rudimentary and even at that basic level often demonstrably wrong.[20] Going a step beyond Compton Mackenzie, one could perhaps ask: 'What should they know of India who only English know?'

Kipling and Gandhi

An unlikely Indian reader of Kipling was Mahatma Gandhi. On 12 November 1904, while in South Africa, he publicised in his weekly journal *Indian Opinion* an appeal for the Edwin Arnold Memorial fund, adding that Kipling was among those on the committee.[21] In 1908, Gandhi played off the government of South Africa for passing the 'Natal Bills', which discriminated against Indians, who were 'British subjects', against the government in London that had approved no such measures, and underlined his argument by invoking strategically the laureate of empire:

> In Kipling's words, the Servant is to be the Master. It is not enough that Natal is to be the Mistress in her own [word missing: 'domain'?], but it is to dictate terms to the Imperial Government.[22]

In 1909, now put in jail by the colonial government for resisting these racially discriminatory regulations, Gandhi advised his followers to undertake both sports and intellectual activity, while noting that Kipling 'has described sportsmen as enemies of the mind',[23] a reference probably to Kipling's jibe about 'the flannelled fools at the wickets and muddied oafs at the goals' in his poem 'The Islanders' (1902).

Back in India in 1915 and back in jail in 1922 to serve a six-year term, Gandhi read a staggering variety of books at a voracious rate, in part of course because he wasn't at liberty to do much else. In his jail diary for the period, he recorded on 21 May 1922: 'Finished reading Kipling's *The Five Nations*',[24] a selection of his poetry from 1896 to 1902 comprising some of his best-known poems including "The Islanders", "Buddha at Kamakura", "The White Man's Burden" and "Recessional." On 17 June, he recorded: 'Finished reading Kipling's Second *Jungle Book*.'[25] The entry on 9 March 1923 is a fair indication of his varied reading agenda: 'Finished reading Kipling's *Barrack-Room Ballads*. Reading Geddes's *Evolution of Cities*. Finished reading the pamphlet on Vedic religion.'[26] Such a juxtaposition, though accidental, helps us 'place' Kipling in the larger context of Gandhi's interests and sensibility, and confirms the fact that by the beginning of the twentieth century Kipling had become part of an almost inescapable climate of opinion not only in England but also in South Africa and India – even if mainly in the form of quotations taken out of context.

On the couple of occasions that Gandhi took more than passing note of Kipling, it was to respond to just such tags. In 1908, speaking of 'the White Man's Burden', Gandhi said that Kipling's writings, 'to my mind, have been very much misunderstood'. He added that Kipling had since

> very considerably, with extended experience [perhaps in light of the Boer War?], revised his views, and he no longer thinks that Coloured people are a menace to the Empire, or that the White man may not co-exist with the Coloured man.[27]

It is not clear what evidence Gandhi had in mind here, and in any case, he went back in 1924 to state that Kipling was not so much misunderstood as himself mistaken: 'Kipling miscalled the white man's yoke [placed repressively on the shoulders of the colonised natives] as the "white man's burden."'[28] And in 1931, just back from the Round Table conference in London, Gandhi reported that, though the conference had not achieved anything, 'wherever I went ... I was surrounded with the greatest amount of affection and I felt that there was no truth in Kipling's saying that the East and West [*sic*] would never meet'.[29] This may suggest that Gandhi too, like innumerable others, had never actually read the poem, for the third line of 'The Ballad of East and West' (1889) begins: 'But there is neither East nor West ...'

Gandhi was not a literary man but his many references to Kipling, however fitful and perfunctory, exist in a wider context in which each was seen as an iconic figure, representative of his respective nation and *its* attitudes towards the other at a time of particular antagonism.[30] Gandhi was the more obvious candidate for such a role, while Kipling, too, more than any British politician, seemed to stand for the British Empire and to articulate a whole set of western views and values which Gandhi opposed not only in terms of colonisation but equally in terms of the entire culture and civilisation that the Empire stood for. This is encapsulated in a remark reportedly made by Gandhi when asked what he thought of western civilisation: 'I think it would be a good idea.'[31]

The postcolonial Kipling

One of the most suggestive and influential discussions of this civilisational binary represented by Kipling and Gandhi is that by Ashis Nandy, a sociologist and clinical psychologist. He delves into Kipling's cherished Indian childhood, which was followed by an 'effeminate, weak' adolescence in England, and sees the outcome as a divided self: 'the hero loyal to Western civilization and the Indianized Westerner who hated the West within him'.[32] Kipling thus developed 'a moral blindness' of great consequence:

> The centrepiece of Kipling's life was a refusal to look within, an aggressive 'anti-intraception' which forced him to avoid all deep conflicts, and prevented him from separating human problems from ethnic stereotypes ... [so that he] saw the bonds of race and blood as more important than person-to-person relationships.[33]

In contrast Gandhi, preserving India's 'androgynous cosmology', put forward 'a transcultural protest against the hyper-masculine world-view of colonialism' through non-violent passive resistance and in so doing 'wanted to liberate the British as much as he wanted to liberate Indians'.[34] This intertwined comparison may not seem quite even-handed to a western reader but perhaps that is precisely where it is truly postcolonial.

Of the better-known trinity of postcolonial theorists and critics – Edward
W. Said, Gayatri Chakravorty Spivak and Homi K. Bhabha – it is, paradoxically, the non-Indian Said who made the most substantial intervention
in Kipling studies through his extended introduction to a Penguin Classics
edition of *Kim*.[35] Spivak and Bhabha, Indians by birth and early education but with doctoral degrees from the west and their entire careers spent
serving the western academy, have taken scant notice of Kipling. It is as if,
condemned already in his own lifetime for his high colonialism, he now has
no right of appeal to a postcolonial court.

Spivak discusses just one short story by Kipling, 'William the Conqueror',
in feminist and 'masculist' terms, considering the heroine as a New Woman.
She describes Kipling's use of 'Hindusthani' [*sic*] as 'always infelicitous,
almost always incorrect', and his use of 'local colour' as an 'effacement of
specificity' rather than the opposite.[36] All the while, Spivak inexplicably keeps
away from what she calls 'the contentious question of Kipling's "imperialism"', while in a passing reference elsewhere, she suggests that a Bengali
author of a book titled *Neo-Hegelianism* (1927) was 'the person mocked by
Kipling in *Kim*', blithely oblivious of the anachronism that Kipling's novel
was published a quarter of a century earlier.[37] And Homi Bhabha has even
less to offer: while he names Kipling among several other authors at the
beginning of two of his essays, with regard to 'mimicry' and to 'a conspiracy
of silence around the colonial truth' respectively, he then moves on and does
not mention Kipling again.[38]

Among other Indians, the egregiously Anglophile Nirad C. Chaudhuri
declared that, in *Kim*, 'its author wrote not only the finest novel in the English
language with an Indian theme, but also one of the greatest of English novels in spite of the theme'.[39] Half a dozen Indian academics have published
either full-length books on Kipling – Francine Krishna (1966), K. Bhaskara
Rao (1967), Vasant A. Shahane (1973) and S. S. Azfar Hussain (1983) – or
studies comparing Kipling with other British writers such as Forster or V. S.
Naipaul – Purabi Panwar (2000) and Christel R. Devadawson (2005). On
the whole, these books do not attempt much that non-Indian critics could
not have produced as well, for they offer little Indian contextualisation of
Kipling based on specialist 'native' knowledge or any distinctly Indian interpretation. Whether published in India or abroad, they have attracted little
international circulation or notice.

Finally, it may be recalled that even when writing about India in India,
Kipling had written exclusively for a 'garrison' readership of other British
men and women living temporarily in India, the Anglo-Indians. He would
have been horrified if someone like Hurree Babu were to read *Kim* – to say
nothing of the Lama, Mahbub Ali or any of the other Indian characters

who could not possibly have read him in English. Despite the early paradisiacal years, or the jaunty later period working and writing there, Kipling remained by language and sensibility an English – and indeed very British – writer. Though he obviously gives simple pleasure to a small segment of the reading public in India – as indeed he does all over the anglophone world – he yet remains to be deconstructed, read against the grain, and enriched in interpretation from distinctly 'Indian' points of view.

Notes

1 Rudyard Kipling, *Something of Myself and Other Autobiographical Writings*, ed. Thomas Pinney (Cambridge University Press, 1990), pp. 3–4. Kipling's breezy account is richly supplemented for the period 1865 to 1899 by Charles Allen, *Kipling Sahib: India and the Making of Rudyard Kipling* (London: Abacus, 2007).

2 Kipling, *Something of Myself*, pp. 5, 6.

3 *Ibid.*, p. 16.

4 Compare W. M. Thackeray (1811–63), who was born in Calcutta, sent to England in 1816, never saw India again, and whose few references to India in *Vanity Fair* are either routine (shawls and elephants) or improbable ('Bogleywallah' as a place-name); George Orwell (1903–50), who was born in Bihar but brought to England at the age of one and later served as a police officer in Burma from 1922 to 1927; and E. M. Forster (1879–1970), who first visited India for six months in 1912–13, when he had already published four novels, and then again for nearly a year in 1921–2, before completing *A Passage to India* (1924). The only British novelist who comes close to matching Kipling in his pattern of to-ing and fro-ing between India and England was Edward Thompson (1886–1946), who was born in India, taken back to England at the age of six, and then returned as an educational missionary to teach in the Wesleyan Methodist College in Bankura in Bengal from 1910 to 1923, after which he taught Bengali and researched Indian history at Oxford University.

5 According to the 2001 Census of India the population of India was 1,028,737,436. See www.censusindia.gov.in/Tables_Published/A-Series/A-Series_links/t_00_003. aspx. The 'Provisional Population Totals' for the 2011 Census of India give the country's population as 1,210,193,422. See censusindia.gov.in/2011-prov-results/ data_files/Figures_At_Glance.pdf. For the distribution by languages from the 2001 census, see www.censusindia.gov.in/Census_Data_2001/Census_Data_Online/ Language/data_on_language.html, especially Statements 1 and 4.

6 Jawaharlal Nehru, *An Autobiography* (1936; Delhi: Oxford University Press, 1980), p. 14.

7 Rudyard Kipling, *Kim*, retold by Richard Shaw, Sunbird Readers Grade 4, Indian Edition (Delhi: Oxford University Press, 1971; 15th impression, 2006).

8 This is confirmed by an informal survey of about 400 college and university teachers of English I conducted on the groupmail of the Indian Association for Commonwealth Literature and Language Studies (at iaclals@yahoogroups.com) in 2007–8. On an elective MPhil. course on 'British Writing on India', which I have taught at the University of Delhi over the last two decades, *Kim* was

initially one of the ten to twelve primary texts, but as it kept ending up among the 'least interesting/challenging texts in the course' in student assessments, I felt obliged to drop it from the course. The main reasons given by the students were that it was exotic, inauthentic and not sufficiently engaging or complex. The University of Delhi also removed *A Passage to India* from its syllabi some ten years ago to make room for more texts in translation from India and continental Europe.

9 Khushwant Singh (ed.), *Kipling's India* (Delhi: Roli Books, 1994).

10 Sudhakar Marathe, personal communication, 9 July 2008.

11 Sudhakar Marathe, Introduction to *Rudyard Kipling: Stories of India* (New Delhi: Penguin Books India, 2003), pp. xi, xv, xvii, xix, xx.

12 In his notes on 'Letters of Marque' in volume I of *From Sea to Sea and Other Sketches* for *The New Readers' Guide to the Works of Rudyard Kipling*, available on the Kipling Society website (www.kipling.org.uk), David Page observes that 'A "Letter of Marque" was a commission issued by a belligerent state to a private person permitting him to employ his vessel as a ship of war. A ship so used was a privateer. The Congress of Paris 1856 abolished privateering which finally became obsolete with the Hague Convention of 1907.'

13 For one of the few available sources on Mukerji, see the (non peer-reviewed) www.en.wikipedia.org/wiki/Dhan_Gopal_Mukerji

14 *Kim* was in the event serialized elsewhere. See Allen, *Kipling Sahib*, pp. 323–4.

15 Quoted in Rimli Bhattacharya, 'Transnational Scouting ("In Search of Perfect Manhood") and Dhan Gopal Mukerji's *Gay-Neck the Pigeon* (1927)', unpublished paper, pp. 15, 37. I am grateful to Dr Bhattacharya, my colleague at the University of Delhi, for drawing my attention to Mukerji and letting me see a copy of her paper.

16 For a lively account from the point of view of British characters of the differences between South India and North-West India, see Kipling's short story 'William the Conqueror' in *The Day's Work* (1898).

17 Graham Greene, 'Introduction' to R. K. Narayan, *The Bachelor of Arts* (1937; London: William Heinemann, 1978; and Mysore: Indian Thought Publications, 1991), n.p. [6 pp.].

18 Quoted and discussed in Susan Ram and N. Ram, *R. K. Narayan: The Early Years: 1906–1945* (New Delhi: Viking, 1996), p. 193.

19 Cited in Susan Ram and N. Ram, *Narayan: The Early Years*, p. 403.

20 For examples, see my notes to *Kim* (London: Penguin, 2011).

21 M. K. Gandhi, *The Collected Works of Mahatma Gandhi*, 100 vols. (New Delhi: Ministry of Information and Broadcasting, Government of India, 1960–94), vol. IV, p. 296. I am grateful to my friend Tridip Suhrud for alerting me to these Gandhi references.

22 *The Collected Works of Mahatma Gandhi*, vol. VIII, p. 236.

23 *The Collected Works of Mahatma Gandhi*, vol. IX, p. 467.

24 *The Collected Works of Mahatma Gandhi*, vol. XXIII, p. 147.

25 *Ibid.*, p. 148.

26 *Ibid.*, p. 179.

27 *The Collected Works of Mahatma Gandhi*, vol. VIII, p. 243.

28 *The Collected Works of Mahatma Gandhi*, vol. XXV, p. 488.

29 *The Collected Works of Mahatma Gandhi*, vol. XL, pp. 451–2.

30 For a visual example, see the cover of Richard Allen and Harish Trivedi (eds.), *Literature and Nation: Britain and India 1800–1990* (London: Routledge/Open University, 2000), which shows Gandhi and Kipling facing each other across a map of India.

31 For a slightly different version of this quotation, see Leela Gandhi, *Postcolonial Theory: A Critical Introduction* (New York: Columbia University Press, 1998), p. 22. For a more comprehensive but no less trenchant critique of western civilisation by Gandhi see his *'Hind Swaraj' and Other Writings*, ed. Anthony J. Parel (Cambridge University Press, 2009).

32 Ashis Nandy, *The Intimate Enemy: Loss and Recovery of Self under Colonialism* (Delhi: Oxford University Press, 1983), p. 68.

33 *Ibid.*, p. 69.

34 *Ibid.*, pp. 48, 51.

35 For Said's introduction and notes to *Kim* see Rudyard Kipling, *Kim*, ed. Edward W. Said (London: Penguin, 1987), pp. 7–46 and 339–66. For a discussion, see my 'Arguing with the Himalayas: Edward Said on Kipling', in Caroline Rooney and Kaori Nagai (eds.), *Kipling and Beyond: Patriotism, Globalization and Postcolonialism* (London: Palgrave Macmillan, 2010), pp. 120–43 and my own introduction and notes to the new Penguin edition of *Kim* (London: Penguin, 2011).

36 Gayatri Chakravorty Spivak, *A Critique of Postcolonial Reason: Toward a History of the Vanishing Present* (Cambridge, MA: Harvard University Press, 1999), pp. 158, 161, 162.

37 *Ibid.*, p. 160 n. 70. Haldar's earliest publication, *Hegelianism and Human Personality* (1910), still postdates *Kim* by nearly a decade.

38 Homi K. Bhabha, *The Location of Culture* (London: Routledge, 1994), pp. 87, 123.

39 Nirad C. Chaudhuri, 'The Finest Story about India – in English', in John Gross (ed.), *Rudyard Kipling: The Man, his Work and his World* (London: Weidenfeld & Nicolson, 1972), p. 28.

FURTHER READING

Kipling's major works (with year of first publication)

Prose

Plain Tales from the Hills (1888)
Soldiers Three, The Story of the Gadsbys, In Black and White (1888)
Under the Deodars, The Phantom Rickshaw, Wee Willie Winkie (1888)
Life's Handicap (1891)
The Light That Failed (1891)
The Naulahka: A Story of West and East (1892)
Many Inventions (1893)
The Jungle Book (1894)
The Second Jungle Book (1895)
'Captains Courageous' (1896)
The Day's Work (1898)
A Fleet in Being (1898)
Stalky & Co. (1899)
From Sea to Sea: Letters of Travel (1899)
Kim (1901)
Just So Stories for Little Children (1902)
Traffics and Discoveries (1904)
Puck of Pook's Hill (1906)
Actions and Reactions (1909)
Rewards and Fairies (1910)
Sea Warfare (1916)
A Diversity of Creatures (1917)
Land and Sea Tales for Scouts and Guides (1923)
The Irish Guards in the Great War (1923)
Debits and Credits (1926)
A Book of Words (1928)
Thy Servant a Dog (1930)
Limits and Renewals (1932)
Something of Myself (1937)

Poetry

Departmental Ditties and Other Verses (1886)
Barrack-Room Ballads and Other Verses (1889–92)
The Seven Seas and Further Barrack-Room Ballads (1891–6)
The Five Nations (1903)
The Years Between (1919)

Collections, editions and reference

Green, Roger Lancelyn (ed.). *Kipling: The Critical Heritage*. London: Routledge and Kegan Paul, 1971.

Kipling, Rudyard. *Early Verse by Rudyard Kipling, 1879–1889: Unpublished, Uncollected, and Rarely Collected Poems*, ed. Andrew Rutherford. Oxford University Press, 1986.

Rudyard Kipling's Verse: Definitive Edition. London: Hodder and Stoughton, 1940.

Something of Myself and Other Autobiographical Writings, ed. Thomas Pinney. Cambridge University Press, 1990.

War Stories and Poems, ed. Andrew Rutherford. Oxford University Press, 1990.

Writings on Writing, ed. Sandra Kemp and Lisa Lewis. Cambridge University Press, 1996.

Pinney, Thomas (ed.). *The Letters of Rudyard Kipling*. 6 vols. Basingstoke: Macmillan, 1990–2004.

Radcliffe, John, *et al. The New Readers' Guide to the Works of Rudyard Kipling* (The Kipling Society). Available from www.kipling.org.uk

Richards, David Alan. *Rudyard Kipling: A Bibliography*. London: The British Library, 2010.

Biographical studies

Allen, Charles. *Kipling Sahib: India and the Making of Rudyard Kipling*. London: Little, Brown, 2007.

Carrington, Charles. *Rudyard Kipling: His Life and Work*. London: Macmillan, 1955.

Gilmour, David. *The Long Recessional: The Imperial Life of Rudyard Kipling*. London: John Murray, 2002.

Lycett, Andrew. *Rudyard Kipling*. London: Weidenfeld & Nicolson, 1999.

Mallett, Phillip. *Rudyard Kipling: A Literary Life*. London: Palgrave Macmillan, 2003.

Orel, Harold (ed.). *Kipling: Interviews & Recollections*. 2 vols. London: Macmillan, 1983.

Ricketts, Harry. *The Unforgiving Minute: A Life of Rudyard Kipling*. London: Chatto & Windus, 1999.

Wilson, Angus. *The Strange Ride of Rudyard Kipling: His Life and Work*. London: Secker & Warburg, 1977.

Criticism

Auden, W. H. 'A Poet of Encirclement'. *Forewords and Afterwords*. London: Faber and Faber, 1973.

Bodelsen, C. A. *Aspects of Kipling's Art*. Manchester University Press, 1964.

Bristow, Joseph. *Empire Boys: Adventures in a Man's World*. London: Unwin Hyman, 1991.

Brogan, Hugh. *Mowgli's Sons: Kipling and Baden-Powell's Scouts*. London: Jonathan Cape, 1987.

Crook, Nora. *Kipling's Myths of Love and Death*. London: Macmillan, 1989.

Eliot, T. S. 'Introduction'. *A Choice of Kipling's Verse*. London: Faber and Faber, 1941.

Gilbert, Elliot, *The Good Kipling: Studies in the Short Story*. Athens: Ohio University Press, 1970.

Green, Roger Lancelyn. *Kipling and the Children*. London: Elek Books, 1965.

Havholm, Peter. *Politics and Awe in Rudyard Kipling's Fiction*. Aldershot: Ashgate, 2008.

Jarrell, Randall. *Kipling, Auden & Co*. Manchester: Carcanet, 1980.

Keating, Peter. *Kipling the Poet*. London: Secker & Warburg, 1994.

Kemp, Sandra. *Kipling's Hidden Narratives*. Oxford: Basil Blackwell, 1988.

Lewis, C. S. 'The Inner Ring'. *They Asked for a Paper*. London: Geoffrey Bles, 1962.

Mason, Philip. *Kipling: The Glass, the Shadow and the Fire*. London: Jonathan Cape, 1975.

McBratney, John. *Imperial Subjects, Imperial Space: Rudyard Kipling's Fiction of the Native-Born*. Columbus: Ohio State University Press, 2002.

McClure, John A. *Kipling and Conrad: The Colonial Fiction*. Cambridge, MA: Harvard University Press, 1981.

Montefiore, Jan. *Rudyard Kipling*. Tavistock: Northcote House, 2007.

Moore-Gilbert, Bart. *Kipling and Orientalism*. London: Croom Helm, 1986.

Nagai, Kaori. *Empire of Analogies: Kipling, India and Ireland*. Cork University Press, 2006.

Orwell, George. 'Rudyard Kipling'. *All Art is Propaganda: Critical Essays*, ed. George Packer. London: Harvill Secker, 2009.

Raine, Craig. 'Introduction'. *Rudyard Kipling: Selected Poetry*. London: Penguin, 1992.

Rooney, Caroline and Kaori Nagai (eds.). *Kipling and Beyond: Patriotism, Globalisation and Postcolonialism*. Basingstoke: Palgrave Macmillan, 2010.

Rutherford, Andrew (ed.). *Kipling's Mind and Art*. Edinburgh: Oliver & Boyd, 1964.

Said, Edward W. *Culture and Imperialism*. London: Chatto & Windus, 1993.

Stewart, J. I. M. *Rudyard Kipling*. London: Gollancz, 1966.

Sullivan, Zohreh T. *Narratives of Empire: The Fictions of Rudyard Kipling*. Cambridge University Press, 1993.

Tompkins, J. M. S. *The Art of Rudyard Kipling*. London: Methuen, 1959.

Walsh, Sue. *Kipling's Children's Literature: Language, Identity, and Constructions of Childhood*. Farnham: Ashgate, 2010.

Wilson, Edmund. 'The Kipling That Nobody Read.' *The Wound and the Bow*. Cambridge, MA: Houghton Mifflin, 1941.

INDEX

Cambridge Companions to...

AUTHORS

TOPICS